P9-CRU-632

THERAPY AS SOCIAL
CONSTRUCTION

INQUIRIES IN SOCIAL CONSTRUCTION

Series editors
Kenneth J. Gergen and John Shotter

This series is designed to facilitate, across discipline and national boundaries, an emergent dialogue within the social sciences which many believe presages a major shift in the western intellectual tradition.

Including among its participants sociologists of science, psychologists, management and communication theorists, cyberneticists, ethnomethodologists, literary theorists, feminists and social historians, it is a dialogue which involves profound challenges to many existing ideas about, for example, the person, selfhood, scientific method and the nature of scientific and everyday knowledge.

It has also given voice to a range of new topics, such as the social construction of personal identities; the role of power in the social making of meanings; rhetoric and narrative in establishing sciences; the centrality of everyday activities; remembering and forgetting as socially constituted activities; reflexivity in method and theorizing. The common thread underlying all these topics is a concern with the processes by which human abilities, experiences, commonsense and scientific knowledge are both *produced in*, and *reproduce*, human communities.

Inquiries in Social Construction affords a vehicle for exploring this new consciousness, the problems raised and the implications for society.

Also in this series

The Social Construction of Lesbianism
Celia Kitzinger

Rhetoric in the Human Sciences
edited by Herbert W. Simons

Texts of Identity
edited by John Shotter and Kenneth J. Gergen

Collective Remembering
edited by David Middleton and Derek Edwards

Everyday Understanding
Social and Scientific Implications
edited by Gün R. Semin and Kenneth J. Gergen

Research and Reflexivity
edited by Frederick Steier

Constructing Knowledge
Authority and Critique in Social Science
edited by Lorraine Nencel and Peter Pels

Discursive Psychology
Derek Edwards and Jonathan Potter

THERAPY AS SOCIAL CONSTRUCTION

F74

EDITED BY
SHEILA McNAMEE and
KENNETH J. GERGEN

SAGE Publications
London • Newbury Park • New Delhi

WITHDRAWN FROM
J. EUGENE SMITH LIBRARY
EASTERN CONN. STATE UNIVERSITY
WILLIMANTIC, CT 06226-2295

Introduction and editorial arrangement © Sheila McNamee
and Kenneth J. Gergen 1992
Chapter 1 © Lynn Hoffman 1992
Chapter 2 © Harlene Anderson and Harold Goolishian 1992
Chapter 3 © Laura Fruggeri 1992
Chapter 4 © Tom Andersen 1992
Chapter 5 © William D. Lax 1992
Chapter 6 © Gianfranco Cecchin 1992
Chapter 7 © David Epston, Michael White and Kevin
          Murray 1992
Chapter 8 © Karl Tomm 1992
Chapter 9 © William Hudson O'Hanlon 1992
Chapter 10 © Annibal Coelho de Amorim and Fatima
           Gonçalves Cavalcante 1992
Chapter 11 © Kenneth J. Gergen and John Kaye 1992
Chapter 12 © Sheila McNamee 1992
Chapter 13 © Jay S. Efran and Leslie E. Clarfield 1992

First published 1992
Reprinted 1993

All rights reserved. No part of this publication may be
reproduced, stored in a retrieval system, transmitted or
utilized in any form or by any means, electronic,
mechanical, photocopying, recording or otherwise, without
permission in writing from the Publishers.

SAGE Publications Ltd
6 Bonhill Street
London EC2A 4PU

SAGE Publications Inc
2455 Teller Road
Newbury Park, California 91320

SAGE Publications India Pvt Ltd
32, M-Block Market
Greater Kailash – I
New Delhi 110 048

British Library Cataloguing in Publication Data

Therapy as Social Construction. –
    (Inquiries in Social Construction Series)
    I. McNamee, Sheila   II. Gergen, Kenneth J.   III. Series
    158.3

    ISBN 0–8039–8302–6
    ISBN 0–8039–8303–4 pbk

Library of Congress catalog card number 92-50277

Typeset by Mayhew Typesetting, Rhayader, Powys
Printed and bound in Great Britain by
Biddles Ltd, Guildford and King's Lynn

This book is dedicated
to the memory of
Harold Goolishian

Contents

Notes on the Contributors

Tom Andersen is a former general practitioner and is currently employed as a psychiatrist. He is also Professor of Social Psychiatry at the University of Tromsø Medical School. He is best known for his innovative 'reflecting position' and is editor of *The Reflecting Team* (1991).

Harlene Anderson, Director of the Houston Galveston Institute, is on the editorial review boards of the *Journal of Strategic and Systemic Therapies* and *Human Systems: the Journal of Systemic Consultation and Management*. She has authored and co-authored numerous professional publications and, along with Harold Goolishian, has a forthcoming book, *A Collaborative Language Systems Approach to Psychotherapy* (Basic Books).

Fatima Gonçalves Cavalcante is a Brazilian gestalt psychologist. She has coordinated, with Dr Amorim, an art therapy group activity which was the origin of her contribution to the present volume. She is currently working with in- and out-patients at the Neuropsychiatric Child Hospital of the Pedro II Psychiatric Center in Rio de Janeiro, Brazil.

Gianfranco Cecchin is currently Co-Director of the Centro Milanese di Terapia della Famiglia and is one of the co-founders of the Milan Model of Family Therapy. He is co-author of *Paradox and Counterparadox* (Aronson), *Milan Systemic Therapy* (Basic Books), and several articles on family therapy.

Leslie E. Clarfield received an M.S. in psychology from Vanderbilt University and is currently completing her doctorate in clinical psychology at Temple University.

Annibal Coelho de Amorim is a Brazilian neurologist and a gestalt psychologist. He has been involved for the past twelve years with mental health and rehabilitation practices in Rio de Janeiro. He is the former Vice-Director of the Childhood Neuropsychiatric Hospital of the National Mental Division/Health Ministry and is presently on staff at this hospital. His work combines the use of constructionist theory with video among adolescents.

Jay S. Efran is Professor of Psychology and Director of the Psychological Services Center at Temple University in Philadelphia. He has served as Director of Clinical Training and is co-author of *Language, Structure, and Change: Frameworks of Meaning in Psychotherapy* (Norton, 1990).

David Epston is Co-Director of the Family Therapy Centre in Auckland, New Zealand. He co-authored, with Michael White, *Narrative Means to Therapeutic Ends* (1990) and *Narrative, Contradiction, Experience, and Imagination* (1992). His *Collected Papers* (1989) were published by Dulwich Centre Publications, Adelaide, South Australia.

Laura Fruggeri teaches Social Psychology at the University of Parma and is a faculty member at the Centro Milanese di Terapia della Famiglia. She is author of several articles and books on systemic thinking and the social constructionist approach applied to the analysis of interpersonal and social relationships.

Kenneth J. Gergen is Professor of Psychology at Swarthmore College. He is the author of, among other works, *The Saturated Self* (Basic Books, 1991) and *Toward a Transformation of Social Knowledge* (Springer-Verlag, 1982). He is a central exponent of the social constructionist movement in modern psychology.

Harold Goolishian was Director Emeritus of the Houston Galveston Institute. He was honored in 1991, just before his death, by the American Association for Marital and Family Therapy for his distinguished professional contributions to family therapy. He is the author of numerous articles, many in collaboration with Harlene Anderson. He was a pioneer in the fields of family and psychotherapy.

Lynn Hoffman is author of several books including *Foundations of Family Therapy* (Basic Books, 1981) and, with Luigi Boscolo, Gianfranco Cecchin, and Peggy Penn, *Milan Systemic Family Therapy* (Basic Books, 1987). She has also written numerous articles on systemic family therapy.

John Kaye is Senior Lecturer in Psychology at the University of Adelaide, South Australia where he is Coordinator of the Master in Applied Psychology Programme. With interests in the Fine Arts, Literature, Metapsychology, Narrative and Discourse Analysis, his teaching and research emerge from a post-foundational orientation to psychology. This orientation also informs his work as a psychotherapist.

William D. Lax is a Core Faculty member at Antioch New England Graduate School, Keene, New Hampshire and Director of Training at Brattleboro Family Institute, Brattleboro, Vermont. He is interested in applying social constructionist thinking within both academic and clinical settings.

Sheila McNamee is Associate Professor and Chair of Communication at the University of New Hampshire. She has published several articles exploring conceptualizations of research as social intervention. She has also written on social constructionist approaches to family therapy.

Kevin Murray specializes in the area of life construction. His Ph.D. thesis at the Department of Psychology, University of Melbourne was on 'Life as Fiction.' He is editor of *The Judgment of Paris: Recent French Thought in a Local Context* (Allen & Unwin, 1991).

William Hudson O'Hanlon has authored or co-authored several books and travels internationally to teach psychotherapy seminars. He has a private practice at the Hudson Center for Brief Therapy in Omaha, Nebraska and is an Adjunct Professor of Psychology at Indiana University of Pennsylvania.

Karl Tomm is a psychiatrist and family therapist who teaches at the University of Calgary. He has a strong interest in postmodernist theoretical developments that have heuristic potential for the clinical process of interventive interviewing. He has published several articles on this topic in *Family Process*.

Michael White is Co-Director of the Dulwich Centre in Adelaide, South Australia. His conceptualization of 'externalizing the problem' in therapy has gained him much recognition. He has written several articles on this topic and is co-author, with David Epston, of *Narrative Means to Therapeutic Ends* (1990) and *Narrative, Contradiction, Experience, and Imagination* (1992).

Introduction

Problems and their solutions do not spring from the soil of simple observation. Whether we locate a problem for which a solution is demanded – for example, an illness for which cure is required – depends not so much on what is before us as behind. That is, we come to the field of observation bearing a lifetime of cultural experience. Most important, we not only bear languages that furnish the rationale for our looking, but also vocabularies of description and explanation for what is observed. Thus we confront life situations with codes in hand, forestructures of understanding which themselves suggest how we are to sort the problematic from the precious. The mental health professions of the present century have largely been guided by a single code of understanding, one that finds its roots in the Enlightenment and its purest form of exposition in scientific foundationalism of the present century. The present volume forms a challenge to the prevailing forestructure, and in doing so attempts to open new vistas for therapeutic theory and practice.

The guiding perspective for most therapeutic endeavors of the present century is committed to the assumption of the individual knower. That is, it is the single individual who possesses the capacity to know the world and to act adaptively within it. If individual capacities and processes are functioning normally, the individual will confront life's challenges as adequately as possible. When there are inadequacies in meeting these challenges, there is reason to believe that the capacities and processes are malfunctioning. From this standpoint, it is the scientist who most fully embodies the virtues of adequate functioning. For it is the scientist who observes most acutely and systematically, who applies the most rigorous and rational procedures in evaluating and synthesizing information. It is the scientist who builds in safeguards against emotions, values, and errant motives, and stands independent from the objects of observation lest his or her conclusions are contaminated. It is this image of the expert, independent, and individual knower that therapeutic practitioners have largely adopted in the present century. It is the therapist who carefully observes and deliberates, and who offers his or her conclusions about the adequacies and inadequacies of independently situated others. And it is the common individual who suffers from inadequacies, who may regain a fulfilling life by giving way to expert knowledge. Interestingly, most of these inadequacies, as the scientist-therapist finds, can be traced to the inabilities (pathologies) of the individual to function as the ideal knower. Thus, for example, Freud wished to replace unconscious processes of the id (sources of malfunction) with the conscious processes of the ego (reason); Horney sought to overcome her patients' basic anxiety through rational insight; object relations specialists and Rogerians looked for processes that would enable the person to become an autonomous actor; behavior modificationists generated technologies to facilitate individual relearning; and cognitive therapists attempt to alter the processes of individual decision making.

The Gathering Storm

Most readers of the present volume will experience a distinct sense of unease with the traditional view of the scientist-therapist. This is largely because the past several decades have been ones of widespread critical reflection within therapeutic circles. The traditional views – often termed 'modernist' – have been actively challenged from a variety of standpoints. Little confidence now remains in the optimistic program of scientifically grounded progress toward identifying 'problems' and providing 'cures.' This is not the context for a full review of the emerging forms of critique and their struggles toward alternatives. However, it is useful to scan briefly the spectrum of discontent:

- Critical therapists locate strong ideological biases within prevailing theories and therapeutic practices. The mental health profession is not politically, morally, or valuationally neutral. Their practices typically operate to sustain certain values, political arrangements, and hierarchies of privilege.
- Family therapists challenge the view that individuals are the centers of malfunction. They locate myriad ways in which 'individual pathology' is but a local manifestation of problems inherent in the functioning of family units – immediate and extended. Informed largely by cybernetic formulations, a variety of systemic alternatives are developed.
- Community psychologists expand the domain of contextual considerations to include various aspects of community life, educational institutions, economic conditions, work life, physical surrounds, and so on as they are implicated in individual disorder. From this standpoint, 'individual pathology' cannot be separated from communal process.

- Feminist scholars locate a variety of ways in which current mental health practices are oppressive and debilitating to women. The system of classifying mental disorders, the pejorative position of the patient, and the tendency of the mental health professions to place the blame for mental dysfunction on the individual woman as opposed to the unsatisfying conditions in which she lives all serve to sustain a patriarchal society.
- Phenomenologists attempt to expunge the therapist of preconceptions about the nature of individual dysfunction (for example, expert knowledge), so that they can understand the client's situation and actions in his or her own terms.
- Constructivists challenge the traditional separation between the knower and the known, arguing that processes inherent in the organism largely determine what is taken to be 'the real.' The scientist is never independent of the observed world.
- Hermeneuticists argue that the traditional view of the therapist as an objective analyst of mental states is misleading and mystifying. Therapeutic interpretation is heavily laden with the presuppositions of the therapist.
- Ex-mental patients organize themselves against the profession of psychiatry, arguing that the current system of classifying pathology is not only oppressive, objectifying, and demeaning, but is also self-serving for the mental health professions.

Each of these domains of critique has also fostered a variety of innovative and absorbing alternatives to the traditional view of scientist-therapist. In our view, some of these alternatives are not wholly satisfying, for while they abandon certain aspects of the traditional view they retain still others (for instance, therapist as expert knower). Also disturbing is the way in which certain alternatives continue to emphasize mechanistic processes of cause and effect (for example, individual action as systems or societally determined). Still others move towards an unacceptable solipsism (such as constructivism), or toward a unilateral and singular conception of the good society. To be sure, many of these struggles toward new visions remain within their infancy, and a final account can scarcely be offered. However, in the meantime a common consciousness is emerging across many of these domains, one that senses the possibility for a form of unification. Is it possible, it is asked, to benefit from these various forms of critique, while simultaneously avoiding a duplication of the past, and sidestepping a variety of other entanglements? It is the possibility for just this kind of common consciousness that the chapters in the present volume set out to explore. The integrative vehicle is social constructionism.

The Emergence of a Constructionist Consciousness

Simultaneous with the growing loss of confidence in vision of scientist-therapist, there has been a generalized falling-out within the academic world with the traditional conception of scientific knowledge. Within the philosophy of science major critiques were launched against the presumption of formal or rational foundations of knowledge. Logical empiricism has largely vanished from serious consideration, critical rationalists are a diminishing breed, and aspirants of a 'new realism' have been unable to articulate an alternative program of science. Since the work of Kuhn and Feyerabend, 'the philosophy of science' has largely been replaced on the intellectual agenda by the history and sociology of knowledge. Both the latter enterprises challenge the view of scientific knowledge as rationally superior, and trace the cultural and historical processes that bring certain conceptions of nature into favor while suppressing others. In effect, it is argued that what we take to be accurate and objective accounts of nature and self are an outgrowth of social processes.

This growing emphasis on the social embeddedness of what we take to be the 'true and the good' is further emphasized and elaborated by widespread developments in literary theory, rhetoric and semiotics. Although this literature is vast and multi-hued, for present purposes there is a primary message to be drawn from these various endeavors: our formulations of what is the case are guided by and limited to the systems of language in which we live. What can be said about the world – including self and others – is an outgrowth of shared conventions of discourse. Thus, for example, one cannot describe the history of a country or oneself on the basis of 'what actually happened;' rather, one has available a repertoire of story-telling devices or narrative forms and these devices are imposed on the past. To fail in employing the traditional modes of telling stories (for examples, stories of progress, change, or failure, with an internal logic, and beginnings and endings) would be to fail in rendering an intelligible account of what occurred. In effect, what we take to be 'the real and the good' are largely products of textual histories.

Yet, for a number of social psychologists, communication theorists, and sociologists, the textual account must be pressed forward in an important way. For, as it is also reasoned, textual histories are not independent of people. Rather, texts are byproducts of human relationships. They gain their meaning from the way they are used within relationships. To be sure, our constructions of the world and ourselves are limited by our languages, but these limitations must be traced at last to us. We generate the conventions of discourse – both in science and everyday life. And, because we have the power to generate agreeable accounts of what is the case, we also have the power of alteration.

This does not mean that there is nothing outside language, nothing beyond what we make it out to be. However, it does argue that because our conjoint formulations of what is the case are typically embedded within our patterns of action, our formulations are enormously important in constructing our future. There is nothing about certain alterations in what we call the human body that necessarily requires the concept of 'death' as a 'finality.' But once this conception is broadly shared, and appropriate mourning practices are established, then the calling becomes a significant precursor to future events. To gain purchase on social change is, then, both to enter into the cultural languages and simultaneously seek their transformation. Yet, this transformation cannot be undertaken by a single will, an all-knowing or all-seeing expert. Rather, transformation is inherently a relational matter, emerging from myriad coordinations among persons.

For many critics of the traditional view of scientist-therapist, this focus on the social construction of the taken-for-granted is highly inviting. It enables critical theorists, feminists, ex-mental patients, and others to continue in their questioning of the current canons of truth within the profession. Constructionism invites the kind of critical self-reflection that might open the future to alternative forms of understanding. With constructivism and phenomenology, constructionism forms (albeit on different grounds) a critical challenge to the subject–object dualism on which the traditional view of the therapist-scientist is based. With family therapists, community psychologists, and cyberneticians, constructionism is also centrally concerned not with individuals but with relational networks. And with all of these orientations, including the hermeneuticists, constructionism challenges the position of transcendent superiority claimed by those operating in the traditional scientific mode.

Precisely how these ends are accomplished is, of course, the subject of most of the present chapters. For convenience we have organized the volume into four parts, each featuring chapters with specific emphases. The divisions are far from pure, as many of the chapters are multiply laminated. However, the first set of chapters elaborates more fully on the theoretical and metatheoretical background of constructionism in the therapeutic context. In the second division, chapters articulate particular forms of practice that illustrate a constructionist sensibility. The four chapters included in this section discuss some of the orientations adopted by constructionist therapists. These chapters differ from those in the following section, where emphasis is placed on actual cases demonstrating some of the creative procedures used to create a discursive space where 'problems' may be differently constructed. The final section of the book questions some elaborations of constructionism and some more popular forms of therapeutic practice. Overall, the chapters here provide a range of reflections on social construction and the therapeutic process.

Note

The authors would like to thank Stuart Palmer, Dean of the College of Liberal Arts, University of New Hampshire, for grants that helped to make this book possible.

PART I

CONSTRUCTING THE THEORETICAL CONTEXT

1

A Reflexive Stance for Family Therapy

Lynn Hoffman

During the past five or six years, a view has emerged among a small sub-group of family therapists that offers something different enough to qualify as a new approach. This approach is more participatory than others and less goal-orientated – some would say it has no goals at all. It enrages some people; others applaud. It is represented by a few groups here and abroad, notably the Galveston group (Anderson and Goolishian, 1988), the Tromsø group (Andersen, 1987), and the Brattleboro group (Lax and Lussardi, 1989), although its adherents are growing. Having been one of the people groping towards this something, I have also been struggling to name it. But so many streams of ideas are flowing together into a larger tributary that it is hard to find one common ancestor.

In certain respects, our present dialogue is congenial to the movement known as postmodernism – with its implication that modernism is now dead and new perspectives are in the making. Without overstating the matter, one could say that many adherents of postmodernism have taken on the project of dismantling the philosophical foundations of Western thought. Sometimes the term 'poststructural' is used as if it were synonymous with postmodern. A poststructural view of the social sciences, for instance, challenges any framework that posits some kind of structure internal to the entity in question, whether we are talking about a text, a family, or a play. In family therapy, this has meant that the cybernetic view that sees the family as a homeostatic system is under attack. Because postmodern and poststructural ideas were originated by people in semiotics and literary criticism, it is becoming increasingly common in talking of social fields of study to use the analogy of a narrative or text.

Within this context, a number of family systems people like Harlene Anderson and Harry Goolishian (1988) have defected from the flag of cybernetics and have adopted the flag of *hermeneutics*. Hermeneutics, referred to with self-conscious grace by some of its adherents as 'the interpretive turn,' is a recently revived branch of textual interpretation. For family therapists who have espoused this view, the feedback loops of cybernetic systems are replaced by the intersubjective loops of dialogue. The central metaphor for therapy thus changes to conversation, reinforced by the fact that the basic medium of therapy is also conversation.

For me, a more useful approach is located in social construction theory (Gergen, 1985). Although many persons, including myself, have frequently confused this theory with constructivism (von Glasersfeld, 1984), the two positions are quite different. There is a common ground in that both take issue with the modernist idea that a real world exists that can be known with objective certainty. However, the beliefs represented by constructivism tend to promote an image of the nervous system as a closed machine. According to this view, percepts and constructs take shape as the organism bumps against its environment. By contrast, the social construction theorists see ideas, concepts and memories arising from social interchange and mediated through language. All knowledge, the social constructionists hold, evolves in the space between people, in the realm of the 'common world' or the 'common dance.' Only through the on-going conversation with intimates does the individual develop a sense of identity or an inner voice.

In addition, the social construction theorists place themselves squarely in a postmodern tradition. They owe much to the textual and political criticism represented by the *deconstructionist* views of literary critics like Jacques Derrida (1978) in France and deriving from the neo-Marxist thinkers of the Frankfurt School. One must add to this intellectual context the writings of the brilliant French social historian Michel Foucault (1975), who has brought the term power back into prominence with his examination of the way relations of dominance and submission are embedded in social discourse.

Due to these influences, we are seeing a revolution in the social sciences: worse yet, a challenge to the idea that students of society ought to call themselves scientists at all. Social researchers like Kenneth Gergen (1991) and Rom Harré (1984) are overturning foundational ideas in modern psychology and sociology. Feminists have joined the attack, finding in the arguments of the postmodern thinkers, especially the theories of Foucault, ample ammunition for their insistence that the very language of therapy is biased against women. And feminist sympathizers like Jeffrey Masson (1990) have made a compelling case for the notion that psychotherapy began as a treatment designed to subjugate women who objected to the way they were treated.

There have been similar explosions in anthropology and ethnography. Ethnographers James Clifford and George Marcus (1986), for instance, take a participatory posture in regard to the people they study, finding in the stance of traditional anthropologists an unconscious colonial mentality. Their critique has profoundly influenced the nature of the research interview and, by extension, the clinical interview as well. The implications of all these challenges to the corpus of beliefs called psychotherapy are mindboggling. In order to explain in detail what I mean, let me describe five sacred cows of modern psychology and the arguments of their critics, many of whom belong to the social constructionist camp.

Five Sacred Cows of Modern Psychology

Objective Social Research

The social constructionists not only challenge the idea of a singular truth, but doubt that there is such a thing as objective social research as well. They charge that we cannot ever really know what 'social reality' is, and that therefore traditional scientific research, with its tests and statistics and probability quotients, is a pious hope if not a downright lie. This claim, if accepted, would obviously threaten the status quo in the mental health profession.

To take only one example, health insurance coverage in the United States for emotional problems is only forthcoming if these problems can be described as biological illnesses. The diagnosis industry is at the heart of our reimbursement system, yet such diagnoses – and the supposedly scientific studies they are based on – are often questionable and flawed. One has only to think of the DSM III category that has recently been invented to characterize women who abuse themselves or cannot leave abusive relationships: Self-defeating Personality Disorder. In a similar category is the diagnosis of Post-traumatic Stress Disorder. This diagnosis evolved because it fitted the flashback problems being experienced by Vietnam veterans, but it is now being used to cover any persons who had a trauma in the past.

My historical sense tells me that now is not a good time to state thoughts like the above, due to the present economics of mental health. In times of crisis, arguments over territory and legitimacy become intense, and we are seeing a rush to define treatable conditions, establish correct ways of treating them, and invent newer and better outcome studies. Never was the idea that reality is socially constructed more evident, but at the same time, never has it been so unwelcome. At the same time, never has it been so necessary.

The Self

Kenneth Gergen presents a compelling case for the 'social construction of the self' (1985) rather than assigning to it a kind of irreducible inner reality represented by words like cognitions or the emotions. Early family therapists were also wary of the idea of the self. They tended to believe that the ideas a person held about his or her self would only change when the ideas held by the people close to this person changed. Twenty years ago, having discovered the family field, I engaged in a project to disappear the individual. Actually, I only replaced the individual unit with the family unit. What was needed was a shift away from structure and a view of the self as a stretch of moving history, like a river or stream.

Accordingly, I came to think of the self as the Australian aborigines think of their 'songlines' (Chatwin, 1987). Songlines are musical roadmaps tracing paths from place to place in the territory inhabited by each individual. A person would be born into one of these songlines but would only know a section of it. The way the Aborigines extended their knowledge of a particular songline was to go on periodic 'walkabouts,' allowing them to meet others living far away who knew a different stanza, so to speak. An exchange of songlines would become an exchange of important knowledge. These songlines would also be tied to the spirits of different ancestors – animals or plants or landmarks – who sprang forth in the 'dreamtime' before people existed. A person might share an ancestor with people who lived in an entirely different part of the territory.

The beauty of this myth is that it presents a picture of individual identity that is not within the person or any other unit. Instead, it consists of temporal flows which can be simple, like a segmented path, or complex, like a moire pattern, but which are realized by singing and walking. The mix of ecological and social understanding afforded by this practice is impressive. I offer it as a poetic example of the social construction of the self.

Developmental Psychology

Social constructionists are the first, to my knowledge, to have questioned the idea of developmental stages. Gergen (1982) offers an extremely cogent argument against developmental theories. He speaks of the danger of assuming that there is any universal standard by which humans can measure their functioning, and states that the whole idea of the normal lifespan trajectory is seriously deficient:

> it is becoming increasingly apparent to investigators in this domain that developmental trajectories over the lifespan are highly variable; neither with respect to psychological functioning nor overt conduct does there appear to be transhistorical generality in lifespan trajectory. . . . A virtual infinity of developmental forms seems possible, and which particular form emerges may depend on a confluence of particulars, the existence of which is fundamentally unsystematic. (Gergen, 1982: 161)

Gergen's words echo the idea, put forth by Ilya Prigogine (1984) and validated later by Chaos theory (Gleick, 1987), that when a system has moved too far from equilibrium – that is, passes over some choice point where a change of state may happen – an element of the random enters in. The trigger event that is operating at that choice point will determine future development, but exactly which trigger will be operative is unpredictable.

In the same way, according to evolution theorists like Stephen Gould (1980), species develop discontinuously and not progressively. A species will evolve slowly according to the interplay between its gene pool and its environment, but at any point some sudden change may take place, like a meteor hitting the path, which will suddenly provide a new trajectory. Then a whole species may die out and a new one take its place. From the work of researchers like these, it becomes harder and harder to argue that within the human personality or within any human group a predetermined and optimal development path can be discerned, and that the failure to achieve this path spells a poor outcome. Yet current psychotherapy practice is to a large part predicated on some version of this idea.

One more question could be asked: how did it come about that modern psychology has so massively adopted a vegetation metaphor based on schedules for growth? One of our sturdiest beliefs about human beings is that there is such a thing as a personality that can be scarred or twisted by a lesion in early life or that by missing some important stage it can be stunted. I call this kind of thinking science by analogy. The trauma theory for emotional problems may in many cases fit the situation, but I do not give it unquestioned status, nor do I feel that it covers every sort of problem.

The Emotions

Rom Harré (1986) has challenged the belief that emotions exist inside people as discrete traits or states and that they are the same all over the world. Many people have no knowledge or record of the emotions we subscribe to; the *idea* of the emotions is comparatively recent even in our own history. Social constructionists view them as just one more part of the complex web of communication between people and do not grant them special status as interior states.

This view has an antecedent in the writings of family therapists. Haley (1963) long ago attacked repression theory, which states that repression of emotions at some early stage could produce symptoms in later life. A version of repression theory now underlies many assumptions of folk psychology: I refer to the widely believed idea that to be healthy one has to 'get in touch' with one's anger or grief. Not expressing your feelings is held to be as dangerous as not eliminating body waste, and many mothers automatically worry if their offspring seem to be holding in their emotions. In fact, the mental health profession has made almost a fetish of this stance in the case of community disasters like floods or adolescent suicides. In the past, people went to one another for comfort, but now there is a perceived need for a professional mourner (often a social worker or a psychologist) to help whole communities 'work through' their emotions. The results of not doing this is said to doom people to live with horrific after-effects, defined vaguely as any kind of psychic or somatic disorder.

Levels

Inspired by this kind of questioning, I have begun to wonder about the idea that there are hierarchical layers of structure embedded within human events. For instance, there is the superficial symptom versus the underlying cause; there is the manifest content versus the latent content; there is the overt communication versus the covert. A very widespread belief of General System Theory is that the natural world is represented by Chinese boxes, one within another, and the more inclusive are more influential than the less inclusive. What if none of these ideas was true? What if all these levels, layers and nests were nothing but sets of different factors influencing one another, all equal to one another, but singled out by us, described by us, and given hierarchical standing by us?

The work of communication researchers Pearce and Cronen (1980) illustrates my point. They divide communication into layers, much as Bateson (1972) used Russell and Whitehead's Theory of Logical Types (1910) to classify messages, but they propose many more layers than he did. Basically, they analyze communication in an ascending order of inclusion (revised from time to time): the speech act, the episode, the relationship, the lifescript, the family myth, the cultural program. They maintain that although the higher levels exert a strong (contextual) force downward, the lower levels also exert a weak (implicative) force upward. Thus, a baby's crying (speech act) could be the context for an offer of feeding (episode) on the part of the mother. Or it could just as well be the other way around.

Where I differ from Pearce and Cronen is that I don't think we need the concept of levels at all. It is enough to think of each category of communication as a possible context for any other category. Which is stronger or higher depends on which one is defined as context for the other one at any given time. This idea greatly appeals to me, because I have been struggling for years to find a way to do without the idea of hierarchies of communication.

So much for the five sacred cows. I would like to consider next a super sacred cow, the nature of the professional relationship itself. To do so, I will call on the metaphor of the colonial official, a metaphor bequeathed to us by the postmodern ethnographers and increasingly used by family therapists as well.

The Colonialism of Mental Health

For me, the most serious challenge to the field of mental health follows the postmodern argument that much 'normal social science' (as these theorists are calling the Western belief in objective social research) perpetuates a kind of colonial mentality in the minds of academics and practitioners. The postmodern ethnographers that I have mentioned point out that many ethnographic researchers in the past have 'studied down,' that is, have chosen to study a less 'civilized' society than their own, or a group seen as limited in respect to ethnic culture or social class. Similarly, a number of researchers in the field of mental health (Kearney et al., 1989) now argue that 'normal psychotherapy' perpetuates a colonial mentality in the minds of its practitioners. To continue with the analogy, the resulting activity could be then called 'practicing down.'

The French historian Michel Foucault (1975) has much to say to us here because of his extremely interesting work on discourse, and particularly the institutionalized kind of talk and writing that is shared by people in a group, a field of study, a profession like law or economics, or an entire country or culture. Being also interested in the mechanisms by which a modern state establishes its rule,

Foucault studies the shift from a designated person or persons monitoring the relations within a society to the *discourse itself* shaping these relations. Once people subscribe to a given discourse – a religious discourse, a psychological discourse, or a discourse around gender – they promote certain definitions about which persons or what topics are most important or have legitimacy. However, they themselves are not always aware of these embedded definitions.

For people involved in the practice of mental health, Foucault's (1975) ideas about the disciplinary use of the 'confessional' are absolutely intriguing. He makes the point that in the Catholic practice of confession, just as in the psychoanalytic practice of free association, the subject is persuaded that he or she has some deep, dark secret – usually sexual – to hide. However, if she confesses it to the proper authority, she can receive absolution, 'work through' the damage to the psyche, or whatever. This unacceptable secret, this 'original sin,' has been accepted by the unsuspecting person as the deepest truth of his or her own heart, and once believed, the idea continues to exert its power of subjugation.

The shift in concept from benign therapist to oppressive professional is one that, fair or unfair, is implied in this view. However, one need not therefore assign blame to a person or group. 'The patriarchy' is not just a collection of males who are dedicated to oppressing women (although it can be perceived as such); it is a way of experiencing and expressing ideas about gender that are cultural givens for both sexes. A corollary of this idea is that therapists of all kinds must now investigate how relations of domination and submission are built into the very assumptions on which their practices are based.

As a result, a new kind of consciousness raising is beginning to take place that does not exempt Marxist therapists because they are champions of the poor, or feminist therapists because they are defenders of women, or spiritual therapists because they follow an other-worldly ideal. These therapeutic discourses can contain the same colonial assumptions as medical approaches. They can all embody oppressive assumptions about personality deficits. They can all offer the client a savior to help them. Spiritualist views about therapy are apt to use the word healing, harking back to shamanistic traditions, while medical views use the word curing, but they both place the client in a submissive place.

This completes the theoretical part of my essay. I turn now to clinical applications of some of the ideas described above. I will describe some reflexive formats, which, because they allow for an alternation of the expert position, interfere with the usual professionalization of the therapeutic enterprise. I will also focus on the postmodern shift in interviewing methods and talk about changes that are affecting the therapeutic conversation itself.

A Growing Dis-ease

About ten years ago, I found myself increasingly haunted by the paradoxes of power that beset the traditional methods of family therapy. They all seemed based on secrecy, hierarchy and control. Even the modulated versions, represented by many Ericksonian practitioners, and the very respectful approach of the Milan Associates, still kept the client at a distance and did not share the thinking of the clinician. There was a good historical reason for this. From its inception, family therapy had a one-way mirror built into its core. The professionals were the observers, the families were the observed. There was never a two-way street. Most first-generation family therapists seemed to support the idea of therapist control, whether exerted openly or secretly. I didn't know which I liked least, pushing clients directly to do what I wanted them to do, or going underground and getting them to do what I wanted them to do under false pretenses.

During this time, what began to happen in my own mind was a shift toward a more collaborative premise. I had read Carol Gilligan's *In a Different Voice* (1982), and had been struck by the idea that in making moral choices, women felt the need to protect relationships while men are more concerned with what is 'right.' Connection seemed to be more highly prized by women than order, justice or truth. This was only the first of many insights that came to me from work that represented what is now being called cultural feminism.

While I did not wish to move back to what we used to call 'chicken soup' therapy, I began to have doubts about the distance between clients and therapists built into the family systems field. This represented a major shift for me. I had been one of the systemic faithful, and believed that family patterns in the present constrained and maintained the symptom. The machinery of pathology did not reside 'in' the individual but rather 'in' the family. My aim in therapy was to disrupt or alter that machinery. Thus, there was no need to develop any more of a personal relationship with people than was necessary to keep them from dropping out of treatment.

As I began to search for this different voice, I became increasingly uncomfortable with this technocratic coldness. Actually, I never entirely bought it. When unobserved, I would show a far more sympathetic side to clients than my training allowed. I would show my feelings, even weep. I called this practice 'corny therapy,' and never told my supervisors about it. But within the past few years I began to feel, 'Why not?' Others, like the researchers at the Stone Center in Wellesley, were making empathy creditworthy again. I began to talk with other women and found that they too used to do secretly what I did and also had pet names for this practice.

I also allowed myself to be influenced by my own previous experiences in therapy. Perhaps I was unlucky, but my encounters with clienthood had usually humiliated and intimidated me. At the very least they reinforced an idea of myself as a poor human being. Partly in reaction to these experiences, I started to look for ways to make clients feel more comfortable. Where appropriate, I would share stories from my own life. I would openly assume responsibility if the client had a complaint about the therapy, rather than treating it as evidence of resistance. I insisted on asking about expectations of therapy the client might have, and invited questions about my own work. If I felt stuck, especially if it seemed that a personal issue of mine were getting in the way, I would throw that idea into the conversation, which often did wonders to move things along.

In addition, I began to see few hierarchical distinctions except those afforded by the difference between positions in a lateral sense. In other words, center and edge replaced up and down. The attempt to honor where people stood and how they saw things became a constant reminder that participants in therapy had their own expertise. A value was placed, thereby, on a participatory experience validated by the expression of many voices, rather than by a reliance on the voice of an expert.

At many points, my evolving position outran my ability to translate it into practice. I continued to 'think Zen' but couldn't always figure out how to 'do Zen.' Then a colleague from Norway, Tom Andersen, came up with an amazing yet simple idea: the Reflecting Team (Andersen, 1987). The expedient of asking the family to listen while the team discussed the family and then asking the family to comment back, suddenly changed everything. The professional was no longer a protected species, observing 'pathological' families from behind a screen or talking about them in the privacy of an office. The assumption of normal social science, that the expert had a superior position from which a correct appraisal could be made, went crashing. For me, at least, the world of therapy altered overnight.

The Word 'Reflexive'

In trying to verbalize what I was experiencing, I found that I was turning increasingly to the word reflexive. This word has been applied to communication theory by Cronen et al. (1982) in their idea of reflexive discourse, and to systemic therapy by Karl Tomm (1987), in his category of reflexive questioning. However, I do not wish to elevate reflexive into another piece of jargon. In *The Random House Dictionary* the word is defined quite simply as 'the bending or folding back of a part upon itself.'

A picture synonym might be a figure eight, which is the sign for infinity and which I saw as an advance on the old idea of the circle or spiral. You had a place for the inner dialogue of persons as well as an intersection representing the forum where they met and spoke. And the figure suggests a moving trajectory when placed in the context of social discourse, congruent with the new emphasis on narrative in the human disciplines and flow in the physical sciences.

Applying the concept of reflexivity to relationships, one could use the ideal of partnership. To me the word implies that there is an equity in regard to participation even though the parties may have different positions or different traits. I have taken this last notion from Riane Eisler's book, *The Chalice and the Blade* (1987), where she presents a partnership model for human societies. An example she gives of this kind of equality is the Olympic Games of the Mycenaean Empire, where men and women competed in jumping over the horns of a bull.

Abandoning attempts at finding a title or a symbol, one might say that the formats that are most characteristic of this new approach all 'fold back upon themselves.' The developments around the Reflecting Team, the use of reflecting conversations and reflexive questioning, the prevalence of 'co-' prefixes to describe a therapeutic conversation ('co-author,' 'co-evolve'), indicate a preference for a mutually influenced process between consultant and inquirer as opposed to one that is hierarchical and unidirectional. In particular, this approach calls into question the high-level status of the professional.

Making the Expert Disappear

My first introduction to the non-expert position was when I first began to watch interviews by Harlene Anderson and Harry Goolishian of the Galveston Family Institute. Their approach has significantly influenced my own, but there was a time when I simply didn't understand what they were doing. I knew they believed that directive therapy models were pathologizing, but their own interviews were so non-goal-oriented that they seemed to do nothing and go nowhere. Their interviewing methods were equally unorthodox. The therapist might talk to one person in a family for a whole session, shocking persons like myself who had been trained in a structural approach. Always looking for the right pigeonhole, I called this new style 'imperceptible therapy.'

Indeed, the hallmark of the Galveston group is a kind of deliberate ignorance. When they describe what they do or how they teach, they state that they come from a position of 'not knowing.' This often irritates people who watch them work, because it seems so clearly not true that they 'don't know.' Their position, however, fits with postmodern ideas about narrative. In relating narrative theory to therapy, Gergen (1991) has observed that traditional therapists believe that there are 'essences' in the human experience that must be captured in some kind of narrative and offered to clients in place of their old, illusory narratives. Going in, the therapist already has some idea of what these essences are.

Postmodern therapists do not believe in essences. Knowledge, being socially arrived at, changes and renews itself in each moment of interaction. There are no prior meanings hiding in stories or texts. A therapist with this view will expect a new and hopefully more useful narrative to surface during the conversation, but will see this narrative as spontaneous rather than planned. The conversation, not the therapist, is its author. This, I think, is the sense in which the Galveston group uses not knowing.

Not knowing in this model is often accompanied by 'not talking' or not talking in the usual way. A good example is the interviewing style developed by Tom Andersen, Anna Margareta Flam, Magnus Hald, and others in Norway. Their questions or comments are marked by tentativeness, hesitancy and by long periods of silence. Often, the voice of the interviewer sinks so low that it is difficult to hear. They tend to begin their sentences with 'Could it be that?' or 'What if?' At first I thought this strange way of talking was due either to their difficulties with our language or else a cultural difference that came from the well-known modesty of the Norwegian personality. This turns out to be untrue. The interviewing method embodies in a most graphic way the deliberate immolation of the professional self, and the effect on clients is to encourage both participation and invention.

Let me end this section by saying that the idea of reducing the status of the interviewer is also a postmodern one. I recently read a collection of studies of research interviewing edited by postmodern researcher Eliot Mishler (1986). In one of his chapters he looks at the methods of Marianne Paget, herself a researcher, and quotes her description of a project in which she asks women artists about their own creative process:

> Reflectively examining the form and quality of her questions, which were not standardized and predetermined by an interview schedule, [Paget] observes that they often have a hesitant and halting quality as she searches for ways to ask about what she wants to learn; they are formulated and reformulated over the course of the interview. She suggests that this way of questioning may allow for and encourage replies that are equally searching, hesitant and formulated in the process of answering; that is, she creates a situation where the respondent too is engaged in a search for understanding. Paget refers also to the significance of her silences for how her respondent comes to tell her story in her own way, noting that at many points, for example, when the respondent paused, she remained silent when she 'might have entered the stream of speech.' (Mishler, 1986: 96–7)

Therapist Narratives

There is above all a reflexive loop between professional and client that includes the therapist's own working philosophy. Social constructionists hold firmly to the idea that there are no incontrovertible social truths, only stories about the world that we tell ourselves and others. Most therapists have a story about how problems develop and are solved or dis-solved.

Ben Furman (forthcoming) challenges this idea when he says that first we find a hypothesis, then we base an intervention on it. He says that the reverse is usually the case. *We go in with an intervention already in mind and then come up with a hypothesis that supports it.* For instance, if a therapist uses a psychodynamic framework, she will assume that her job is to help someone work through a trauma of the past and will therefore look for a narrative that shows a developmental deficit. Or a family therapist may believe that problems are related to improper hierarchies in the family structure and will propose altering coalitions between members who are in different generation lines. There are many such examples of therapist narratives.

I was playing with this idea in relation to Pearce and Cronen's levels of communication, mentioned above, which they divide into speech act, episode, relationship, lifescript, family myth, and cultural program. Each of these levels can be viewed horizontally, that is, as contexts for one another. A particular sequence between two people can be the context for a child's temper tantrum or it can be the other way around. The segment of communication a therapist most characteristically focuses on will tell us more about the therapist than about the family.

To cite instances, some therapists, like the Milan Associates, go after what they see as a family myth. Others target the individual's lifescript. Still others go in at the level of the speech act, reflecting back a word used by the client and racheting it bit by bit toward one that opens up more possibilities. I saw a videotape of Goolishian and Anderson speaking with a client who had been viewed as a 'young bag lady' and who spent much of her time sitting in a dark closet. During the conversation, the woman changed her complaint from a 'boredom sensation' to feeling 'unhappy' or 'depressed.' This was one of the events of the session that made it possible to alter the description of the client from a 'crazy' person to someone who was suffering from being alone.

Considerations about which level of communication a therapist goes in on can explain some conflicts in the field. Take the objection raised by feminist family therapists to systemic practice. They feel that in cases of battering, seeing the couple together absolves the man from responsibility and blames the woman. This view is congruent with going in on the level of the *episode*. In this context, the violence is wrong and must stop. The woman should not be seen together with the man lest it be implied that she is as responsible for the battering as he is. But if one goes in on the level of the *relationship*, which is what systemic therapists do, then one sees the interlock of behaviors over time. This view may empower the woman to be able to do some things differently; at the very least it relieves her of the title of victim.

Of course, no level is more true than the other; it is just that a different solution to the problem falls out of which one is focused on. It may be that the episode level will supersede the relationship level because stopping the violence takes priority. There are also feminists who prefer going in at the level of the cultural program, saying that to treat the woman as a person who needs therapy is to remain apolitical and to inadvertently support the status quo.

Associative Forms

But the danger in any scheme that divides up social interaction is that we too often choose one category and then start to believe in it. We need a method that prevents us from making such a choice except as intention and context cause us to do so. In therapy, one way to build in the requisite doubt is to set up a situation where a plurality of stories is encouraged and associative formats keep meanings unfixed. This is happening all over now. It is striking how many therapists are showing a new interest in reflecting modes, associative modes and metaphoric modes of doing therapy.

Tom Andersen, for instance, often uses images to describe people's views and actions. I am thinking of an interview of a couple, one of whom was Buddhist and the other Christian. During a team reflection, Tom offered an image of 'two beautiful smiling suns.' He followed this idea with an incantation that went: 'Let go the sun, let rise the sun.' To my literal mind, he was suggesting that a solar system with two suns might have a problem, and indeed they did seem to be locked into a struggle of wills. Now, I know that I am only imposing my own understanding. According to a follow-up, the couple merely remembered the interview as being very useful, and did not comment on the symbolism at all. The reflection stayed ambiguous, allowing the couple to associate to the images according to their own views.

I, myself, encourage people to play with stories, and will offer some of my own to push the idea along. I admit that my stories tend to be positive and transformative, meaning that I try to turn what is experienced as a difficulty into something that contains some hope. Often, in the New Age community where I live, the idea of karma comes up. I might then describe a couple's problem as a 'karmic issue' and suggest that it might have to do with a dilemma that did not get resolved in past generations, if not past lives. For good or ill, they have the opportunity to work on it with each other. If they are successful, the children of the next generation can move on to a new challenge.

This playing with associative forms – stories, ideas, images, dreams – has always been part of therapy, but only now has it had a foundation in one of the descriptive human disciplines, which is what I take social constructionism in its widest form to be. As I continue to check in with the work of persons who are experimenting with these newer models, I am struck by the emphasis on linguistic play, and wonder if we are not seeing a new *Gestalt* for systemic consultation. The Galveston group is currently using the term 'collaborative language systems' approach; Gergen has suggested 'narrative therapy;' I and others have been using the word 'reflexive.' Yet other terms are undoubtedly being tested out, as the social and linguistic process that forms new fields of study wends its way through time.

An Ethic of Participation

In ending, I would like to return to the contribution of the postmodern ethnographers. Clifford and Marcus (1986) take the idea of the transcendental or objective observer and replace it with the idea of a collaboration in which no one has the final word. Implicitly, the nature of the conversation changes. In their words:

> Because post-modern ethnography privileges 'discourse' over 'text,' it foregrounds dialogue as opposed to monologue, and emphasizes the cooperative and collaborative nature of the ethnographic situation. . . . In fact, it rejects the ideology of 'observer–observed,' there being nothing observed and no one who is observer. There is instead the mutual, dialogical production of a discourse, of a story of sorts. (Clifford and Marcus, 1986: 126)

Statements like these suggest that an ethic of participation rather than a search for 'the cause' or 'the truth' is now emerging as a central value of social thought and action. Applied to therapy, this would put our goals in a frankly political light. But I would resist the idea that we should espouse a new kind of Marxism. Even in espousing emancipation, nobody has the corner on what the ideal discourse should be or which social problem is the most pressing. In general, our aim should be a critical stance that favors becoming aware of the power relations hidden within the assumptions of any social discourse, including critical discourse itself. Thus, not just our theory but our practice should reflect an awareness of hidden power relationships. It is not sufficient simply to stop blaming women or to empower ethnic groups. Activism, especially in a 'good cause,' runs the risk of reinforcing the illusions of power of the professional herself.

Here I return finally to the dangers of professionalism. Masson (1990), as I have said, questions the elevated status of the health professional. He quotes from *Profession of Medicine* (1972) by medical sociologist Eliot Freidson:

> It is my own opinion that the profession's role in a free society should be limited to contributing the technical information men [sic] need to have to make their own decisions on the basis of their own values. When he preempts the authority to direct, even constrain men's [sic] decisions on the basis of his own values, the professional is no longer an expert but rather a member of a new privileged class disguised as expert. (Freidson, 1972: 382)

I respectfully agree with that statement, except for the use of the word 'men' to represent all people. As Masson points out elsewhere in his book, the subjects of the early versions of the talking cure we call psychotherapy were mostly women, and still are. In a free society, women as well as men must have access to the thinking of the persons they consult, in order to prevent 'professionals disguised as experts' from making their choices for them. The reflexive, reflecting and reflective formats I am addressing in this chapter go part of the way to make this possible.

References

Andersen, T. (1987) 'The reflecting team', *Family Process*, 26: 415–28.
Anderson, H. and Goolishian, H. (1988) 'Human systems as linguistic systems', *Family Process*, 27: 371–95.
Bateson, G. (1972) *Steps to an Ecology of Mind*. New York: Ballantine.
Chatwin, B. (1987) *The Songlines*. London: Jonathan Cape.
Clifford, J. and Marcus, G. (1986) *Writing Culture*. Berkeley, CA: University of California Press.
Cronen, V.E., Johnson, K.M. and Lannamann, J.W. (1982) 'Paradoxes, double-binds, and reflexive loops', *Family Process*, 21: 91–112.
Derrida, J. (1978) *Writing and Difference*. Chicago: University of Chicago Press.
Eisler, Riane (1987) *The Chalice and the Blade*. New York: Basic Books.
Foucault, M. (1975) *The Archeology of Knowledge*. London: Tavistock.
Foucault, M. (1977) *Discipline and Punish*. London: Allen Lane.
Freidson, E. (1972) *Profession of Medicine*. New York: Dodd Mead.
Furman, B. (forthcoming) 'Hindsight – the reverse psychology of the therapist', *Journal of Family Therapy*.
Gadamer, H. (1975) *Truth and Method*, tr. G. Barden and J. Cumming. New York: Continuum.
Geertz, C. (1983) *Local Knowledge*. New York: Basic Books.
Gergen, K. (1982) *Toward Transformation in Social Knowledge*. New York: Springer-Verlag.
Gergen, K. (1985) 'The social constructionist movement in modern psychology', *American Psychologist*, 40: 266–75.
Gergen, K. (1991) *The Saturated Self*. New York: Basic Books.
Gilligan, C. (1982) *In a Different Voice*. Cambridge, MA: Harvard University Press.
Gleick, J. (1987) *Chaos*. New York: Penguin Books.
Gould, S.J. (1980) *The Panda's Thumb*. New York: W.W. Norton.
Haley, J. (1963) *Strategies of Psychotherapy*. New York: Grune & Stratton.
Harré, R. (1984) *Personal Being*. Cambridge, MA: Harvard University Press.
Harré, R. (1986) *The Social Construction of Emotions*. New York: Basil Blackwell.
Kearney, P., Byrne, N. and McCarthy, I. (1989) 'Just metaphors: marginal illuminations in a colonial retreat', *Family Therapy Case Studies*, 4: 17–31.
Lax, W. and Lussardi, D. (1989) 'Systemic family therapy with young children in the family: use of the reflecting team', in J.J. Zilback (ed.), *Children in Family Therapy*, New York: Haworth.
Masson, J. (1990) *Against Therapy*. New York: Fontana Paperbacks.
Mishler, E. (1986) *Research Interviewing: Context and Narrative*. Cambridge, MA: Harvard University Press.
Pearce, W.B. and Cronen, V.E. (1980) *Communication, Action and Meaning: the Creation of Social Realities*. New York: Praeger.
Prigogine, I. and Stengers, I. (1984) *Order out of Chaos*. New York: Bantam Books.
Shotter, J. and Gergen, K. (eds) (1989) *Texts of Identity*. London: Sage.

Tomm, K. (1987) 'Interventive interviewing: Part II. Reflexive questioning as a means to enable self-healing', *Family Process*, 26: 167–84.

von Glasersfeld, E. (1984) 'An introduction to radical constructivism', in P. Watzlawick (ed.), *The Invented Reality*. New York: W.W. Norton.

Whitehead, A.N. and Russell, B. (1910–13) *Principia Mathematica*, 2nd edn (3 vols.). Cambridge: Cambridge University Press.

2

The Client is the Expert: a Not-Knowing Approach to Therapy

Harlene Anderson and Harold Goolishian

That is an interesting and complicated question. If a person like you had found a way to talk with me when I was first going crazy . . . at all the times of my delusion that I was a grand military figure . . . I knew that this [delusion] was a way that I was trying to tell myself that I could overcome my panic and fear. . . . Rather than talk with me about this, my doctors would always ask me what I call conditional questions. . . . [To which the therapist inquired, 'What are conditional questions?']

You [the professionals] are always checking me out . . . checking me out, to see if I knew what you knew rather than find a way to talk with me. You would ask, 'Is this an ashtray?' to see if I knew or not. It was as if you knew and wanted to see if I could . . . that only made me more frightened, more panicked. If you could have talked with the 'me' that knew how frightened I was. If you had been able to understand how crazy I had to be so that I could be strong enough to deal with this life threatening fear . . . then we could have handled that crazy general.

The words are those of a revolving-door treatment failure, a thirty-year-old man, Bill, who had been hospitalized on several occasions for what had been diagnosed as paranoid schizophrenia. His previous treatment contacts had been unsuccessful. He had remained angry and suspicious, and he had been unable to work for some time. Through much of his adult life he was sporadically on 'maintenance doses' of psychoactive medication. At the time he first consulted one of the authors he had once more been fired from a teaching job. More recently, the man had greatly improved and had been able to hold down a job. He insisted that his current therapist was different from the others and that he now felt more capable of managing his life. It was this conversational context that influenced the question, 'What, if anything, could your previous therapists have done differently that would have been more useful to you?'

In this conversation Bill was referring to his experience of therapy as practiced by the authors and their colleagues at the Houston Galveston Family Institute. This is a therapy that has been evolving over the last twenty-five years. During this time the thinking has undergone a major shift away from the usual theories of social science that typically inform psychotherapy. The ideas in this chapter represent a current interest in an interpretive and hermeneutic approach to understanding therapy. Specifically, the therapist position of 'not-knowing' and its relevance to the notions of therapeutic conversation and conversational questions is discussed.

From Social Structure to the Generation of Human Meaning

Over the last several decades, developments in the systemic therapies have attempted to develop a conceptual framework that bypassed the earlier empiricism of theories of therapy. These developments shifted family therapy thinking to what is called second-order cybernetics and ultimately constructivism. Of late it has been our conclusion (Anderson and Goolishian, 1988, 1989, 1990a) that there are serious limits to this cybernetic paradigm as it informs therapy practice. These limits are principally in the mechanical metaphors underlying cybernetic feedback theory. We note that within this metaphor there is little opportunity to deal with the experience of an individual. We also see limited utility in the increasingly popular cognitive and constructivist models that ultimately define humans as simple *information-processing machines* as opposed to *meaning-generating beings* (Anderson and Goolishian, 1988, 1990a; Goolishian and Anderson, 1981).

Meanwhile, our developing theories of therapy are rapidly moving toward a more hermeneutic and interpretive position. This is a view that emphasizes 'meanings' as created and experienced by individuals in conversation with one another. In pursuit of this new theoretical base, we have developed a number of ideas that move our understanding and explanations of therapy into the arena of shifting systems that exist only in the vagaries of discourse, language and conversation. It is a position that is nested in the domains of semantics and narrative. Our current position leans heavily on the view that human action takes place in a reality of understanding that is created through social construction and dialogue (Anderson and Goolishian, 1985; Anderson et al., 1986a; Anderson and Goolishian, 1988). From this position, people live, and understand their living, through socially constructed narrative realities that give meaning and organization to their experience. It is a world of human language and discourse. Earlier, we have talked about these ideas, about systems of meaning, under the rubric of problem-determined systems, problem-organizing dissolving systems, and language systems (Anderson and Goolishian, 1985; Anderson et al., 1986a, b; Anderson and Goolishian, 1988; Goolishian and Anderson, 1987).

Our current narrative position leans heavily on the following premises (Anderson and Goolishian, 1988; Goolishian and Anderson, 1990).

First, human systems are language-generating and, simultaneously, meaning-generating systems. Communication and discourse define social organization. A socio-cultural system is the product of social communication, rather than communication being a product of structural organization. All human systems are linguistic systems and are best described by those participating in it, rather than by outside 'objective' observers. *The therapeutic system is such a linguistic system.*

Secondly, meaning and understanding are socially constructed. We do not arrive at, or have, meaning and understanding until we take communicative action; that is, engage in some meaning-generating discourse or dialogue within the system for which the communication has relevance. *A therapeutic system is a system for which the communication has a relevance specific to its dialogical exchange.*

Thirdly, any system in therapy is one that has dialogically coalesced around some 'problem.' This system will be engaged in evolving language and meaning specific to itself, specific to its organizations and specific to its dis-solution around 'the problem.' In this sense, the therapy system is a system that is distinguished by the evolving co-created meaning, 'the problem,' rather than an arbitrary social structure, such as a family. *The therapeutic system is a problem-organizing, problem-dis-solving system.*

Fourthly, therapy is a linguistic event that takes place in what we call a therapeutic conversation. The therapeutic conversation is a mutual search and exploration through dialogue, a two-way exchange, a criss-crossing of ideas in which new meanings are continually evolving toward the 'dis-solving' of problems, and thus, the dissolving of the therapy system and hence the *problem-organizing problem-dis-solving system.*

Fifthly, the role of the therapist is that of a conversational artist – an architect of the dialogical process – whose expertise is in the arena of creating a space for and facilitating a dialogical conversation. *The therapist is a participant-observer and a participant-facilitator of the therapeutic conversation.*

Sixthly, the therapist exercises this therapeutic art through the use of conversational or therapeutic questions. The therapeutic question is the primary instrument to facilitate the development of conversational space and the dialogical process. To accomplish this *the therapist exercises an expertise in asking questions from a position of 'not-knowing' rather than asking questions that are informed by method and that demand specific answers.*

Seventhly, problems we deal with in therapy are actions that express our human narratives in such a way that they diminish our sense of agency and personal liberation. Problems are concerned or alarmed objection to a state of affairs for which we are unable to define competent action (agency) for ourselves. In this sense, *problems exist in language and problems are unique to the narrative context from which they derive their meaning.*

Eighthly, change in therapy is the dialogical creation of new narrative, and therefore the opening of opportunity for new agency. The transformational power of narrative rests in its capacity to re-relate the events of our lives in the context of new and different meaning. *We live in and through the narrative identities that we develop in conversation with one another.* The skill of the therapist is the expertise to participate in this process. Our 'self' is always changing.

These premises place heavy emphasis on the role of language, conversation, self, and story as they influence our clinical theory and work. Today there is much interest among therapists about these issues in the continuing attempts to understand and describe clinical work. There are, however, very different views emerging. Some writers emphasize the stability over time of the personal narratives that we work with in therapy. We, on the other hand, emphasize the always changing, evolving, and dialogical basis of the story of the self. In taking this position, we find ourselves emphasizing the therapist position of *not-knowing* in the understanding that develops through therapeutic conversation. The concept of not-knowing is in contrast to therapist understanding that is based in pre-held theoretical narratives.

Not-knowing requires that our understandings, explanations, and interpretations in therapy not be limited by prior experiences or theoretically formed truths, and knowledge. This description of the not-knowing position is influenced by hermeneutic and interpretive theories and the related concepts of social constructionism, language, and narrative (Gergen, 1982; Shapiro and Sica, 1984; Shotter and Gergen, 1989; Wachterhauser, 1986). This hermeneutic position represents the theory and practice of interpretation. Fundamentally, it is a philosophical stance that 'maintains that understanding is always interpretive . . . that there is no privileged standpoint for understanding' (Wachterhauser, 1986: 399) and that 'language and history are always both conditions and limits to understanding' (Wachterhauser, 1986: 6). Meaning and understanding are socially constructed by persons in conversation, in language with one another. Thus, human action takes place in a reality of understanding that is created through social construction and dialogue. These socially constructed narrative realities give meaning and organization to one's experience (Gergen, 1982; Shotter and Gergen, 1989; Anderson and Goolishian, 1988).

Therapeutic Conversation: a Dialogical Mode

The process of therapy based on this stance, on this dialogical view, is what we call a therapeutic conversation. Therapeutic conversation refers to an endeavor in which there is a mutual search for understanding and exploration through dialogue of 'problems.' Therapy, and hence the therapeutic conversation, entails an 'in there together' process. People talk 'with' one another and not 'to' one another. It is a mechanism through which the therapist and the client participate in the co-development of new meanings, new realities, and new narratives. The therapist's role, expertise, and emphasis is to develop a free conversational space and to facilitate an emerging dialogical process in which this 'newness' can occur. The emphasis is not to produce change but to open space for conversation. In this hermeneutic view, change in therapy is represented by the dialogical creation of new narrative. As dialogue evolves, new narrative, the 'not-yet-said' stories, are mutually created (Anderson and Goolishian, 1988). Change in story and self-narrative is an inherent consequence of dialogue.

Achieving this special kind of therapeutic conversation requires that the therapist adopt a *not-knowing* position. The not-knowing position entails a general attitude or stance in which the therapist's actions communicate an abundant, genuine curiosity. That is, the therapist's actions and attitudes express a need to know more about what has been said, rather than convey preconceived opinions and expectations about the client, the problem, or what must be changed. The therapist, therefore, positions himself or herself in such a way as always to be in the state of 'being informed' by the client ('client' in this chapter refers to one or more persons). This 'being informed' position is critical to the assumption in hermeneutic theory that the dialogical creation of meaning is always a continuing process. In not-knowing the therapist adopts an interpretive stance that relies on the continuing analysis of experience as it is occurring in context.

The therapist does not 'know,' a priori, the intent of any action, but rather must rely on the explanation made by the client. By learning, by curiosity, and by taking the client's story seriously, the therapist joins with the client in a mutual exploration of the client's understanding and experience. Thus the process of interpretation, the struggle to understand in therapy, becomes collaborative. Such a position allows the therapist always to maintain continuity with the client's position and to grant primary importance to the client's world views, meanings, and understandings. This allows clients room for conversational movement and space, since they no longer have to promote, protect, or convince the therapist of their view. This relaxing, this releasing process, is similar to a notion attributed to Bateson: specifically, in order to entertain new or novel ideas, there has to be room for the familiar. This does not mean that the therapist develops and offers the new ideas or the new meanings. They emerge from the dialogue between the therapist and the client and thus are co-created. The therapist simply becomes part of the circle of meaning or hermeneutic circle (for discussions of the circle of meaning or the hermeneutic circle, see Wachterhauser, 1986: 23–4; Warnke, 1987: 83–7).

In therapy, the hermeneutic circle, or circle of meaning, refers to the dialogical process through which interpretation begins with the therapist's preconceptions. The therapist always enters the therapeutic arena with expectations about the issues to be discussed that are based on the therapist's prior experiences and the referral information. Therapy always begins with a question based on this already created meaning. The meaning that emerges in therapy is understood from this whole (the therapist's preconceptions), but this whole is, in turn, understood from the emerging parts (the client's story). Therapist and client move back and forth within this circle of meaning. They move from part to whole to part again, thus remaining within the circle. In this process, new meaning emerges for both therapist and client.

To 'not-know' is *not* to have an unfounded or unexperienced judgment, but refers more widely to the set of assumptions, the meanings, that the therapist brings to the clinical interview. The excitement for the therapist is in learning the uniqueness of each individual client's narrative truth, the coherent truths in their storied lives. This means that therapists are always prejudiced by their experience, but that they must listen in such a way that their pre-experience does not close them to the full meaning of the client's descriptions of their experience. This can only happen if the therapist approaches each clinical experience from the position of not-knowing. To do otherwise is to search for regularities and common meaning that may validate the therapist's theory but invalidate the uniqueness of the clients' stories and thus their very identity.

The development of new meaning relies on the novelty and the newness, the not-knowing of what it is that the therapist is about to hear. This requires that the therapist have a high capacity simultaneously to attend to both inner and outer conversation. Gadamer has stated:

> A person trying to understand a text is prepared for it to tell him something. That is why a hermeneutically trained mind must be, from the start, sensitive to the text's quality of newness. But this kind of sensitivity involves neither 'neutrality' in the matter of the object nor the extinction of one's self, but the conscious assimilation of one's own bias, so that the text may present itself in all its newness and thus be able to assert its own truth against one's foremeanings. (1975: 238)

Interpreting and understanding, then, is always a dialogue between therapist and client and is not the result of predetermined, theoretical narratives that are essential elements of the therapist's world of meaning.

Central to the many linguistic and socially derived narratives that operate in behavioral organization are those that contain within them the elements articulated as self-descriptions, or first-person narratives. The development of these self-defining narratives takes place in a social and local context involving conversation with significant others, including oneself. That is, people live in and through the ever-changing narrative identities that they develop in conversation with one another. Individuals derive their sense of social agency for action from these dialogically derived narratives. Narratives permit (or inhibit) a personal perception of freedom or competency to make sense and to act (agency). The 'problems' dealt with in therapy can be thought of as emanating from social narratives and self-definitions that do not yield an agency that is effective for the tasks implicit in their self-narratives. Therapy provides opportunity for the development of new and different narratives that permit an expanded range of alternative agency for 'problem' dis-solution. It is the accomplishment of this new narrative agency that is experienced as 'freedom' and liberation by those who view therapy as successful.

At the same time this liberation requires a shift away from the traditional concept of therapist–client separation. We view client and therapist as being together in a system that evolves over the course of the therapeutic conversation. Meaning becomes a function of their relationship. From this perspective, client and therapist are seen as mutually affecting each other's meaning, and meaning becomes a byproduct of mutuality. Client and therapist are dependent in the moment-to-moment creation of new understandings. In effect, they generate a dialogically shared meaning that exists only at the moment in the therapeutic conversation which continues to change throughout time.

Conversational Questions: Keeping Understanding *on the Way*

Traditionally, questions in therapy are influenced by the therapist's expertise, an expertise reflective of a theoretical understanding and knowledge of psychological phenomenon and human behavior. That is, the therapist explains (diagnoses) and intervenes (treats) the phenomenon or behavior from this prior knowledge base, from generalized theory. In doing this therapists emphasize (and protect) their own narrative coherence rather than the client's. This knowing position is similar to what Bruner (1984) distinguishes as a 'paradigmatic posture' versus a 'narrative posture.' In the paradigmatic posture the interpreter focuses on explanation that emphasizes a denotative understanding, general categories, and broader rules. For example, the use of concepts such as 'id,' 'super ego,' or 'symptom functionality' are the type of broad categories often developed in the process of therapeutic understanding. To ask questions in therapy from a knowing position fits with Bruner's paradigmatic posture in that the response is limited to the therapist's pre-held theoretical perspective. In contrast, the not-knowing position – similar to Bruner's 'narrative posture' – suggests a different kind of expertise; one that is limited to the process of therapy rather than to the content (diagnosis) and change (treatment) of pathological structure.

The therapeutic or conversational question is the primary tool that the therapist uses to express this expertise. It is the means through which the therapist remains on the road to understanding. Therapeutic questions always stem from a need to know more about what has just been said. Thus, the therapist is always being informed by the client's stories and is always learning new language and new narrative. Questions that are overly directed by a methodology risk squelching the therapist's opportunity to be led by the clients into their own worlds. The basis of therapeutic questioning is not simply to interrogate the client or to gather information for validating or supporting hypotheses. Rather, the aim is to allow the client to lead the therapist's own range of understanding into question.

In this hermeneutic sense, during the process of psychotherapy, the therapist is not applying a method of questioning but rather is continually adjusting his or her understanding to that of the other person. Thus, the therapist is always in the process of understanding, always on the way to understanding and always changing. Not-knowing questions reflect this therapist position and this therapeutic process. Thus, the therapist does not dominate the client with expert psychological knowledge so much as he or she is led by, and learns from, the expertise of the client. The therapist's task, therefore, is not to analyze but to attempt to understand, to understand from the changing perspective of the client's life experience. The object in hermeneutic understanding is to let the phenomena lead. Bill's words at the beginning of this chapter seem indeed a lament for just this sort of understanding.

Local Meaning and Local Dialogue

The process of questions generated from the position of 'not-knowing' results in the development of a locally (dialogically) constructed understanding and a local (dialogic) vocabulary. Local refers to the language, the meaning, and the understanding developed between persons in dialogue, rather than broadly held cultural sensibilities. It is through local understanding that one makes intimate sense out of memories, perceptions, and histories. Through this process the space for continuing new narrative with new history – and thus new future – remains open.

The issue of local meaning and local language is important because it seems that there is a range of experiences and a way of knowing these experiences that is sufficiently different from 'knower' to 'knower' which will vary from therapy to therapy. Garfinkel (1967) and Shotter (1990) make the strong point that in any conversation the participants will refuse to understand what is being said other than within the meaning rules which have been negotiated within the context of the immediate dialogical exchange itself. Meaning and understanding is, according to Garfinkel, always a matter of negotiation between the participants. The traditional paradigmatic language of general psychological and family theory can never be sufficient to explain or understand locally derived meaning. To attempt to understand the first-person experiences that therapists deal with in therapy through the use of general psychological and family models as well as the associated vocabularies leads to a reduction to stereotypical, theoretical concepts. In using such concepts, such pre-knowledge, to understand the client's narrative, therapists often lose touch with the client's locally developed meanings and can constrain the client's narrative. The therapist, therefore, becomes an expert in asking questions about the stories told in therapy in a way that the questions relate to the reasons for consultation (for example, the problem as reported). To do this requires that the therapist remain attentive to the development of, and understand within the client's language, the narrative and the metaphors that are specific to the problem.

What Therapeutic Questions are *Not*

Therapeutic questions from a not-knowing position are in many ways similar to so-called Socratic questions. They are not rhetorical or pedagogical questions. Rhetorical questions give their own answers; pedagogical questions imply the direction of the answer. Questions in traditional therapy are often of this nature; that is, they imply direction (correct reality), and leave the client a hint in order to reach the 'correct' answer.

In contrast, not-knowing questions bring into the open something unknown and unforeseen to the realm of possibility. Therapeutic questions are impelled by difference in understanding and are drawn from the future by the as-yet unrealized possibility of a community of knowledge. In asking from this position the therapist is able to move with the 'not-yet-said' (Anderson and Goolishian, 1988). Therapeutic questions also imply many possible answers. Conversation in therapy is the unfolding of these 'yet-unsaid' possibilities, these 'yet-unsaid' narratives. This process accelerates the evolution of new personal realities and agency that emerge from the evolving of new narratives. New meaning, and therefore new agency, is experienced as change in individual and social organization.

A Case Example: 'How long have you had this disease?'

A frustrated psychiatric colleague requested a consultation on an impenetrable case – a forty-year-old man who chronically felt he had a contagious disease and was perpetually infecting others, even killing them, with it. Multiple negative medical consultations and psychotherapies had failed to relieve the man of his conviction and fear about his infectious disease. Although he talked of difficulties in his marriage (his wife didn't understand him) and his inability to work, his primary concern was his disease and the ever-spreading contamination. He was frightened, distraught, and unable to be at peace because of the harm and destruction that he knew he was spreading.

Early in his story, wringing his hands, he told about being diseased and infectious. The consultant (Goolishian) asked him, 'How long have you had this disease?' Looking astonished and after a long pause, the man began to tell his story. It began, he said, when he was a young merchant seaman. While in the Far East he had sexual contact with a prostitute. Afterwards, remembering the lectures on sexually transmitted diseases that were given to the crewmen on the boat, he feared that his lust had exposed him to one of these horrible sexual diseases and that he required treatment. Panicked, he went to a local clinic for consultation. At this clinic, he explained his fears to a nurse who was from a religious order. She sent him away saying that they did not treat sexual perverts there – that he needed confession and God, not medicine. For a long time after that, ashamed and guilt-ridden, he kept his concerns to himself and confided in no one.

When he returned home from sea he was still frightened that he had contracted some disease but he could not bring himself to confide in anyone. He would appear at various medical clinics, ask for a physical examination and be told that he was in excellent shape. These negative reports convinced him that his disease was much worse because it was unknown to medical science. As his concerns grew he began to think that he was infectious and that he was contaminating others. This contamination of others became such a problem that he eventually realized that he was infecting others indirectly; for example, by viewing television or by listening on the radio. He continued to consult physicians, but the physical and laboratory examinations were always negative. By now he was being told, not only that he did *not* have a disease but that he *did* have a mental condition, and he was referred on several occasions for psychiatric consultation. Over time he became convinced that no one understood the seriousness of his contamination, the extent of his disease, nor the destruction he was causing.

As the consultant continued to show interest in his dilemma, the man became more relaxed. Somewhat animated, he elaborated his story and joined with the consultant's curiosity. The consultant did not simply take a history or re-collect events of the static past. His curiosity remained with the man's reality (the disease and contamination problem). The intent was not to challenge the man's reality or the man's story, but rather to learn about it, and to let it be re-told in a way that allowed the opportunity for new meaning and new narrative to emerge. In other words, the consultant's intent was not to talk or manipulate the man away from his ideas, but rather through not-knowing (non-negation and non-judgment) to provide a starting point for dialogue and the opening of conversational space.

Colleagues viewing the interview process were quite critical of this collaborative position and of questions like 'How long *have you had* this disease?' They feared that such questions have the effect of reinforcing the patient's 'hypochondriacal delusion.' Many suggested that a safer question would have been, 'How long *have you thought* you had this disease?'

The not-knowing position, however, precludes the stance that the man's story was delusional. He said he was sick. Thus, it was necessary to hear more, to learn more about his sickness, and to converse within this languaged reality. Being sensitive to and trying to understand the man's reality was an essential step in a continuous process towards establishing and maintaining a dialogue. It was critical that the consultant remain within the rules of meaning as developed in the local conversation and to talk and understand in the familiar language and vocabulary of the client. This is not the same as condoning or reifying another's reality. It is a conversational moving within the 'sense' of what has just been said. It moves with the narrative truth of the client's story rather than challenging it, and remains within the locally developed and locally negotiated meaning system.

To have asked a safer question like 'How long is it that you *think* you have been diseased?' would only have served to impose the consultant's predetermined or 'knowing' and 'paradigmatic' view that the disease was a figment of the man's imagination or a delusion and distortion in need of correction. In response to such a question the suspicious man would have been left to operate from his own preconceived ideas and expectations of the consultant. Most likely, once again, he would have felt misunderstood and alienated. The consultant would have been just one more in the line-up of professionals who could not believe and who asked 'conditional' questions. Misunderstanding and alienation are ingredients that close rather than open dialogue.

Upon leaving this interview, the man was asked by the referring psychiatrist (who had been observing) how the interview went. His immediate response was, 'You know, he believed me!' In a follow-up conversation, the psychiatrist described the continuing effect that the interview had on himself and the client. He said that the therapy sessions seemed less difficult and that the man's life situation was much better. Somehow, he said, whether or not the man was infected was no longer an issue. The man was now dealing with his marriage and unemployment problems and there had even been some conjoint sessions with the man's wife. The consultant's not-knowing opened a starting point for, a possibility for, a dialogical exchange between the client and himself, between the client and the psychiatrist, and between the psychiatrist and himself.

This does not suggest that the consultant's questions produced a miracle cure. Nor is it to suggest that any other question would force a further therapeutic impasse. No magical question or intervention can singularly influence the development of a life. No one question can open a dialogical space. Nor does the question itself cause someone to shift meaning, to have or not to have a new idea. But, rather, each question is an element of an overall process.

The therapist's central task is to find the question to which the immediate recounting of experience and narrative presents the answer. Such questions cannot be pre-planned or pre-known. What has just been told, what has just been recounted, is the answer to which the therapist must find the question. The developing therapeutic narrative is always presenting the therapist with the next question. From this perspective, questions in therapy are always driven by the immediate conversational event. To not-know means that the accumulated experience and understanding of the specific therapist is always undergoing interpretive change. It is in this local and continuing process of question and answer that a particular understanding or a particular narrative becomes a starting point for the new and 'not-yet-said.'

Summary

Therapeutic conversation and therapeutic questions that stem from the position of not-knowing become a collaborative effort of generating new meaning based on the linguistic and explanatory history of the client, as his or her story is continually retold and elaborated through the therapeutic dialogue. This kind of dialogical exchange facilitates the change in first-person narrative that is so necessary to change in therapy. New futures result from developing narratives that give new meanings and understandings to one's life and enable different agency. In therapy this is best accomplished by questions born of a genuine curiosity for that which is 'not-known' about that which has just been said.

Telling one's story is a re-presentation of experience; it is constructing history in the present. The re-presentation reflects the teller's re-description and re-explanation of the experience in response to what is not-known by the therapist. Each evolves together and influences the other, as well as the experience, and thus, the re-presentation of the experience. This does not mean that in the course of therapy therapists simply narrate what has already been known. They do not recover some identical picture or story. Rather, therapists explore the resources of the 'not-yet-said.' People have imaginative memory. Past accounts are retrieved in such a way that the power of countless new possibilities is invoked, and thus new fiction and new history are created. Imagination is constituted in the inventive power of language through the active process of conversation; the searching for the 'not-yet-said.'

In therapy, interpretation, the struggle to understand, is always a dialogue between client and therapist. It is not the result of predetermined theoretical narratives essential to the therapist's world of meaning. In attempting to understand the client the assumption must be made that the client has something to say, and that this something makes narrative sense, asserts its own truth, within the context of the client's developing story. The therapist's response to the sense of the client's story and its elements is in contradiction to the traditional position in therapy which is to respond to the nonsense, or pathology, of what has been said. In this process the newly co-authored narrative understanding must be in the ordinary language of the client. A therapeutic conversation is no more than a slowly evolving and detailed, concrete, individual life story stimulated by the therapist's position of not-knowing and the therapist's curiosity to learn. It is this curiosity and not-knowing that opens conversational space and thus increases the potential for the narrative development of new agency and personal freedom.

References

Anderson, H. and Goolishian, H. (1985) 'Systems consultation to agencies dealing with domestic violence', in L. Wynne, S. McDaniel and T. Weber (eds), *The Family Therapist as Consultant*. New York: Guilford Press.

Anderson, H. and Goolishian, H. (1988) 'Human systems as linguistic systems: evolving ideas about the implications for theory and practice', *Family Process*, 27: 371–93.

Anderson, H. and Goolishian, H. (1989) 'Conversations at Sulitjelma', *Newsletter, American Family Therapy Association*, Spring.

Anderson, H. and Goolishian, H. (1990a) 'Beyond cybernetics: comments on Atkinson and Heath's "Further thoughts on second-order family therapy"', *Family Process*, 29: 157–63.

Anderson, H. and Goolishian, H. (1990b) 'Chronic pain: the individual, the family, and the treatment system', *Houston Medicine*, 6: 104–10.

Anderson, H., Goolishian, H., Pulliam, G. and Winderman, L. (1986a) 'The Galveston Family Institute: some personal and historical perspectives', in D. Efron (ed.), *Journeys: Expansions of the Strategic and Systemic Therapies*. New York: Brunner/Mazel.

Anderson, H., Goolishian, H. and Winderman, L. (1986b) 'Problem determined systems: towards transformation in family therapy', *Journal of Strategic and Systemic Therapies*, 5: 1–14.

Bruner, J. (1984) 'Narrative and paradigmatic modes of thought', Invited address, American Psychological Association, Toronto, Aug.

Gadamer, H. (1975) *Truth and Method*. New York: Continuum.

Garfinkel, H. (1967) *Studies in Ethnomethodology*. Englewood Cliffs, NJ: Prentice-Hall.

Gergen, K. (1982) *Toward Transformation in Social Knowledge*. New York: Springer-Verlag.

Gergen, K. (1985) 'The social constructionist movement in modern psychology', *Amercian Psychologist*, 40: 266–75.

Gilligan, C. (1982) *In a Different Voice: Psychological Theory and Woman's Development*. Cambridge, MA: Harvard University Press.

Goolishian, H. (1990) 'Family therapy: an evolving story', *Contemporary Family Therapy: an International Journal*, 12 (3): 173–80.

Goolishian, H. and Anderson, H. (1981) 'Including non-blood related persons in treatment: who is the family to be treated?' in A. Gurman (ed.), *Questions and Answers in Family Therapy*. New York: Brunner/Mazel.

Goolishian, H. and Anderson, H. (1987) 'Language systems and therapy: an evolving idea', *Psychotherapy*, 24 (3S): 529–38.

Goolishian, H. and Anderson, H. (1990) 'Understanding the therapeutic system: from individuals and families to systems in language', in F. Kaslow (ed.), *Voices in Family Psychology*. Newbury Park, CA: Sage.

Shapiro, G. and Sica, A. (1984) *Hermeneutics*. Amherst, MA: University of Amherst Press.

Shotter, J. (1990) 'The myth of mind and the mistake of psychology', in W. Baker, M. Hyland, R. van Hezewijk and S. Terwee, *Recent Trends in Theoretical Psychology* vol. 2. New York: Springer-Verlag.

Shotter, J. and Gergen, K.J. (eds) (1989) *Texts of Identity*. London: Sage.

Wachterhauser, B.R. (1986) *Hermeneutics and Modern Philosophy*. New York: State University of New York Press.

Warnke, G. (1987) *Gadamer: Hermeneutics, Tradition and Reason*. Stanford, CA: Stanford University Press.

3

Therapeutic Process as the Social Construction of Change

Laura Fruggeri

The recognition of the constructive role of the observer in any process of observation, description, or knowledge represents a turning point in the broader scientific domain and, specifically, in the social sciences. In fact, the acknowledgement of the constructive function individuals have in their relationships with the world constitutes the foundation for unbinding scientific discourse from mechanistic elements as well as from the use of timeless logical and mathematical metaphors (Bateson, 1972, 1979; Bateson and Bateson, 1987). Knowledge emerges as an on-going self-referential construction; a recursion of descriptions that generate other descriptions (von Foerster, 1981). Individuals, in their processes of constructing the world, are bound by the beliefs, maps, and premises that they have about the world (Bateson, 1972; Maturana and Varela, 1987). The definition of knowledge as a self-referential process is the starting point for the elaboration of a scientific paradigm that cannot rely on objectivity, on one descriptive and accurate language, or on a universal conceptual framework (Ceruti, 1986). It is a paradigm that does not separate the study of an object from the study of the knowing subject (Morin, 1977).

This epistemological perspective is a revolutionary point of view that has much influenced the clinical field. Paraphrasing Varela (1979), we can say that it became very clear that psychotherapy, as all human affairs, is based on the hermeneutic circle of interpretation–action. As 'at each stage, the observer relates to the system through an understanding, which modifies his relationship to the system' (Varela, 1979: 57), so the psychotherapists construct, through their own understanding and descriptions, the interactional process they are involved in with patients.

The challenge represented by this thinking has been taken up by scholars who operate from a wide range of therapeutic models. For example, cognitive therapy was initially anchored to the behaviorist tradition. However, many cognitive therapists are now moving to a systemic-constructivist perspective (Guidano, 1987). In the psychoanalytic field, many integrate the typically hermeneutic tradition with an approach where the construction of the patient–

therapist relationship is seen as the fundamental element of the psychoanalytic process (Bion, 1983, 1984). Systemic theory emancipated itself from the reductionist pragmatic perspective of the sixties. A convincing critique to the directive, instrumental, control-oriented therapeutic models was developed (Dell, 1982; Keeney, 1983; Hoffman, 1986). At the same time, a non-instrumental framework based on constructionist principles began to emerge. The interactional processes that construct social meanings have become a crucial issue in the theory and practice of psychotherapy (Cronen et al., 1982; Fruggeri et al., 1985; Ugazio, 1985; Anderson et al., 1986; Goolishian and Anderson, 1987; Andersen, 1987; Cecchin, 1987; McCarthy and Byrne, 1988; Hoffman, 1988; Fruggeri and Matteini, 1988; Fruggeri et al., 1991).

In the systemic approach, social constructionism has generated conceptual and methodological revisions. Many therapists, starting from pragmatic, strategic, and structural backgrounds, are now in the middle of a transitional phase. They are attempting to integrate old and new models, old certainties and new sets of premises. The new scientific paradigm raises some questions that do not merely pertain to therapeutic techniques. Instead, they challenge the very notion of psychotherapy and the identity of the therapist. It is, in fact, a thinking that questions the foundations on which psychotherapy, both as a scientific and as a social phenomenon, is based.

It is an epistemological perspective that questions the premises according to which therapists define themselves, elaborate theories and practices, models and techniques, develop interpersonal, social, and institutional relationships. In this transition, therapists have found themselves faced with many dilemmas. These dilemmas center on important issues, including (1) a questioning of the medical model upon which psychotherapy was developed; (2) a demystification of the therapist's transformative skills; and (3) a confusion surrounding the ethical and professional responsibilities of the therapist.

The Potent become Impotent

The self-reference that characterizes the process of knowledge implies that the relationships between the individual and the environment or other individuals cannot be instructive interactions. That is to say that 'no one can do anything to anybody.' This is exactly the opposite of the basis upon which the therapist–client encounter takes place and on which the therapist bases his or her actions. It is, in fact, contrary to the statement that concedes to therapists the power to change clients through their use of technical tools. The concept of non-instructive interaction involves a revision of the causal paradigm through which the phenomenon of psychotherapy is explained. The demise of the therapist's potency opens an empty space: what is left of psychotherapy if one of its constitutive elements is gone?

The Medical Model is Pushed Aside

To assume that individuals construct their realities opens a discussion that pertains to the issue of the description of normal or pathological mechanisms. The constructionist approach holds that the regularities of individuals or families functioning are not features of that person or of that family, but of the therapist's descriptions. As Dell (1982) says, there are an infinity of features of a person or of a family, and each one is defined by a form of describing. Such descriptions are not of the client; they are something that the therapist brings to the client.

However, the medical model, upon which many of the psychotherapeutic, heuristic principles are based, teaches us that the cure of all states of discomfort is linked to the precise identification of the pathological mechanism. This mechanism should, in fact, be destroyed with the proper treatment. Thus, if we claim that the therapist cannot have access to the objective knowledge of any pathological mechanism, how can we still define the therapist as a healer and still call the practice a cure?

The Wand is Broken

Starting from the idea that individuals' behaviors are a function of their cognitive and symbolic processes, their interpersonal behaviors cannot be considered mere answers to what others do, but functions of the meanings that the individuals attribute to their own and others' behaviors. The therapist's interventions then do not have an effectiveness in themselves, since their efforts are linked to the meanings that the clients attribute to them. What then is the significance of the therapist's tools? What sense does it make to learn or use a technique whose reliability is not defined a priori; a technique that cannot even be considered a therapeutic tool until the client 'recognizes' it?

The Ethical-Professional Doubt Appears

If the direction of change is not unilaterally determined, therapists are, in a way, dispossessed of controlling the effectiveness of their technical tools. In this frame, how can therapists be responsible for their interventions? Where is the space for the responsibility that socially, institutionally, and legally they are requested to take? What is the therapist responsible for? In sum, these dilemmas raise important questions.

The Identity Crisis Breaks Out

How is it possible to specify the therapist's intentionality? In what ways do his or her conversations, dialogues, relationships with the client differ from any other conversations, dialogues, or relationships?

Toward the Construction of a New Identity

Confronted with these dilemmas some therapists reject the constructionist view, accusing it of solipsism; others feel impotent. Many authors, particularly von Foerster (1981) and von Glasersfeld (1984), have attempted to support the constructionist view against the critique of solipsism. Given the historical context in which their ideas emerged, von Glasersfeld and von Foerster emphasized the observer or the knower. We can clearly recognize the important shift this emphasis represented. However, we can now – in *our* historical context – see that an increased emphasis on the observer can lead to recapitulation of the same dualistic subject/object schema presented by traditional orientations focused on the observed. We need to move the focus from this dualistic tradition of subject and object to treat the *process of knowledge*. In doing so we must emphasize that knowledge is a social construction. We cannot ignore that the hermeneutic circle of interpretation–action does not take place in a vacuum. The descriptions of the observer/therapist cannot be considered abstractions; they are socially constructed realities. Let us not forget that every day each one of us has to cope with constructed realities and still we do not experience an abstracted world. The beliefs that construct these realities are not ideas in the minds of people, they are generated in communication processes (Moscovici, 1961, 1982, 1984, 1988). Therefore the hermeneutic circle of interpretation–action can be described as follows: beliefs held by individuals construct realities and realities are maintained through social interaction which, in turn, confirm the beliefs that are then socially originated.

By abandoning a dualistic epistemology we find it possible to overcome the sense of paralysis the earlier dilemmas engender.

The dualistic epistemology presents choices between control and impotence, effectiveness and ineffectiveness, objective knowledge and non-knowledge. In other words, the logic of dualities rigidly identifies the absence of control with impotence, science with objectivity. Thus the absence of objectivity is identified with non-knowledge, and utility with effectiveness. That is, effectiveness is rigidly associated with objectivity and control. The constructionist approach offers the possibility to draw a new framework in which all sorts of dualisms can be overcome. In fact, constructionism is an observer's point of view in which movement for the observer is from the considering of self looking at a universe to the recognition of self as part of a social multiverse. It is a complementary, non-dualistic perspective. It does not substitute a concept with its opposite; it holds that the organizational closure of systems is maintained through interactions, that change occurs through stability, that autonomy takes place through constraints, and that in limits we find possibilities.

Taking this particular view, I shall reconsider the clinical issues laid out above. According to the principle of self-reference that characterizes the processes of knowledge, the analysis that the therapist makes of the client's situation and of the client's relationships cannot be considered an objective description. There is no description that is more exact or more accurate; there are no tools to be used for more correct observation. Therapists' descriptions are, in fact, linked to their maps, and therapists will see what their viewpoint allows them to see. Yet, this is not solipsism. The observer's/therapist's descriptions are *constrained* by the descriptions of the client's own descriptions. The social process, therefore, where client's and therapist's descriptions converge act as constraints and/or possibilities to continuing their individual viewpoints or changing them. This constraint renders self-reference a constructing process instead of a mere solipsistic game. The observation of the therapist is limited by the viewpoint of the client and vice versa (Fruggeri, 1990). Thus therapists' constructions are linked to the way their actions are interpreted by the client, to the way their questions, comments, and interventions are 'heard' by the client.

Let us take the typical situation in which a family therapist, because of the maps he or she uses to describe the family, 'sees,' among many possible features, that there is a conflict between the parents. Let us also assume that the therapist is free from lineal maps such as 'the parents' conflict is the cause of the child's symptom.' The connection that the therapist will draw between the parents' conflict and the child's suffering is not only determined by the maps of the therapist, but also by the *meaning* that the family members will attribute to the search for a connection between these 'events.' If the family uses lineal explanations, no matter what intentions or maps the therapist uses, the family will 'hear' that the parent's conflict causes the child's suffering.

Research conducted on the professional–client relationship in different contexts of intervention (Fruggeri, 1988, 1991) has identified that the recurrent pattern summarized as 'the more the professional helps the more the problem persists and amplifies' is linked to the family's idea that they are inadequate, bad, or wrong. This idea for the family, however, developed in their interactions with the professional. It does not come from a wrong interpretation of the given situation; rather, it comes from a right interpretation, according to the specific belief systems of the persons involved. That is, it emerges from the belief systems that the family generates through their experience, as members of a cultural and social community. In particular, the identified recurrent pattern is not correlated to the presenting problem, to the type of intervention, to the referring modalities, nor to the way either the client, the family, or the professional approaches the presenting problem. The pattern is not even connected to the way they all relate with one another. Instead, it emerges as the result of a coordination of actions and of meanings attributed to the actions on behalf of everyone involved in the situation.

Psychotherapy emerges here as a communication process in which the different partners construct the reciprocal roles and together construct an interpersonal context within a consensual domain. In this perspective the definition of knowledge as an operation of discovery is dismissed. In addition, the viewing of psychotherapeutic practice as manipulation disappears. With this, the distinction between knowing and acting is erased. Knowing becomes, in fact, an act for which meaning emerges through the coordination of client's and therapist's beliefs.

This casts a new light on the different phases of the therapeutic process. The distinction between an interview aimed at understanding the client's dynamics and an interview aimed at modifying these dynamics seems to be artificial. The interview conducted by the therapist is simultaneously information taking and information giving. For example, when I begin therapy I usually ask the questions, 'What brought you here?' and 'How do you see the situation?' I ask these two questions to everyone in the family. I can think of many different ways of starting a dialogue with the clients. I select these questions out of many possible opening questions. I could ask of behaviors instead of opinions, of symptoms instead of explanations, and I could ask the questions to only one family member (the client or one of the parents). The fact that I ask the two specific questions instead of others is not random. It is linked to the theoretical model I refer to. But this is not the only reason. To ask the question, 'How do you see the situation?' to everyone is not only an action coherent with the constructionist theoretical model, but it also contributes to recognizing the interview as a construction process. Similarly, we can see that the question, 'What is your problem?' asked to only one person is not only an expression of an objectivist framework (it assumes a problem exists), but it may also contribute to construct with the family the problem as objective. The word 'may' is used here in order to underline that the kind of reality brought forth is, in a final analysis, a co-construction. The therapist is not an observer who is simply aware of the reflexivity between his or her actions and beliefs, but is an observer of the self at the same time as constructing the situation that is being observed (Fruggeri, 1990). This translates into a methodological approach that sees the therapist constantly hypothesizing about the meanings that her or his actions can assume in the interactive context shared with the client.

The obvious question at this point is, 'How does the therapist know what meanings the client attributes to the therapist's actions?' The short answer would be that the therapist does not, according to the framework developed here. However, I think this would be a denial of the methodological issue implied in the question. Each therapist makes, at each stage of the interview, decisions about what to do, how to do it, and whether to do it, in order to help the client. All therapists use some criteria in making these decisions. The effort to make one's criteria explicit contributes to the specification of a methodology of psychotherapy and helps the therapist to reflect on ways of constructing the therapeutic reality.

This methodological guideline (for example, questioning one's own criteria) does not imply a search for truth or objectivity, not even an approximation to it. While considering the unintended consequences of all social interactions (Shotter, 1990), this methodology underlines the responsibility that the therapist has for his or her constructions. Therefore, if the short answer to the above question is that therapists cannot know the meanings attributed by the client to his or her actions, the long answer is that therapists cannot know them in an objective way, but it is through hypothesizing about this question that they construct the therapeutic context. The awareness of the criteria upon which therapists constantly hypothesize becomes a therapeutic tool. An even broader answer would be that therapists cannot avoid addressing the issue of the social construction of belief systems and, therefore, they cannot escape from studying these processes, in which they are also deeply involved.

Let us return to the therapist's dilemmas. The discomfort emerging from the acknowledgement that 'no one can do anything to anybody,' or from the ethical-professional doubt that derives from the recognition that it is impossible to control how the client evolves, vanishes if we connect these with the methodology discussed above. The therapist does not have the power to change nor unilaterally to determine the direction of change. It is the redefinition of psychotherapy as a context of constructing social realities that re-establishes the therapist's responsibility. Therapists find themselves in a position requiring that they deal with the intrinsic non-neutrality of their way of being in the relationship (Marzari, 1991). The belief systems connected with the therapist's practice, and the way they coordinate their actions with the client's, cannot be taken for granted. Nor can they remain invisible any more. The development of the therapeutic process and its results are strictly interdependent with them.

The therapist's power and responsibility become thus redefined. They are freed from the notion of unilateral control and are instead placed in the dynamic of the systemic co-construction. The theoretical perspective that opposes power to responsibility ends up with giving only a moralistic interpretation of these two concepts, where power is always bad and responsibility is always good. On the other hand, too much emphasis on responsibility outside of an interpersonal-social context ends up as omnipotence, if not power, thereby reproducing a control-orientated epistemological framework. Power should be neither celebrated nor demonized. Power and responsibility could instead be reconsidered, using Bateson's distinction between 'the whole' and 'the being part of.' In essence, one could say that the problem for a therapist is neither to be powerful nor to succumb to power. Rather, the therapist should take responsibility for his or her power of construction within the constraints of the relational/social domain.

The constructionist framework, on one hand, challenges us to consider manipulation as an illusion. On the other hand, it requires reflecting on the possibility that also the unilaterally defined democratic, egalitarian attitude can represent a manipulation, therefore an illusion. As power is not unilaterally determined, egalitarianism and the respect for others are not unilaterally determined. They are the result of an interactive process, in which both the offering of respect and the same acceptance/recognition of the offer are necessary.

New Questions Emerge

From a constructionist viewpoint, psychotherapy can be theoretically redefined. Unbound from the mechanistic characterization that confines it in the realm of techniques, psychotherapy emerges as an interpersonal construction process. As such, psychotherapy cannot be abstracted from the social context in which it takes place and by which it is determined. Psychotherapy is socially defined as a context for problem solving, evolution and change. Every time one or more persons refer to a therapist by expressing their problem, they also implicitly ask for help. They come with expectations about what they will receive. The therapist cannot avoid operating with the aim of overcoming the presenting problem. The therapist cannot avoid acting as the 'designated agent of change' for a 'designated patient' who asks for an intervention (Marzari, 1991).

To manage the psychotherapeutic situation effectively entails, from this perspective, dealing with the social designation that defines the therapist's identity (that is, as an 'expert'). At the same time, however, effective management also requires keeping in mind the theoretical principle that relational change cannot be unilaterally created or governed. The idea of a therapist as an architect of change can be abandoned without any trauma if we also abandon the correlated idea of a client resisting change.

In a constructionist framework not only psychotherapy, but also pathology, are re-conceptualized. The core of the issue is not the etiology of symptoms, but rather the interpersonal and social processes and dynamics that maintain the symptoms. Research does not refer to the causes of a problem. It pertains to the strange loops (Cronen et al., 1982) that emerge from the reciprocal determination of beliefs and behaviors in the personal and interpersonal experience. Attention is paid to the function of amplification and maintenance of the strange loops through the social and scientific communities, cultural values, and diagnostic and therapeutic practices.

In this view, as Keeney suggests, psychotherapy is aimed at modifying the way the problematic system changes in order to remain stable. Therefore, 'therapeutic change involves change of change – a change of how a system's habitual process of change leads to stability' (Keeney, 1983: 177). Psychotherapy can then be defined as a process of deutero-learning (Bateson, 1972); that is, a process of co-constructing a context in which a change in the *set* of alternatives from which choice is made becomes possible.

According to this definition, the therapist is described as the person who takes part in the construction of interpersonal realities that have the characteristics of being different from the reality that the client and the client's significant system have constructed in their history/experience/practices. The therapist triggers a process of change if he or she is successful in interfering with the repetition of the same experience that brought the client to therapy (Maturana, 1988; Anderson et al., 1986; Fruggeri et al., 1985; Fruggeri and Matteini, 1988; Fruggeri et al., 1991).

Thus the methodological guidelines of psychotherapy are identified in the following: (1) the introduction of differences; (2) the proposal of different descriptions of some event; (3) new ways of connecting behaviors and events; and (4) the introduction of reflexivity.

These pivotal methodological principles can remain at a superficial level if we do not address how individuals, who are closed in a circuit of premises and interpersonal behaviors that do not allow them to make a choice out of that set of premises (Bateson, 1972), 'see' the differences proposed by the therapist. Difference, novelty, reflexivity are not intrinsic characteristics of the therapist's questions or comments. The intervention which introduces differences is only the one that is 'recognized' as such by the client. Should we say that no matter what the therapist does, the result of the therapeutic process will always be determined by the client who selects what is useful for his or her change? I see this as a position which re-invents, in its opposing form, the claim that the therapist determines the results of the psychotherapeutic process. And, if the latter leads to a control-oriented approach, the former leads to a very loose definition of the phenomenon that we call psychotherapy.

This is, in my opinion, a central issue for the constructionist approach to psychotherapy. In order to address it, rigorous research is needed. We still do not have answers to how beliefs are socially generated, and we are even further away from a description of how beliefs change. We claim that successful psychotherapy is a process in which the clients change their premises or change the conversations they are involved in, or change their narratives. We imply that the narratives, conversations, and premises that should be changed are the context in which the problem is brought forth. However, we still do not have descriptions, coherent with the autopoetic or endogenic perspective we refer to, that account for the process of change in premises, or in conversations, or in narratives. What makes a relationship a process of deutero-learning? What makes a conversation that particular type of conversation that changes all the other conversations? What makes a narrative a special kind of a narrative that generates new narratives? My opinion is that therapists should answer these questions in the name of a non-control-oriented constructionist thinking.

One very first step in this direction is research that I, together with a colleague, started (Fruggeri and Matteini, 1991). We have conducted a systematic analysis of family therapy sessions, with the aim of identifying eventual regularities in correlations between changes in the way the clients (individuals or family groups) describe, explain, attribute meaning to their experience and specific kinds of interventions (questions or comments) of the therapist. The study has, up to now, taken into consideration a limited number of sessions. The following are the regularities that consistently emerged from the analysis.

First, the therapist's interventions to which the family members respond with a different description, explanation, or attribution are questions or comments that challenge the coherence between descriptions, explanations, and attributions and maps, premises, and belief systems. Additionally, every time that the therapist offers a different description, explanation, or attribution, the family members tend to integrate such interventions in their belief systems, maps, and premises. It seems that, in a therapeutic relationship, the challenge to the coherence between descriptions and beliefs constitutes a perturbation which challenges the individuals to generate a new coherence.

Secondly, the most significant change in conversations (that is, a change in the type of descriptions, explanations, attributions) occurs in correspondence with an intervention of the therapist that connects the multiple descriptions, explanations, attributions offered by the individuals in the course of the conversation. In this sense, we could hypothesize that it is not sufficient to offer a multiplicity of points of view, but the therapist has to offer the possibility for the family members to see them all connected. That is an occurrence that happens only after the family members have experienced the possibility of generating different points of view.

Conclusion

Some methodological guidelines emerge from the above considerations.

First, the practice of therapists working from a constructionist framework is characterized by the acknowledgement of their premises, point of view, biases. It is through this acknowledgement that they can observe their own way of constructing the phenomena they are observing and their relationship to them.

Secondly, therapists decide their actions in consideration of the meaning that their way of constructing the observed processes assumes in the co-construction of the relationship with the others. The story of the patients, their expectations, the referring modalities, the request for help, eventual previous experiences with therapeutic institutions, the beliefs that they share in a social domain, all constitute the context of meanings within which the therapist's actions are constructed by the patients.

Thirdly, therapists act in order to create differences or novelty. We need further research in order to say what this means from a methodological point of view. From the observations conducted thus far it is proposed that differences and novelty are generated by the patient when the therapist challenges the coherence of the reflexive circle between beliefs and actions (constructions) and when the therapist takes a different point of view. The context of observation/construction is different not when therapists change the object of observation, but when they change the way of observing. A different type of viewpoint does not merely move from individuals to relationships, from content to process, from patient to therapist, from actions to meaning. The movement from this perspective, which is still dualistic, is to the consideration of the relationship between individual and family, to the imbrication of content and process, to the reflexivity of actions and meanings, to the co-construction of therapist and client.

In this light it is not a mere matter of principle that therapists are responsible for their power of construction. The power of construction emerges as a responsibility that is scientific and, at the same time, ethical and social.

References

Andersen, T. (1987) 'The reflecting team', *Family Process*, 26: 415–28.

Anderson, H., Goolishian, H. and Winderman, L. (1986) 'Problem determined systems: toward a transformation in family therapy', *Journal of Strategic and Systemic Therapies*, 5: 14–19.

Bateson, G. (1972) *Steps to an Ecology of Mind*. New York: Ballantine.

Bateson, G. (1978) 'Afterword', in J. Brockman (ed.), *About Bateson*. London: Wildwood House. pp. 235–47.

Bateson, G. (1979) *Mind and Nature: a Necessary Unity*. New York: Dutton.

Bateson, G. and Bateson, M.C. (1987) *Angels Fear*. New York: Macmillan.

Bion, V.R. (1983) *Attenzione e interpretazione*. Rome: Armando.

Bion, V.R. (1984) *Discussioni con Bion*. Turin: Loescher.

Cecchin, G. (1987) 'Hypothesizing, circularity and neutrality revisited: an invitation to curiosity', *Family Process*, 26: 405–13.

Ceruti, M. (1986) *Il vincolo e la possibilità*. Milan: Feltrinelli.

Cronen, V., Johnson, K. and Lannamann, J. (1982) 'Paradoxes, double binds and reflexive loops: an alternative theoretical perspective', *Family Process*, 21: 91–112.

Dell, P. (1982) 'Beyond homeostasis: toward a concept of coherence', *Family Process*, 21: 21–40.

Fruggeri, L. (1988) 'I sistemi di significato nello sviluppo delle relazioni fra educatori, genitori, bambino nell asilo nido', in W. Fornasa (ed.), *Nido futuro: strategie e possibilità*. Milan: Angeli. pp. 65–101.

Fruggeri, L. (1990) 'Metodo, ricerca, construzione: il cambiamento come costruzione per la conoscenza', in M. Ingrosso (ed.), *Itinerari sistemici nelle scienze sociali*. Milan: Angeli. pp. 247–64.

Fruggeri, L. (1991) 'Servizi sociali e famiglie: dalla risposta al bisogno alla construzione delle competenze', *Oikos*, 4: 175–90.

Fruggeri, L., Dotti, D., Ferrari, R. and Matteini, M. (1985) 'The systemic approach in a mental health service', in D. Campbell and R. Draper (eds), *Applications of Systemic Family Therapy*. London: Grune & Strutton. pp. 137–47.

Fruggeri, L. and Matteini, M. (1988) 'Larger systems? Beyond a dualistic approach to the process of change', *Irish Journal of Psychology*, 9: 183–94.

Fruggeri, L. and Matteini, M. (1991) 'La struttura della narrazione terapeutica', in V. Ugazio (ed.), *Soggetto, emozioni, sistema*. Milan: Vita e Pensiero. pp. 67–83.

Fruggeri, L., Telfner, U., Castellucci, A., Marzari, M. and Matteini, M. (1991) *New Systemic Ideas from the Italian Mental Health Movement*. London: Karnac Books.

Goolishian, H. and Anderson, H. (1987) 'Language systems and therapy: an evolving idea', *Psychotherapy: Theory, Research and Practice*, 24: 529–38.

Guidano, V.F. (1987) *Complexity of the Self*. New York: Guilford Press.

Hoffman, L. (1986) 'Beyond power and control: toward a "second order" family systems therapy', *Family Systems Medicine*, 4: 381–96.

Hoffman, L. (1988) 'A constructivist position for family therapy', *Irish Journal of Psychology*, 9: 110–29.

Keeney, B. (1983) *Aesthetics of Change*. New York: Guilford Press.

McCarthy, I. and Byrne, N. (1988) 'Moving statutes: re-questioning ambivalence through ambiguous discourse', *Irish Journal of Psychology*, 9: 173–82.

Marzari, M. (1991) *La costruzione della differenza*. Bologna: Clueb.

Maturana, H. (1988) 'Reality: the search for objectivity or the quest for a compelling argument', *Irish Journal of Psychology*, 9: 25–82.

Maturana, H. and Varela, F. (1987) *The Tree of Knowledge*. Boston, MA: New Science Library.

Morin, E. (1977) *La méthode: la nature de la nature*. Paris: Seuil.

Moscovici, S. (1961) *La psychanalise, son image et son public*. Paris: Presses Universitaires de France.

Moscovici, S. (1982) 'The coming era of representations', in J.P. Codol and J.Ph. Leyens (eds), *Cognitive Analysis of Social Behavior*. The Hague: Nijhoff.

Moscovici, S. (1984) 'The phenomenon of social representations', in R. Farr and S. Moscovici (eds), *Social Representations*. Cambridge: Cambridge University Press.

Moscovici, S. (1988) 'Notes towards a description of social representations', *European Journal of Social Psychology*, 18: 211–50.

Shotter, J. (1990) *Knowing of the Third Kind*. Utrecht: University of Utrecht.

Ugazio, V. (1985) 'Oltre la scatola nera', *Terapia Familiare*, 19: 75–83.

Varela, F. (1979) *Principles of Biological Autonomy*. New York: North Holland.

von Foerster, H. (1981) *Observing Systems*. Seaside, CA: Intersystems Publications.
von Glasersfeld, E. (1984) 'An introduction to radical constructivism', in P. Watzlawick (ed.), *The Invented Reality*. New York: Norton.

PART II

FORMS OF PRACTICE

4

Reflections on Reflecting with Families

Tom Andersen

This book has given me the privilege to re-walk my own tracks over the years in order to describe and understand what might be defined as my professional evolution. My way of describing and understanding has shifted over time. So, the telling of my professional story has to start at the end, namely with what I think today about descriptions, their corresponding understandings, and how I construct them.

What I Think Today

I see life as the moving of myself and my surroundings and the surroundings of those surroundings towards the future. The shifts of life around me come by themselves, not by me. The only thing I can do is to take part in them. To take part is to learn to use the repertoire of understandings and actions that have come from the various experiences I have had over the years. What seems to be most important is to learn what I shall *not do again*. This idea has been stimulated strongly from the exchanges I have had with Harold Goolishian.[1] He says, 'If you know what to do it limits you. If you know more what not to do, then there is an infinity of things that might be done.' How I use my repertoire is related to how I understand the moment of life I take part in, and my understanding is related to how I describe it. What I describe is what I pay attention to and focus on. Life, every moment of it, is so rich and full that it is impossible to pay attention to and focus on everything at the same time. I have to select what to focus on; if I will it or not, from moment to moment. Therefore, I *cannot* describe those parts of life that I *do not* pay attention to and thus *do not* focus on. My descriptions and understandings are formed in language, and I can only make them according to the language I have in my repertoire. Therefore I can only pay attention to and focus on that for which I have a language to describe and understand.

When life comes to me, it touches my skin, my eyes, my ears, the bulbs of my tongue, the nostrils of my nose. As I am open and sensitive to what I see, hear, feel, taste, and smell I can also notice 'answers' to those touches from myself, as my body, 'from inside,' lets me know in various ways how it thinks about what the outside touches; what should be concentrated on and what not. This state of being open and sensitive to the touches from the 'outside life' and at the same time being open and sensitive to the answers from the 'inside life' is what I prefer to call 'intuition.' At this point in time my intuition seems to be what I rely on the most. In re-walking my professional tracks, my intuition tells me that I shall take part first, and then sit down and think about the taking part; not sit down and think first and thereafter take part. As I am sure that my thinking is with me as I take part, I have felt comfortable following what my intuition has suggested to me.

This might correspond to some ideas which Thomas Kuhn (1970) discusses about theories. He says that all research that defines aims and means within a given paradigm will most often produce 'findings' that support the theory upon which the research was primarily based. Indirectly, Kuhn suggests that one might wait with the applications of theory and let the practice be as free as possible in its search for 'relevant' descriptions and understandings. Thereafter one might discuss these 'findings' (descriptions and understandings) against the background of various existing theories. This might 'challenge' and maybe even expand these theories as well. I have organized this chapter according to such thinking. That means that I will speak from practice first and, thereafter, now and then, stop to discuss and theorize about the described practice. This might also comply with my understanding of certain key ideas that have emerged from the discussion of postmodern philosophy. Baynes et al. (1987) state that theory is itself a narrative. So, if my narrative is told within the framework of my 'old' narrative – as, for instance, a repetition – it loses its freedom.

The Early Years: Family Physician

After finishing medical school in the southern part of Norway (Oslo), I moved to the arctic part of the country to be a country family physician for four years.

Those four years created many questions and concerns. Two became prominent. One was about the social effect of illness. When a person, particularly a child, was sick, I wondered how I could understand all the activities in the sick child's surroundings that the sickness created. I thought psychiatry might be a field that could provide answers, and I entered that field. The second question was about all the aches and pains in the moving parts of patients for which my examinations did not suffice. How could all these be understood? I did not know where the route was to be found. I could only wait until the route one day would come by itself.

Psychiatry gave no answer to the first question. It actually raised new concerns: could there be alternatives to the beliefs that 'mentally ill patients' can be steered into health? Could there be alternatives to separating the 'mentally ill' from their family, friends, jobs, and so forth? (To be hospitalized in north Norway often means to find oneself very far from home.) Could 'patients' be called something other than 'patients'? Could alternatives to standard treatment (namely, being locked behind closed doors, given medication against one's will, behavior modification, and so on) be more coherent with the context of 'patient'–family–friends–job–neighborhood? These were only some of many questions.

Searching for Alternatives

Some of us came together informally in the early 1970s on weekends once a month. We read Minuchin (1974), Haley (1963) and Watzlawick et al. (1974). We tried to apply their techniques. However, we were not very successful in making the kind of changes we envisioned.

I always felt uncomfortable at that time, when we, convinced of having a better understanding of the problems than the families themselves, provided a new and 'smart' understanding of the problem or provided a 'smart' instruction how to handle it.

Watzlawick et al. (1967) turned our attention to Gregory Bateson. We were fortunate, and it was a great relief, to be acquainted with the Milan team's approach (Selvini et al., 1980) through two members of the team, Gianfranco Cecchin and Luigi Boscolo. In addition, Lynn Hoffman and Peggy Penn from the Ackerman Institute in New York helped us elaborate our understanding of Bateson's work (Bateson, 1972, 1978, 1979) in general, and the Milan approach in particular.

The Milan approach consists of a team meeting with the family. A member of the team talks with the family while the rest of the team follows the conversation from behind a one-way mirror. The person who talks with the family has a preliminary idea of how the problem can be understood, a hypothesis, which guides their interview. During the interview the interviewer leaves the family to join the remainder of the team to discuss possible interpretations that are different from the family's. The interviewer then disconnects with the team and reconnects with the family to give this new understanding. This is called 'the intervention.'

When my various colleagues and I tried to apply the Milan approach, I always felt uncomfortable delivering the intervention to the family. It was always hard to say, 'This is what we see,' or 'This is what we understand,' or 'This is what we want you to do.' Presenting the intervention this way gave me the feeling that we, the therapy team, had a better way to see and understand the problem. We also seemed to be assuming that we had a better proposal for how the family should handle their problem than they had themselves.

In order to avoid these problems we started in the last part of 1984 to say, 'In addition to what you saw we saw this,' or 'In addition to what you understood we understood this,' or 'In addition to what you have tried to do yourself, we wonder if you might try to do this.' It did not take long to realize that we had shifted from an 'either–or' to a 'both–and' stance. I felt greatly relieved to make this shift. It seems that the state of feeling discomfort has been a major contributor to change in my work.

A Major Shift: Reflecting

Aina Skorpen, a mental health nurse I was working with, and I had been discussing a certain idea since late 1981. This idea was connected to our observation of what people often told us when we met them the first time. They would typically say, 'We do not know *what* to do! What shall we do?' In our discussions we began to consider why we left the families during the breaks in the sessions? Why did we hide away our deliberations about the families? Perhaps we should stay with the families and let them see and hear what *we* did and how *we* worked with the question? Perhaps, by giving them access to our process, they would more easily find their own answers. At first we did not dare to make our discussions 'public' because we thought that the language we used contained too many 'nasty' words. For example, a team member might say, 'I am glad I am not a member of a family with such a talkative mother!' or 'What is it like to be married to such a stubborn man?' We thought that those words would come into the open easily if we talked in front of the families. In spite of these fears, everything was brought into the open one day in March 1985. On that particular day, a team[2] who had followed the conversation from behind the one-way mirror, proposed to those in the therapeutic conversation (a family and an interviewer) that we talk for a while with them listening to us. We said that we could talk about what we had been thinking while we listened to the talk they had just had. My early fears were not fulfilled. The 'nasty' words did not appear, nor did this conversation require any strong effort from us to avoid 'nasty' words. From that day the team was called 'the Reflecting Team.'[3]

When we suggested to the family that we share our ideas, it was natural for us to say, 'Maybe our talk will bring ideas that could be useful for your conversation.' We did not say, 'useful for you,' but 'useful for *your conversation*.' I have since then been thinking of the languages professionals use. I am deliberately saying 'languages' (in the plural) because there will naturally be a 'public' language for conversation with the families present and a 'private' language when the professionals are alone. The 'private' language will easily attract 'nasty' words and also all the 'intellectual,' 'academic,' and 'foreign' words and concepts that professionals often share when they are left alone. I have been wondering how easy is it for professionals to make the shift from 'private' language at one moment to 'public' language at the next? If there are difficulties in distilling the 'public' talk from 'private' elements, how will that effect the conversations with clients?

The open-reflecting-team mode of working tended to move professional language towards daily language. This language contained only words and concepts we could all use in common. This way of relating to the clients comprised more than a shift of language.

Modes of Procedure

In what follows I shall lead the reader towards the practical part of the work, although there will be some mention of the corresponding thinking.

Introducing Not Too Unusual Differences

When I was a GP, questions about patients' aches and pains found answers when I met with physiotherapist Gudrun Øvreberg who introduced me to her teacher Aadel Bülow-Hansen, another physiotherapist. Bülow-Hansen had noticed that patients who are tense tend to flex their bodies towards a 'creeping-together' position. As they do so they also restrict their breathing. In order to be helpful to them, Bülow-Hansen stimulated them to stretch out and 'open up' their bodies. One way to do so was by inducing pain in the patient. She had noticed that if a muscle, for example, on the back side of the calf, is held with a painful grip, the pain will stimulate the person to stretch the body. When the body stretches, deeper inhalation is stimulated. This deeper inhalation will, in its turn, stimulate more stretching, which, in its turn, stimulates more stretching, and so on, until the chest is filled according to its flexibility. When the air is exhaled, some tension in the body disappears. She noticed, however, that if her grip was too soft, nothing happened to either the stretching or the breathing. If her grip was too rough or her hold was too long, the patient would respond with a deep inhalation but the breathing would stop as the person held the air back without letting it go. If her hand was appropriately painful and her hold appropriately long, there would be an expansion of the breathing without stopping it.

What I learned from Aadel Bülow-Hansen was a variation on Gregory Bateson's famous sentence, 'the elementary unit of information – is a difference that makes a difference' (Bateson, 1972: 453). Those who do not know what to do, need something different (unusual), but this something should not be too different (unusual). That applies to *what* we talk with families about and *how* we talk with them and what the *context* of the talking is. How can we know when our contributions are too unusual? The answer is found by noticing the client's way of participating in the conversation. Are there signs in the conversation that tell that it is uncomfortable for the client to take part? Those signs might differ from person to person. We are thereby challenged to be acquainted with and sensitive to those particular signs the various individuals send us. We must rely on our intuition in noticing those signs.

These ideas of not being too unusual correspond well with the ideas of Humberto Maturana and Fransisco Varela's perturbations (disturbances) (1987). We need to be 'disturbed' since disturbances keep us alive and make us able to change in correspondence with the shifting world around us. But if the disturbances are too different from what our repertoire is able to integrate, we disintegrate if we include them.

Either–or versus Both–and
After starting the reflecting-team mode of working, spontaneous changes in our procedures occurred. The team behind the screen, which before had talked together when observing the therapy session, became increasingly silent. We understood later that this

listening in silence helped the team create many more ideas than before. When we previously talked, the team concentrated primarily on only one or a few ideas.

We also developed some rules of procedure. The first was that the team's reflections should be based on and start with something expressed during the conversation, not from another context. We might begin our reflections by saying, 'When I heard . . .,' or 'When I saw . . . I had this idea.' We often started by stating our uncertainty, 'I am not sure but it seemed to me . . .,' or 'I am not sure but I had the feeling . . .,' or 'Maybe you heard something else but I heard . . .' Then we followed, 'My thinking of that made me wonder . . .,' or 'Thinking of her speaking of this or that I saw . . .,' or 'When I thought of this or that this question came to my mind . . .,' or 'I noticed that they had done this or that, I wonder what would happen if they did . . .' We placed a strong emphasis on the family's autonomy of choice. The listening families are invited to 'take in' what they like. At present I prefer to say the following just before such reflections start, 'When they [that is, the team] talk, you might listen to them if you want, or think of something else if you want, or just rest, or do whatever you prefer to do.' It seems important to let them know that this is just an offer, and not something they must pay attention to. It is very important to give the listener the possibility of turning away from that with which they feel uncomfortable. It is very important for them to have the ability *to say no*.

A second rule is that the team, when talking 'publicly,' should restrain themselves from giving 'negative' connotations. Nothing is negative in itself; it becomes negative when the listener perceives it as negative. We keep these thoughts in mind when we say what we say. A member of the reflecting team commenting, for example, 'I cannot understand why they did not try this or that,' will most probably be heard as criticizing. Rather, one could say 'I wonder what would happen if they tried this or that?'

The last and third rule concerns the reflecting mode when all – both family and the whole team – are in the same room, which happens when no one-way mirror is available. When the team reflects, they are encouraged to look at one another when they talk and not look at those who listen. This gives the listeners the freedom to *not* listen.

After the team has shared their reflections, the conversation is turned over to the family and the interviewer. The interviewer offers the opportunity for the family to discuss their thoughts as they listen to the team's talk. However, the interviewer does not necessarily press the family if they prefer to keep their thoughts private. We hope that thoughts will be shared that might be starting points for new conversations or for finding new descriptions and understandings. Such shifts might happen once or twice during a meeting, perhaps even more often. The way of working that has been outlined so far implies that there are always many versions of a situation, which means that there are many ways to describe it and therefore many ways to understand it. Those who consult us are often equipped with the idea that there is *one* right way to understand a situation and many wrong ones.

The pair of words *either–or* seem to be a heritage from Plato. He and many followers searched for the Truth and the Good. The task was to forge descriptions which were *representations* of that Truth. Those representations, they thought, would give us *knowledge* to *explain* and *predict*. There would be knowledge that was right and knowledge that was wrong. The discussion that has been introduced by postmodern philosophy has questioned the position of either–or (Baynes et al., 1987; d'Andrade, 1986). That discussion yields other concepts in addition to those which have dominated thought for a long while, including mythos in addition to truth, metaphor in addition to concept, figurative in addition to literal, imagination in addition to reason, rhetoric in addition to logic, and narrative in addition to argument.

Most of all, these new discussions introduce the idea that we relate to life based on our perceptions, descriptions and understandings of the world. Squarely spoken, we do not relate to life 'itself' but to our understanding of it. This represents a major shift in thinking, and this view is coherent with constructivist thinking (also called second-order cybernetics) which states that we strongly participate in creating our understanding of life (Maturana, 1978; von Foerster, 1984; von Glasersfeld, 1984). These authors also strongly emphasize that there are as many versions of a situation as there are persons to understand it. The reflecting team mode tries to include as many versions as possible. Below are some examples.

The first two questions in the meeting 'How would you like to use this meeting?' This question, which is one of my first questions in a meeting, seems to have become a natural consequence of making the conversations 'public.' It feels more comfortable to avoid fixing any plan about what one should talk about and how one should talk before the session begins. Including those in therapy creates a more equal relationship.

'What is the history of the idea behind this meeting?' This is the second question. The answers to who was the first to have the idea for a meeting, and how the various participants were touched by the idea also clarifies who is most eager to talk and who is more reserved. Which issues the eager ones want to talk about become the point of immediate focus. The more reserved family members are invited to participate as they feel comfortable.

Talk about this talk We also find it useful to 'talk about how we shall talk.' For example, we explore what are the best circumstances for the talk; at home or in an office? Should there be a reflecting team or not? Who might (indirectly asking who should not) talk with whom about which issue at which point in time? These are only three of many possible procedural questions that are important. The function of this conversation is to provide a context within which the participants feel comfortable.

Talk about past and future talks Anderson et al. (1986) have introduced the useful concepts of a 'problem-creating and problem-dissolving system.' They say that a problem very often attracts many persons who want to contribute to its solution. In order to try to solve it they create their meanings as to how it can be described and understood, and how it can be acted on. When those meanings are *not* too different, the exchange of opinions may create new and useful meanings. If, however, the meanings are too different, the exchanges stop. By asking about previous talks we can learn which ones should not be repeated. By asking the question, 'Who can talk with whom about this issue at this point in time?' we may probably find more useful conversations. Those with appropriately different meanings will, when they talk, often come up with new meanings. Those who hold meanings that are too different will have a hard time talking together and will often rather stick to the meanings they already have, even when these meanings have proved not to be useful. I do not encourage people who have very different views to talk to each other, but rather talk to me since I try hard *not* to have any meanings about their meanings.

Inner and outer conversations The reflecting-team mode offers the various persons present the possibility to shift back and forth between listening and talking about the same issues. These two different positions in relation to the same issues seem to provide two different perspectives, and these two perspectives of the same will most probably create new perspectives. There are infinite ways to organize a conversation so that the shift back and forth between talking and listening can occur. The reflecting-team mode is only one of many ways. The simplest one is without a team. A professional might talk with one in the group, for a while, often five minutes, sometimes ten, with the others listening to that talk. Then, he or she turns to the others to ask what they had been thinking as they heard the talk. After this talk with 'the others,' one may again turn back to the first speaker and ask what that person was thinking as they heard what the others had been thinking. The best 'name' at present for these shifting talks is *the reflecting process.* This process provides shiftings between 'inner' and 'outer' talk. The idea of 'inner' and 'outer' talk is as old as human history. The reflecting process is only to highlight something we long have had in hand but not yet 'organized' in daily conversations. When I talk with others, I partly talk with the others, partly to myself. Very much of my 'inner' talk is about those ideas taking place in the 'outer' talk that I might 'take in,' and how I eventually might use those ideas.

The Flow of Conversation: Questions and Co-presence
When we enter the scene of a problem it is important to locate the existing meanings and opinions and we do so best by asking questions (Penn, 1982, 1985). Questions also tend to open up a conversation that has stopped. If a professional offers his or her meanings and opinions, this will often provoke already existing meanings to stand even more firmly fixed. The questions which are the safest to ask are those that are strongly connected to what the person one speaks with has just said. I prefer at present to wait with my question(s) until the person I speak with has finished talking *and* thinking. My question usually focuses on something *my intuition* tells me is significant for the person to continue to talk about. My intuition also helps me find the question I shall ask and how I shall ask it. I boldly refer the reader to what I have written before about such questioning (Andersen, 1991).

While listening to the speaker's answers, I try to develop a sense of co-presence. This kind of listening became central to me as I met with a group from the inner part of Finnmark county. They belong to the Sami people (in English literature often called Lapps) who originally followed their reindeer herds on their migration between the interior in winter and the coast of the Arctic Ocean in summer. In their tradition, the extended family comes to the house of those who have been visited by a harsh destiny, an unexpected death. They often sit quietly without speaking. Those who grieve know that their close ones are there, co-present and available for talking, if needed. Might *that* be the most significant of our contributions: to listen to the quietness of the troubled one's thinking?

Language and the Constitution of Being

Many people carefully search for words to express themselves. They search, at *every moment of time*, for the words that are most meaningful for them. I find myself increasingly engaged in talking with them about the language they use. Often unnoticed shades and nuances in the words emerge through such talk and, very often, this 'nuancing' of their words and language contributes to shifts of the descriptions, understandings, and meanings that the language attempts to clarify.

David E. Leary (1984) says that we use metaphors to construct all our talking:

> our vision or understanding – in science and medicine as well as in everyday life – is structured by metaphor. All comprehension, I believe, is based upon a process of comparing the unknown with the known, of aligning the unfamiliar with the familiar, of using categories of understanding from one realm of experience as templates or grids upon which to analyze experience from some other realm. That is what I mean by metaphor and metaphorical thinking. Metaphor in this broad sense is simply the giving to one thing or experience a name or description that belongs by convention to something else, on the grounds of some proposed similarity between the two. According to this definition, which goes back to Aristotle and would be endorsed by most contemporary scholars who study figurative speech and thought, metaphor is logically indistinguishable from trope in general, and thus encompasses analogy, simile, metonymy, and so on, as well as metaphor more narrowly construed. At the same time, such things as fables, parables, allegories, myths, and models – including scientific models – can be understood, through this definition, as extended or sustained metaphors.

From Leary's article, I conclude that we not only construct our talking on metaphors, but also our thinking. Martin Heidegger (1962) and Hans Georg Gadamer (Warnke, 1987) put much emphasis on the use of language as part of that process. And, as I understand, Kenneth J. Gergen (1985, 1989) advocates the view that a person's self-expression through language contributes strongly to the person's being who he or she is. Talking with oneself and/or others is a way of defining oneself. In this sense the language we use makes us who we are in the moment we use it. Those who first put these views into clinical practice were Harlene Anderson and Harold Goolishian (1988).

One might say that the search for new meanings, which often comprises searching for a new language, is a search for us to be *the* selves with which we feel most comfortable. So-called 'therapeutic' talk might be regarded as a form of search; a search for new descriptions, new understandings, new meanings, new nuances of the words, and ultimately for new definitions of oneself.

This understanding of the meaning of conversation has made it difficult for me to interrupt a person's talking and thinking, since that process of talking and thinking constitutes a search for the new and part of that new is the search for being what the person wants to be.

It is not difficult any more to listen to another's talking even if it takes forty-five minutes before I can say my first word. My meetings with Aadel Bülow-Hansen and Gudrun Øvreberg have also offered a valuable background to think of talking and language alternatively. They say that the phase of exhaling is our expressing ourselves and also our releasing inner tension. Every word and every expressed emotion go by exhaling. Our sad crying, our shouting anger, our whispering fears are all brought by the stream of air that leaves us. That stream of air is produced by the muscles in the abdominal wall and the lower part of our backs. These muscles might make slow and weak or rapid and strong air-streams with correspondingly soft or strong expressions.

Every person has his or her own rhythm and speed, which I must take into consideration when I participate in a conversation. As the stream of air passes the larynx its height or depth of the tone is modulated, and when it passes the oral and nasal cavities the muscles there act on it to make words composed of vowels and consonants. The activities of the muscles of the tongue, the lips, the palate, the jaws, and the nose influence the stream of air variously. The consonants are made by these muscles interfering with the stream. The hard consonants (such as *k*, *p*, and *t*) are made by sudden interruptions as the softer consonants (*m*, *n*, and *l*) are made by softer interruptions. The air-streams making vowels are not interrupted and will therefore float freely. Making the various vowels is achieved by varying the openings of the cavities of mouth and nose.

There is an interesting correspondence between the metaphor and the air-stream and its formation. Some words, when spoken, and consequently heard by the speaker, might immediately influence the abdominal wall's activity either to the softer or the stronger. Thus, if the talking in a conversation is a process where a person searches for being the person he or she wants to be, that search is not only a mental but a physiological search as well. And one might say that talking is a mental (metaphorical) and physiological definition of oneself. One might also say that pain and aches and stiffness in the body are related to obstructing the free flow of air through the body. In other words, they are connected to persons being in a state of not expressing themselves. With that in mind, it becomes even more important for me to not interrupt a person's talking and thinking. Sometimes as I listen I can hear the small sighs that come when some tension somewhere in the body goes and thereby lets the air go out more easily. The more one listens, and the more one listens with intensity, the more such small sighs can be heard. I was very excited when I learned from Aadel Bülow-Hansen that if there is tension in those muscles of the nose, palate, jaw, tongue, and lips that participate in the making of words there is a corresponding inhibition of the movements of breathing in the abdomen and chest.

The final words allow a metaphor:

> The abdominal wall is the organ's bellow, the larynx the shifting organ pipes and the cavities of mouth and nose our cathedrals, our shifting cathedral. Some of the words that come to these cathedrals are sacred, sometimes so sacred that they can not be spoken but only thought.

Closing Words

The open conversations that constitute 'the Reflecting Process' have brought clients and professionals toward more egalitarian relationships. In such a relationship it has become natural to focus primarily on what they have in common; the conversation between them. During the long process that has followed the launching of 'the Reflecting Process' it has emerged that questions are better tools for a professional than meanings and opinions. It has become natural to search for all the immanent but not yet used descriptions and understandings of the defined problems. And in doing so it has become of central interest to focus on the language that is used to describe and understand. The language that a person uses is very personal as it contains carefully selected metaphors. When the words are expressed, the words themselves and all the emotions that are embedded in them are brought to others through the physiological act of breathing. This act of breathing, which is part of the act of creating meaning, is very personal. It sets the air in motion and creates a wind that touches others with its words and emotions.

The listener is not only a receiver of a story but also, by being present, an encouragement to the act of making the story. And that act is the act of constituting one's self.

Notes

1. The exchanges of ideas that I have had the privilege to have with Harold Goolishian and his colleague Harlene Anderson, Galveston Family Institute, Texas, have very strongly influenced my thinking and practice. This chapter would not have had the form and content it ended up with without those exchanges.

2. This was one of two teams, which during the years 1984–88 comprised these members who took part at different periods: Carsten Bjerke, Eivind Eckhoff, Bjørn Z. Ekelund, John Rolf Ellila, Anna Margrete Flåm, Magnus Hald, Torunn Kalstøl Per Lofnes, Torill Moe, Trygve Nissen, Lorentz Notø, Tivadar Scüzs, Elsa Stiberg, Finn Wangberg, and Knut Waterloo.

3. Reflecting refers here to the same meaning as the French word *réflexion* (something heard is taken in, thought over, and the thought is given back) and not the English meaning (replication or mirroring).

References

Andersen, T. (ed.) (1991) *The Reflecting Team: Dialogues and Dialogues about the Dialogues.* New York: Norton.

Anderson, H. and Goolishian, H. (1988) 'Human systems as linguistic systems: preliminary and evoking ideas about the implications for clinical theory', *Family Process*, 27: 371–94.

Anderson, H., Goolishian, H. and Winderman, L. (1986) 'Problem determined systems: towards transformation in family therapy', *Journal of Strategic and Systemic Therapy*, 5: 1–11.

Bateson, G. (1972) *Steps to an Ecology of Mind.* New York: Ballantine.

Bateson, G. (1978) 'The birth of a matrix, or double bind and epistemology', in M. Berger (ed.), *Beyond the Double: Communication and Family Systems, Theories, and Techniques with Schizophrenics.* New York: Brunner/Mazel.

Bateson, G. (1979) *Mind and Nature: A Necessary Unity.* New York: Bantam.

Baynes, K., Bohman, J. and McCarthy, T. (1987) *After Philosophy: End or Transformation?* Cambridge, MA: MIT Press.

d'Andrade, R. (1986) 'Three scientific world views and the covering law model', in D.W. Fiske and R. Shweder (eds), *Metatheory in Social Science.* Chicago, IL: University of Chicago Press.

Gergen, K.J. (1984) 'Theory of the self: impasse and evolution', *Advances in Experimental Social Psychology*, 17: 49–115.

Gergen, K.J. (1985) 'The social constructionist movement in modern psychology', *American Psychologist*, 40 (3): 266–75.

Gergen, K.J. (1989) 'Warranting voice and the elaboration of the self', in J. Shotter and K.J. Gergen (eds), *Texts of Identity.* London: Sage.

Haley, J. (1963) *Strategies of Psychotherapy.* New York: Grune & Stratton.

Heidegger, M. (1962) *Being and Time.* New York: Harper & Row.

Kuhn, T.S. (1970) *The Structure of Scientific Revolution.* Chicago: University of Chicago Press.

Leary, D.E. (1984) 'The role of metaphor in science and medicine', Paper presented as part of the Program for Humanities in Medicine Lecture Series at the Yale University School of Medicine, 19 Oct.

Maturana, H. (1978) 'The biology of language: the epistemology of reality', in

G. Miller and E.H. Lenneberg (eds), *Psychology and Biology of Language and Thought*. New York: Academic Press.

Maturana, H. and Varela, F. (1987) *The Tree of Knowledge*. Boston: MA: New Science Library.

Minuchin, S. (1974) *Families and Family Therapy*. London: Tavistock.

Penn, P. (1982) 'Circular questioning', *Family Process*, 21: 267–80.

Penn, P. (1985) 'Feed-forward: future questions, future maps', *Family Process*, 24: 299–311.

Selvini, M., Boscolo, L., Cecchin, G. and Prata, G. (1980) 'Hypothesizing-circularity-neutrality: three guidelines for the conductor of the session', *Family Process*, 19: 3–12.

von Foerster, H. (1984) 'On constructing a reality', in P. Watzlawick (ed.), *The Invented Reality*. New York: Norton.

von Glasersfeld, E. (1984) 'An introduction to radical constructivism', in P. Watzlawick (ed.), *The Invented Reality*. New York: Norton.

Warnke, G. (1987) *Gadamer: Hermeneutics, Tradition and Reason*. Stanford, CA: Stanford University Press.

Watzlawick, P., Beavin, J. and Jackson, D.D. (1967) *Pragmatics of Human Communication*. New York: Norton.

Watzlawick, P., Weakland, J. and Fisch, R. (1974) *Change: Principles of Problem Formation and Problem Resolution*. New York: Norton.

5

Postmodern Thinking in a Clinical Practice

William D. Lax

What stories can do, I guess, is make things present.

(Tim O'Brien, 1990: 204)

During the past ten years the social sciences have undergone significant changes through the increasing influence and acceptance of postmodern thinking.[1] This thinking challenges many accepted ideas regarding the theory and practice of psychotherapy, particularly family therapy. This chapter discusses some of these challenges, and explores the implications of these transitions for family therapy, both theoretically and practically. Particular focus will be on deconstruction theory and the roles of narrative, text, and reflexivity as they relate to clinical discourse. I will present a narrative view of therapy, proposing that the ways in which clients describe their lives limit them in developing new ideas or approaches regarding their life situations. Psychotherapy is the process of shifting the client's current 'problematic' discourse to another discourse that is more fluid and allows for a broader range of possible interactions. While embracing the narrative view, I will discuss how the text analogy from literary criticism is limited in its application to human systems, and will conclude with a discussion of current work practiced at the Brattleboro Family Institute that exemplifies many of these ideas in clinical practice.[2]

Postmodern Thinking

Writings on postmodernism frequently focus on ideas regarding text and narrative, with attention to the importance of dialogic/multiple perspectives, self-disclosure, lateral versus hierarchical configurations, and attention to process rather than goals. In addition, such writing is often characterized by the following emphases: the self is conceived not as a reified entity, but as a narrative; text is not something to be interpreted, but, is an evolving process; the individual is considered within a context of social meaning rather than as an intrapsychic entity; and scientific knowledge or what would be considered undeniable 'facts' about the world yields to narrative knowledge with emphasis placed more upon communal beliefs about how the world works (see Gergen and Davis, 1985; Lyotard, 1988; Sampson, 1989; Sarup, 1989).

While family therapy recognizes the individual in-a-context rather than simply as an intrapsychic entity, most current thinking still carries a more 'modern' perspective rather than postmodern.[3] This modern perspective views family structures as inherently hierarchically arranged, considers the family as existing independent of an observer, sees the therapist as maintaining an expert position, and holds 'normative family development' as the benchmark of healthy family growth and functioning (see Haley, 1976; Bowen, 1978; Minuchin, 1974).

Recently, with the advent of the Milan Associates and their return to Bateson's thinking (Selvini et al., 1980; Boscolo et al., 1987), along with the pioneering work of theorists and therapists like Tom Andersen (1987, 1991), Harold Goolishian and Harlene Anderson (1987, 1990), Lynn Hoffman (1988, 1990), and Michael White (White, 1989; White and Epston, 1990), the field has begun to take a more postmodern turn. This transition incorporates several significant changes. Universal truths or structures give way to a multiverse or plurality of ideas about the world (Maturana and Varela, 1987). The view of families as homeostatic systems yields to one of social systems being generative and states of disequilibrium as being productive and normal (Elkaim, 1982; Hoffman, 1981). Families are conceptualized as social systems composed of meaning-generating, problem-organizing systems (rather than systems in which symptoms serve functions) with problems existing in and mediated through language (Anderson and Goolishian, 1988, 1990; Epstein and Loos, 1989). Additionally, hierarchical, expert-orientated models of therapy are shifting to ones of lateral configuration, with both clients and therapists having a more equal responsibility for the therapeutic process (see Andersen, 1991; Caesar and Roberts, 1991). These shifts call for a re-evaluation of much of our traditional thinking about family therapy. The family no longer becomes the object of treatment, viewed independent of an observer or as a source of problems, but as a flexible entity composed of people with shared meanings (Jorgenson, 1991).

Narrative, Deconstruction, and the Text

A major feature of this emerging perspective is the understanding of the role of narrative in clinical practice. Sarbin (1986) provides an essential transition with his distinction of narrative as a root metaphor in human experience. The narrative view holds that it is the process of developing a story about one's life that becomes the basis of all identity and thus challenges any underlying concept of a unified or stable self.

The development of a narrative or story is something that we do in conjunction with others (see Gergen, 1989; Shotter, 1989). It is the process of defining who we are in interaction with other people's perceived understandings of us. This is a recursive process. We shape the world in which we live, thereby creating our own 'reality' within a context of a community of others. The boundaries of our narratives are constructed through political, economic, social, and cultural constraints and potentials, with our choice of narratives not limitless, but existing within prescribed contexts. This narrative or sense of self arises not only through discourse with others, but *is* our discourse with others. There is no hidden self to be interpreted. We 'reveal' ourselves in every moment of interaction through the on-going narrative that we maintain with others. According to philosopher Emanuel Levinas (in Kearney, 1984), 'the I does not begin with itself in some pure moment of autonomous self-consciousness, but in relation with the other, for whom it remains forever responsible.' A permanent self is merely an illusion that we cling to, a narrative developed in relation to others over time that we come to identify as who we are.[4]

I find it most useful to view this emphasis on narrative in conjunction with theories of literary deconstruction. Jane Flax, in her commentary on postmodern thinking, states that all postmodern discourses are basically deconstructive 'in that they seek to distance us from and make us skeptical about beliefs concerning truth, knowledge, power, the self, and language that are often taken for granted and serve as legitimation for contemporary Western culture' (1990: 41). Deconstruction theory is rooted in a philosophical tradition arising particularly from the works of Kant, Husserl, Heidegger, and Wittgenstein (see Eagleton, 1983; Taylor, 1986). These thinkers continually address the questions of how we can know the world (reality) and what the role of language is in our descriptions of the world.

According to French deconstruction theorist Jacques Derrida (1976, 1978), language is a system of signs that do not have an inherent positive or negative value. Values are given to them only through our meaning making. The existence of a word automatically includes all those distinctions of both itself and its relationship to other words that are not present. Thus, multiple understandings are always available through the distinction of what is present in the text in relation to opposing words and ideas that are not present. These other possible understandings can be understood as traces in the text, 'always already' available to be called forth. Following the 'reader response' perspective (see Culler, 1982), these new distinctions are not like artifacts, waiting to be discovered, but different views available to each reader based on that person's perspective within which she views the text.

As psychologist Edward Sampson points out, there are marked similarities between Derrida's ideas of *différance* – which Derrida describes as 'neither a word nor a concept' (1986: 400) – and Bateson's notions of difference: both 'describe relations, not entities' (Sampson, 1989: 11). *Différance*, however, takes on an additional quality to the Batesonian idea of difference. Derrida proposes that there is both what is said and what is not said, and the tension between the two is *différance*. This tension creates the potential for a new understanding to emerge. This new understanding is not a duality of either/or between words and meanings, but a shift, at a minimum, to a both/and position. With this interplay of the said and the not-said, the present and the not-present, there is always the potential of another position or perspective, which has not yet been distinguished, to emerge. It is this other position for which Derrida further suggests we continually look: a description that is even outside of the both/and perspective. For Derrida, another view is there for us, and we should always attempt to deconstruct our world as we know it, looking for the unexpected that might replace that view.

In therapy new narratives/perspectives can arise through the interplay of the client's metaphors and phrasings with those of the therapist. Thus, the therapist can attend to what is not said by the clients and offer a different view back to them as a reflection. For example, we saw a couple in therapy who talked about feeling 'lost' with each other.[5] The therapy team observing the session made some comments in the presence of the clients. They wondered what it would be like to be 'found,' and talked about journeys in which people and ideas can be both lost and found. They considered what the couple might find on such a trip and the road signs they might encounter along the way. After these reflections, the couple began to talk differently about their journey and discussed what signs they thought they might find. Their feelings of desperation quickly changed to hopefulness as they began to develop a new 'course' for themselves, which included aspects of both being lost and found as well as new ideas of their own. They said that the team's comments enabled them to develop a new picture of their situation.

The team's different story was not intended to replace the couple's story. It allowed a *différance* or tension to be generated between the two. This tension was the beginning of the development of a new narrative by the couple, one that was neither one's story nor the other's. It was potentially both something new and an integration/variation of the other stories already developed. This couple's new story about their lives could be viewed as existing as a trace for them already in their repertoire, only not yet distinguished.

From Literary Texts to Human Systems

The examination of the text as an analogy for human systems has become popular recently in different disciplines. Geertz (1973) and Ricoeur (1979) both extol the use of text as a metaphor for human experience. In clinical practice the text analogy has been utilized by White and Epston (1990) and Penn and Sheinberg (1991). Gergen also examines the text analogy, but questions it as a useful metaphor. He both challenges the role of looking for any underlying intentions in human interaction and asks 'if persons are texts then who are the readers?' (1988: 43). He proposes that one can never truly know either one's own or another's intentions. The only possibility is for multiple interpretations, 'no one of which is objectively superior' (1988: 35). Understanding arises not through an examination of deep structure, latent or unconscious material, but through interaction between individuals. Thus Gergen emphasizes the role of context and relationship between individuals in the unfolding of meaning and intention in human behavior. The challenge, thus, is to shift the concept of understanding from that of the individual to the arena of interaction between the observer and observed: a process of co-construction of understanding.

Following this perspective, the text analogy for human systems takes on much greater complexity than it does in literature. Clients are not passively inscribed texts waiting to be interpreted by a reader, even if the interpretation is not a fixed, right, or privileged view. Each reading is different, given the interaction between the client and therapist. The client, in essence, does not have a singular 'true' story independent of a 'reader' to whom she is telling that particular story. The interaction itself is where the text exists and where the new narrative of one's life emerges. The unfolding text is always something that occurs *between* people. Clients unveil the story of their lives in conjunction with a specific reader/therapist, therefore the therapist is always a co-author of the story that is unfolding, with the client(s) as the other co-author(s). The resulting text is neither the client's nor the therapist's story, but a co-construction of the two.

This narrative view is not to imply that the client does not have a story independent of the therapist. However, the story always unfolds in conjunction with an observer (present or implied), and who may be the person herself. The story can change over time as we develop 'insights' about ourselves, and reinterpret and embellish our life history in the context of the other, with history continually being recreated/constructed rather than 'remembered.' Real events do happen in our lives, but we then develop a narrative around them that sometimes freezes them. As we develop a new perspective about the event and our interaction with it, we change our narrative about it. From this perspective, insight can be considered merely a new understanding which makes sense to the person at that moment in time: it is not the discovery of some truth about one's existence, it is the development of a new story that one can utilize for the future until a new insight emerges.

If the therapist is a co-author/co-constructor, and his or her job is to co-generate a new text or story, how is this done? I find it most useful here to think in terms of shifting the discourse in which the client is currently engaged to another discourse in which the problem does not exist. This narrative view of therapy proposes that the ways that clients describe their lives limit them in developing new ideas or approaches regarding their life situations. The therapist's job is to join with them in the development of a new story about their lives that offers them a view that is different enough from their situation, yet not too different, to further the conversation. This view does not solidify problems, side with any one participant as being more 'right' than another, nor tell people what the 'correct' response, attitude, or behavior should be. Therapy is a process of continuing to engage in a conversation with the *intention* of facilitating/co-creating/co-authoring a new narrative with the clients without imposing a story on them. The starting point is always the client's story about his or her understanding of the world in the context of telling us as an observer/participant. It cannot be our story on top of theirs. The therapist is no longer seen as an expert, with a privileged story or view, but as a facilitator of this therapeutic conversation, a master or mistress of the art of conversation (Goolishian, personal communication, 21 June 1989).

Narrative Therapy: Discourse and Reflexivity

Of central importance to this view of changing/co-constructing narratives are the ideas of discourse and reflexivity. We continually live in discourse. In therapy we can engage with clients in discourses about experiences they have had. These may be *content* discussions examining specific resources they may have developed in solving a particular problem or *process* discourses examining the therapeutic relationship and how it is similar to or different from other relationships or ideas. We may choose to engage in a discourse regarding the present, past, or future, depending upon our orientation and our exchange with our client. Regardless of the choice, discourses continually delineate and objectify our world. What discourse we choose depends on what clients 'bring to us' and what orientation or discourse we as therapists bring to the therapeutic interaction which includes those of gender, culture, theoretical perspectives, and life experiences. Each type of conversation is a different discourse arising through the interaction of ourself with another. The uniqueness and quality of our work is dependent upon these multiple discourses. They should never be fixed and should be deconstructed by both clients and therapists, and subsequently reconstructed together.

Thus, discourse is conversation with others and is a social process. It does not mirror reality, but is a functioning element in the social process itself (Rorty, 1979). Following the work of Anderson and Goolishian (1990), conversation can be defined as any interaction between people in which there is some 'shared space' and there is mutual interaction within this space. Within this shared space there is a sense of understanding in which meanings of one another's thoughts, feelings, and actions are generated.

Reflexivity is 'the capacity of any system of signification to turn back upon itself, to make its own object by referring to itself' which is also understood as ideas which fold back on themselves (Ruby, 1982: 2). It is the act of making oneself an object of one's own observation. Through reflexive conversations, in which a person makes her prior conversation an object of her own observation, one shifts discourse and thus perspective. One is able to 'step aside' from the discourse one was initially engaged in and view it from another perspective.[6]

This process was made very evident to us in working with a mother and her youngest of eleven children.[7] She had come to us because her thirteen-year-old son, James, had been having difficulties in school. The school recommended therapy, saying that he was always moving about in the room, talking with other children, not turning in homework assignments and often sick, necessitating his being sent home. The school was beginning to consider him hyperactive and wanted a medical consultation. Mother described her son as 'very young,' frequently sick, and seemingly 'finding trouble.' She felt that many of his problems had to do with his being so 'little.' However, she also said that he was very caring, greatly concerned about her health and not as restless around the home.

In our initial conversations she told us that she and the boy's father had never been married and no longer lived together, although James saw his father daily. She explained that she was in very poor health, needing periodic 'emergency' attention from the local rescue service for breathing problems. James's father was also in poor health with high blood pressure, and had a life-long prescription drug addiction from which he had only recently been withdrawn.

The therapist, Judy Davis, talked with them about who might participate in the therapy, and both mother and son agreed that it might be useful to include father. He came to the next session, but somewhat reluctantly. Each parent had a different view of their son and said that it was difficult to have discussions with him. Judy discussed different ways of talking, with one suggestion being that they talk about their different views while their son watched and listened from behind the one-way mirror with me. All agreed. They returned for the next session, but father said that he had a lot on his mind and that therapy was making his life harder rather than easier. He could not deal with his problems as well as those of his son. Judy again raised the idea of the format discussed at the last meeting, and they proceeded with that arrangement. Although father continued to discuss his difficulties with therapy, the conversation quickly shifted as Judy asked what it might be like for them if they were to discuss their different views of their son. They both responded that they wished to do this, and James and I went behind the mirror to observe their conversation. Mother said that she saw her son as little and young, needing much care and attention; father saw him as older and more capable of receiving increased responsibility.

James and I then changed rooms with them, having the two of them and the therapist watch and listen to us discuss our observations of the interview. He talked at length about his feelings of wanting to help both of them, how he did that by being readily available to each, and about his plans for the future. He said that he wanted to work as a 'rescueman, a fireman or someone who can help other people.' He also said that he did not want to go very far from home.

We switched rooms again and Judy asked the parents their views of their son's comments. With tears, mother talked about how impressed she was: 'My little boy grew up out there in front of my eyes.' Father also responded emotionally and said that he had never heard his son talk with anyone 'the way that he did with Bill.' His new respect for his son was visible. Furthermore, father announced that he liked this process very much and wished to continue in therapy. Ideas about future conversations were discussed including talking about the mother's feelings about her last child leaving home.

Eight months after therapy ended, we met with the family at the mother's home. Both mother and father said that their son was doing much better at school, was working after school at a local hospital, and there had been only one incident since therapy ended: their son had set off a fire alarm and as 'restitution' had to do some community work at the fire station. While he had completed his requirements for this service, he continued at the fire station as a volunteer.

We believe that one aspect of this work that made it useful to the family was the shifting of discourses that the parents and son were able to take due to the reflexivity of their watching and listening to each other's conversations. Prior to this they had been engaged in only one discourse without any other perspective. The separation enabled each to observe the content of the original discourse from a new position and engage in a different discourse about the former. Neither parent had to convince the other that their son was old or young, and the son did not have to defend his position regarding what he was doing at school or at home.

In our therapeutic interactions, we often rely on reflexivity for new conversations to take place between individuals and for all participants to experience a certain degree of understanding of themselves and the other. Therapists are continually translating their clients' words into their own, sharing these with them, and seeing if there is a correspondence to their language/meaning-making system. Thus, understanding rather than explanation offers the possibility of new narratives to unfold, as it offers a slightly different view of the initial situation/description. In clinical practice this can be seen when a therapist tells a client her version/picture of the client's situation and it 'fits' for the client, even though it is different from the client's original story. The client often responds, 'You understand me.' To illustrate further, I was talking with a woman who described herself as 'agoraphobic . . . a lifelong illness.' I asked her what it would be like for her if I had some different views of her situation, and she said that it 'depended on how strange they were.' I told her that they might be strange, but they were only ideas and we could discard them if they were too strange! She said that I could tell her. I said the following, not directly to her, but as a conversation with myself (see Wangberg, 1991):

I wonder if your agoraphobia is like a kite on a string that is attached to your belt at the back of your pants. You forget that it is there, but are always pulling it along with you as you go through life. Sometimes it is windier than other times and you are reminded about it, and it keeps you from going too far into stormy weather. What would it be like to let go of the string and let the kite go on its own? How would things be different for you? Have there even been times when you forgot that the kite was attached to you?

She listened quietly to my story. She said that my story was relevant to her, and we then continued to have a discussion about my story and hers, that focused on both kites and freedom as well as agoraphobia and constraints. She said that she now had the beginnings of a new perspective on her situation which was not so restrictive.

I believe that she had the perceived experience of being understood by me which enabled both of us to begin to develop a new story between the two of us. Again, the presentation of my different story was not an attempt to 'give' her a new story of her life. By talking in the way I did, she was placed in a reflexive position to her previous conversation with me. However, I was engaged in a different discourse than the one in which she and I were involved before this reflection. In her listening, she was able to shift her own position and discourse to another one. Our two 'conversations' folded over each other, like the kneading of bread dough, generating a new position that was new to both of us which included the ideas of both freedom and constraint.

Our Current Work

Our work at the Brattleboro Family Institute integrates ideas from postmodern thinking into clinical practice. We have been strongly influenced by the work and writings of Lynn Hoffman (1988, 1990) and the 'reflecting position' developed by Tom Andersen (1987, 1991) and his colleagues in the north of Norway. Our work specifically focuses on the reflexivity between the participants in conversation, including both the clients and the therapists. In practical application we use questions, reflections, and shifting positions as the main clinical approaches of the therapy. The interview between the therapist and the family follows the questioning model first introduced by the Milan Associates and which has been expanded by Penn (1982, 1985) and Tomm (1987). Questions are often directed toward what Bateson described as information or differences. These are not intended to provide a new solution, but to create a tension that may lead to an integration of the differences and/or the development of a new narrative.

Throughout the interview attention is given to who can be talking with whom, about what, and how (Andersen, 1991). Our intention is to maintain the therapeutic conversation and not continue in a manner that is too different from the client's style, pace, or willingness to proceed. If the conversation were to be either too similar or too different from their usual mode of interaction and understanding, the conversation might come to a halt. The therapist initially asks questions regarding the context of the meeting and the history of the idea of coming in terms of relationships among those present and their ideas. 'How did the idea to come to therapy come about? Who had that idea first? Who agreed the most/least with it? If you had that idea in the past, how do you explain that you did not come in then? If we were to talk about these issues now, what might that be like for each of you? Is there anyone else who you think it might be useful to include in this conversation?'

In asking questions, the therapist maintains a perspective that there are no hierarchical arrangements in conversations. It is not an 'onion-skin' approach to therapy with conversations striated in concentric circles with the therapist having the job of traversing the layers until the 'real' material is reached. Each discourse is considered relevant if the participants consider it so, with the context of the conversation given an equal value to the content. One discourse is not necessarily more or less encompassing than another one. It may have more 'significance' to the participants, but this has more to do with the extent of the meanings that each ascribes to the discourse rather than its inherent nature.

As an interview progresses and other ideas are considered by the interviewer, team or clients, they can be 'put on the table' to be considered by the other participants. In the case described earlier of the mother, father, and son, ideas regarding membership in future meetings and formats for conversation were suggested, with the therapist's ideas made known to the family. In this manner the idea of potentially talking about issues can be considered, not necessarily with the goal of getting the clients to talk about them, but to engage in this discourse itself. New ideas can continually be introduced from this position, and this process allows both clients and therapist to determine what ideas and questions can and cannot be considered. The therapist may even have direct suggestions or ideas for the client. These too can be introduced *as an idea*, even a strong one, to be considered by the clients. The clients can be asked what their thoughts are about both the ideas/suggestions and about the therapist even introducing these strong ideas.

When shifting perspectives and introducing new ideas, some descriptions/discussions are not always able to be included in a conversation. As in literary criticism, there may be contextual limits to the extent of the narratives which can be understood or generated. For example, in some families where there is a difference in opinion about whether alcohol abuse is taking place, a detailed conversation about alcohol may be too different from what they are capable of discussing at that time. A conversation about the possibility of discussing alcohol and an examination of their differences about the issue may be more possible for them and may allow them to continue in therapy. Once a therapist begins to press them beyond what they can be engaged in, they may not return to therapy. This does not mean that therapists needs to handle them with 'kid gloves.' They can introduce the difficult topics to be discussed from their own point of view and ask what it would be like to discuss them.

A comment that is frequently raised in our training programs with students pertains to the appropriate moment for addressing 'content' in our conversations. We are often asked: 'You are always "talking about talking" as if you are at the edge of the pool always testing the water. When do you get into the pool? Initially I thought that we first needed to meet the clients 'where they were' and move into the 'pool' slowly, going only as quickly as they could, being respectful of their processes. I believe now that when we are in conversation with our clients, we are *always* in the pool. The pool is the intersubjective interaction between us, the on-going discourse of the moment. It is neither more nor less important than any other; it merely is. Therefore, we should not assume any rights to direct the course of a conversation from any privileged position, nor can we predict where or how a conversation should unfold. While we may have an idea about what might take place or what has been useful to other clients in the past, this is only one view. These other views can be discussed, but should not be imposed on our clients.

This perspective on therapy is consistent with postmodern ideas in several significant ways. It is a shift from other models in the field, as it introduces the thinking of the therapist in a very overt way. There are no secret conversations behind clients' backs. Instead, all conversations are held in front of the clients, whether this is done through the team coming out from behind the mirror or a single therapist having a conversation with herself. The therapist is included fully as a participant in the therapeutic system, making her ideas about the therapy known to the clients. There are always other conversations that could take place, but the one the participants are engaged in is considered primary. For the therapist to say that one conversation is more important than another is merely the therapist's 'bias.' This bias is not to be discounted but considered as another perspective within the on-going conversation. To illustrate, in situations of violence or sexual abuse, the therapist may have a particular view about the situation, such as 'women should never be hit by men.' Rather than ignore this view and allow it to be a possible underlying lens which covertly influences the conversation, one approach is to make this view overtly known to the participants in the therapy. The therapist can put this view 'on the table' for discussion with a question or comment, such as, 'in situations like this I often have a strong reaction like . . . What would our meeting be like if I were to maintain this perspective in our conversation? Who would have difficulty with it?' In this way the ideas are shared, externalized, and participants can comment on them, potentially leading to a different way of discussing the situation. This approach maintains a respectful perspective of all members as equal collaborators in the process of making distinctions and choices as to which idea is attended to next.

There is an emphasis on process rather than goals. As stated above, one never knows when a new narrative will emerge, and sessions are not predetermined or outlined to proceed according to any set treatment plan or preordained 'steps.' Client and therapist are on a mutual exploration rather than on a goal-directed course with a specified outcome in mind or with the therapist intent on maintaining an expert position. Therapy focuses on the conversation between the client and therapist; as Rorty states, 'the point of edifying philosophy is to keep the conversation going rather than to find objective truth' (1979: 377).

If there were any goals at all, they would be to continue the conversation and distinguish aspects that were potentially available, but previously not examined, until a new narrative is developed. The therapist is always looking for other ways of introducing differences, whether through a story, reframe, metaphor or rephrasing of a single word. It is not finding a 'true' meaning, nor offering a new story. There is no metaposition or metaview of the therapist, and there is a continual questioning of assumptions on both parts. The new narrative that emerges from this interaction is one developed by all participants.

Summary

This chapter has identified several distinctions that are inherent in postmodern thinking and has related them to therapy. It is to be hoped that these will only serve to stimulate further conversation rather than offer another 'way' of doing therapy. Obviously this vein of thinking and clinical practice has serious clinical implications for the role of therapist as expert, and the meaning of diagnosis and treatment planning. This model contends that we can never know when a new narrative will be developed, and therefore other models of therapy that suggest specific stages of treatment are directly challenged, as well as those which ascribe to a therapist-oriented, hierarchically constructed approach. As Tom Andersen (1991) implies in his excellent commentary on his own work, this is a way of thinking that does not have a set formulation or fixed model of work. I believe that we have only seen the beginnings of a radical departure of therapy as we have known it over the past thirty years, one which it is to be hoped will challenge the expert model, socially, politically, and culturally.

Notes

My appreciation to my colleagues at the Brattleboro Family Institute and Antioch New England Graduate School for assisting me in formulating the ideas in this chapter. My thanks also to Sydney Crystal, Judy Davis, Eugene Epstein, Margit Epstein, Ken Gergen, Lynn Hoffman, Joan Laird, Lindy Norlander, Sheila McNamee, and Joe Pumilia for comments on earlier drafts of this chapter.

1. Postmodern thinking is evident principally in the social sciences of anthropology/ethnography (Geertz, 1973), cybernetics (von Foerster, 1981), feminism (Flax, 1990; Hare-Mustin and Maracek, 1988; Fraser and Nicholson, 1990), hermeneutics (Ricoeur, 1979; Gadamer, 1975), literary criticism (Barthes, 1979; Derrida, 1976, 1978, 1986; Lyotard, 1988), and social psychology (Gergen, 1985, 1989; Sampson, 1989; Shotter, 1989).

2. The clinical work at the Brattleboro Family Institute has been strongly influenced by Lynn Hoffman (1988, 1990) and by the reflecting team perspective developed by Tom Andersen (1987, 1991) and his colleagues in Tromsø, Norway. This work has been discussed elsewhere (see Davidson et al., 1988; Davidson and Lussardi 1991; Lax, 1989, 1991; Lax and Lussardi, 1988; Miller and Lax, 1988).

3. The modern perspective referred to here is one of a philosophical nature that privileges the subject in the construction of meaning. It assumes positions of expertise and authority (see Barnaby and Straus, 1989; Reiss, 1982).

4. Similar thinking can be found in other domains. Buddhist thought and teachings, particularly Theravada Buddhism, for example, claims that what we 'see' is only our concepts, not what is really there. These concepts are not context-free, but arise through our interactions (both present and past) in the world with others. All of life is seen as impermanent, including any sense of oneself.

5. The therapists were William Lax and Randye Cohen, and the team consisted of Ron Hollar and Perry Williamson.

6. This process of utilizing one discourse to observe another one is familiar to therapists from many different theoretical perspectives. Some psychodynamic therapists strive to develop an 'observing ego' in their clients; cognitive-behavioral therapists utilize ideas of thought-stopping, facilitating this same shift in discourse;

and solution-focused therapists develop a new discourse of 'unusual outcomes' or 'exceptions.' Hoffman (this volume) considers this process central to all good therapies and describes it as 'context resonance.'

7. The therapist was Judy Davis and the team consisted of William Lax and Joe Pumilia.

References

Andersen, T. (1987) 'The reflecting team: dialogue and meta-dialogue in clinical work', *Family Process*, 26 (4): 415–28.

Andersen, T. (ed.) (1991) *The Reflecting Team: Dialogues and Dialogues about the Dialogues*. New York: Norton.

Anderson, H. and Goolishian, H. (1988) 'Human systems as linguistic systems', *Family Process*, 27 (4): 371–95.

Anderson, H. and Goolishian, H. (1990) 'Some fundamental assumptions'. Unpublished paper, Galveston Family Institute.

Barnaby, B.B. and Straus, B.R. (1989) 'Notes on postmodernism and the psychology of gender', *American Psychologist*, 44 (10): 1328–30.

Barthes, R. (1979) 'From work to text', in J. Harari (ed.), *Textual Strategies*. Ithaca, NY: Cornell University Press.

Boscolo, L., Cecchin, G., Hoffman, L. and Penn, P. (1987) *Milan Systemic Family Therapy*. New York: Basic Books

Bowen, M. (1978) *Family Therapy in Clinical Practice*. New York: Jason-Aronson.

Caesar, P.L. and Roberts, M. (1991) 'A conversational journey with clients: therapist as tourist not tour guide', *Journal of Strategic and Systemic Therapies*, 10 (3/4): 38–51.

Culler, J. (1982) *On Deconstruction*. Ithaca, NY: Cornell University Press.

Davidson, J., Lax, W., Lussardi, D., Miller, D. and Ratheau, M. (1988) 'The reflecting team', *Family Therapy Networker*, 12 (3).

Davidson, J. and Lussardi, D. (1991) 'Use of the reflecting team in supervision and training', in T. Andersen (ed.), *The Reflecting Team: Dialogues and Dialogues about the Dialogues*. New York: Norton.

Derrida, J. (1976) *Of Grammatology*, tr. G.C. Spivak. Baltimore, MD: Johns Hopkins University Press.

Derrida, J. (1978) *Writing and Difference*, tr. A. Bass. Chicago: University of Chicago Press.

Derrida, J. (1986) 'Différance', in M.C. Taylor (ed.), *Deconstruction in Context*. Chicago, IL: University of Chicago Press.

Eagleton, T. (1983) *Literary Theory: an Introduction*. Minneapolis, MN: University of Minnesota Press.

Elkaim, M. (1982) 'Non-equilibrium, chance and change in family therapy', *Journal of Marital and Family Therapy*, 7 (3): 291–7.

Epstein, E.S. and Loos, V.E. (1989) 'Some irreverent thoughts on the limits of family therapy', *Journal of Family Psychology*, 2 (4): 405–21.

Flax, J. (1990) 'Postmodernism and gender relations in feminist theory', in L.J. Nicholson (ed.), *Feminism/Postmodernism*. New York: Routledge.

Fraser, N. and Nicholson, L.J. (1990) 'Social criticism without philosophy: an encounter between feminism and postmodernism', in L.J. Nicholson (ed.), *Feminism/Postmodernism*. New York: Routledge.

Gadamer, H.G. (1975) *Truth and Method*. New York: Continuum.

Geertz, C. (1973) *The Interpretation of Cultures*. New York: Basic Books.

Gergen, K.J. (1985) 'The social constructionist movement in modern psychology', *American Psychologist*, 40 (3): 266–75.

Gergen, K.J. (1988) 'If persons are texts', in S.B. Messer, L.A. Sass and R.L. Woolfolk (eds), *Hermeneutics and Psychological Theory*. New Brunswisk, NJ: Rutgers University Press.

Gergen, K.J. (1989) 'Warranting voice and the elaboration of self', in J. Shotter and K.J. Gergen (eds), *Texts of Identity*. London: Sage.

Gergen, K.J. and Davis, K.E. (eds) (1985) *The Social Construction of the Person*. New York: Springer-Verlag.

Goolishian, H. and Anderson, H. (1987) 'Language systems and therapy: an evolving idea', *Psychotherapy*, 24: 529–38.

Goolishian, H. and Anderson, H. (1990) 'Understanding the therapeutic system: from individuals and families to systems in language', in F. Kaslow (ed.), *Voices in Family Psychology*. Newbury Park, CA: Sage.

Haley, J. (1976) *Problem Solving Therapy*. San Francisco, CA: Jossey Bass.

Hare-Mustin, R.T. and Maracek, J. (1988) 'The meaning of difference: gender theory, postmodernism, and psychology', *American Psychologist*, 43 (6): 455–64.

Hoffman, L. (1981) *Foundations of Family Therapy*. New York: Basic Books.

Hoffman, L. (1986) 'Beyond power and control', *Family Systems Medicine*, 3: 381–96.

Hoffman, L. (1988) 'A constructivist position for family therapy', *Irish Journal of Psychology*, 9 (1): 110–29.

Hoffman, L. (1990) 'Constructing realities: an art of lenses', *Family Process*, 29 (1): 1–12.

Jorgenson, J. (1991) 'How families are constructed'. Unpublished doctoral dissertation, University of Pennsylvania.

Kearney, R. (1984) *Dialogues with Contemporary Continental Thinkers*. Manchester: Manchester University Press.

Lax, W. (1989) 'Systemic family therapy with young children in the family: use of the reflecting team', *Psychotherapy and the Family*, 5 (3/4): 55–73.

Lax, W. (1991) 'The reflecting team and the initial consultation', in T. Andersen (ed.), *The Reflecting Team: Dialogues and Dialogues about Dialogues*. New York: Norton.

Lax, W. and Lussardi, D. (1988) 'The use of rituals with adolescents and their families', in E.I. Black, J. Roberts and R. Whiting (eds), *Rituals in Families and Family Therapy*. New York: Norton.

Lussardi, D.L. and Miller, D. (1990) 'A reflecting team approach to adolescent substance abuse', in T.C. Todd and M. Selekman (eds), *Family Therapy with Adolescent Substance Abuse*. New York: Allyn & Bacon.

Lyotard, J.-F. (1988) *The Postmodern Condition: a Report on Knowledge*, tr. G. Bennington and B. Massumi. Minneapolis, MN: University of Minnesota Press.

Maturana, H. and Varela, F. (1987) *The Tree of Knowledge*. Boston, MA: New Science Library.

Miller, D. and Lax, W.D. (1988) 'Interrupting deadly struggles: a reflecting team model for working with couples', *Journal of Strategic and Systemic Therapies*, 7 (3): 16–22.

Minuchin, S. (1974) *Families and Family Therapy*. Cambridge, MA: Harvard University Press.

O'Brien, T. (1990) *Things They Carried with Them*. Boston, MA: Houghton Mifflin.

Penn, P. (1982) 'Circular questioning', *Family Process*, 21: 267–80.

Penn, P. (1985) 'Feed-forward: future questions, future maps', *Family Process*, 24: 299–311.

Penn, P. and Sheinberg, M. (1991) 'Stories and conversations', *Journal of Strategic and Systemic Therapies*, 10 (3/4): 30–7.

Reiss, T.J. (1982) *The Discourse of Modernism*. Ithaca, NY: Cornell University Press.

Ricoeur, P. (1979) 'The model of the text: meaningful action considered as a text', in P. Rabinow and W.S. Sullivan (eds), *Interpretative Social Science*. Berkeley, CA: University of California Press.

Rorty, R. (1979) *Philosophy and the Mirror of Nature*. Princeton, NJ: Princeton University Press.

Ruby, J. (1982) *A Crack in the Mirror*. Philadelphia, PA: University of Pennsylvania Press.

Sampson, E.E. (1989) 'The deconstruction of the self', in J. Shotter and K.J. Gergen (eds), *Texts of Identity*. London: Sage.

Sarbin, T.R. (1986) *Narrative Psychology: The Storied Nature of Human Conduct*. New York: Praeger.

Sarup, M. (1989) *An Introductory Guide to Post-structuralism and Postmodernism*. Athens, GA: University of Georgia Press.

Selvini, M.P., Boscolo, L., Cecchin, G. and Prata, G. (1980) 'Hypothesizing – circularity – neutrality: three guidelines for the conductor of the session', *Family Process*, 19 (1): 3–12.

Shotter, J. (1989) 'Social accountability and the social construction of "You"', in J. Shotter and K.J. Gergen (eds), *Texts of Identity*. London: Sage.

Taylor, M.C. (1986) *Deconstruction in Context: Literature and Philosophy*. Chicago, IL: University of Chicago Press.

Tomm, K. (1987) 'Interventive interviewing: Part II. Reflexive questioning as a means to enabling self-healing', *Family Process*, 26: 167–84.

von Foerster, H. (1981) *Observing Systems*. Seaside, CA: Intersystems Publications.

Wangberg, F. (1991) 'Self reflection: turning the mirror inward', *Journal of Strategic and Systemic Therapies*, 10 (3/4): 18–29.

White, M. (1989) *Selected Papers*. Adelaide: Dulwich Centre Publications.

White, M. and Epston, D. (1990) *Narrative Means to Therapeutic Ends*. New York: Norton. (Also printed as *Literate Means to Therapeutic Ends*, 1989, Adelaide: Dulwich Centre Publications.)

6

Constructing Therapeutic Possibilities

Gianfranco Cecchin

In the field of family therapy we can notice a slow but continuous movement from an epistemology based on cybernetic principles to an epistemology based on the notion that human relationships emerge through their socially produced stories. Particular family narratives come into being in the social domain. From this perspective we can say that interactions provide the opportunities and the limits to our worlds.

In this chapter I will reconstruct one story of the evolution from cybernetic principles to social construction and suggest that this process has been happening through the constant questioning and curiosity of beliefs, models, and particular forms of practice. I also want to suggest that by being both a strategizer and a non-instrumental clinician, the therapist can avoid the certainty of ultimate truth.

It is interesting to hypothesize about the movement from principles of cybernetics to those of social construction. Any form of stability creates the condition for new changes which creates a new stability, and so on. With this in mind, it is revealing to look at what has taken place in the family therapy field, particularly with my own involvement in the evolution of the Milan Systemic model. I was one of four people in Milan in 1971–72 who tried to do therapy in a different way. After several years of trying to work therapeutically using the psychoanalytic model, we felt dissatisfied and began looking for a new model and a new way to work. Several conceptual shifts marked our development of the systemic model: the shift from (1) energy to information; (2) entities to social constructions; and (3) a focus on family to therapist.

From Energy to Information

As a team, we were confronted with new ideas presented by Watzlawick et al., 1967. These ideas appeared to constitute a magnificent theory. According to this theory there was no longer any need to use the concept of energy. Everything was communication. Everything was a message.

We found a new freedom, a freedom not to look at what we can find inside a person but at how people fit together in a communication net where everyone is doing something and at the same time responding to somebody else. What emerged were stories and games, most of them beautifully dramatic and even sometimes very comic. We became fascinated by games and began looking for ways to bring out the 'real' game in every family. It was an enjoyable and fascinating experience to talk to a family and spend time with our colleagues finding out what kind of games people were playing. Of course, having chosen this stand, certain consequences emerged.

Some disturbances and contradictions began to appear. First, we noticed that the more pathological the family was, the easier it was to describe the family or to describe its game. We adopted a stance that allowed us to see families as mechanistic systems regulated by feedback. The doubt crept in, 'Is our theory good for systems which, in some ways, resemble a machine? What about other human systems that do not resemble machines?' Secondly, because we were seduced by the idea of games, our descriptions very often ended up portraying people as coming together for the sole purpose of competing with one another, outsmarting one another, or defining their relationships from an 'up' position (as was in the common language of the time). Sometimes we felt that people would stay together in order to fight because episodes of fighting provided opportunities for 'winning.' In the couple or in the family, we could see tremendous competition and, when everything was quiet, we thought it was a simple, temporary, apparent equilibrium in a situation of permanent battle.

Naturally, the battle was not only between the members of the family, but when they came to us, the battle began to include us. Therapists would often go behind the mirror to plan their strategy with colleagues in order to fight back. We used the language of warfare, saying, for example, 'This family is organizing some kind of trap for us,' and 'What kind of maneuver can we create to fight back?' Also, 'I think the son is making an alliance with the therapist perhaps in order to put down the parents.' Lastly, 'The wife is very charming but she is trying to humiliate her husband,' and so on.

Every move became a maneuver and every statement was understood in ten different ways. When the family came to us, the questions we asked were, 'What kind of game are they playing with each other?' 'What kind of game are they playing with us?' and 'What kind of different game could we play with them?' Usually we wanted to win these games, and we were convinced that in this manner we could persuade them to give up their power struggle. If this was impossible, we might succeed in convincing them to change their game, or bring it to a more tolerable level not necessitating symptoms. In this context, it was necessary for the therapist to have control over the session. For example, if we invited four people and they showed up with only three, we would send them home until all four could come. If we gave in it was like losing a battle. The relationship was one of confrontation instead of cooperation.

One of the 'weapons' we used at that time was what we called the 'paradoxical intervention' (Selvini et al., 1978). We could observe that in families and couples people were battling against one another using paradoxical communication. Paradox was a way to gain control but at the same time it was a way to bring the battle to a standstill or to a kind of apparent truce. The families were also behaving in a paradoxical way with us. It was a way to make peace as well as to make war. So we became experts in creating paradoxical situations springing from the intensity of the therapeutic relationship. Also here there was nothing new, we were simply applying the ideas provided by Watzlawick et al., 1967. But in some way we got stuck with the reputation of being the ones who do 'paradoxical therapy.' Many times when someone came to visit or some student was observing a therapy session, at a certain moment this person would ask, 'Where is the paradox?' We would ask a family a simple question like, 'How are you?' and someone would ask, 'How can you make that paradoxical?' We became stuck with the 'label' of paradox. Everything had to be paradoxical. And of course, everything was in the frame of a power play. After a while, we recognized another conceptual shift. This shift was marked by our own observation that we, as team members, were fighting with one another and generally feeling discomfort. Something had to change.

What helped us to overcome this impasse was, again, another theory. We discovered Bateson's *Steps to an Ecology of Mind* (1972). We saw that the Palo Alto Group (Watzlawick et al., 1967) had drawn inspiration from Bateson's work. So, we began picking from the different ideas of Bateson, in their original form, in order to move beyond our own impasse.

From Entities to Social Constructions

Building upon the shift from energy to information, we recognized communication as a relational process wherein information is socially constructed. Bateson articulated this position in his discussion of power. Power, says Bateson, is an idea, a construction.

People create the idea of power and then behave as if power existed. Power is created by the context and is invented by the protagonists of the situation.

Adopting this idea, we moved from seeing family members' actions as maneuvers within a game for power. We began to see people as involved in staying together, not to control one another or to control their relationship, but to make sense *with* one another. This was an interesting conceptual shift. Husbands and wives, parents and children are not there to try to outsmart one another. They are trying to make sense of their relationship. In some way it was a more 'human' position for the therapist. Fighting and competing for power was only one of the many ways people try to make sense. We could call it an attempt to make sense when other options to do so are not available or are not seen.

This shift provided the opportunity for a renewed interest in what the therapist was doing in the therapeutic context. Once the metaphor of a game or battle was dismissed, the need to win was also dismissed. Now we could engage in a self-reflexive process. Once we identified this shift, we became aware of an interesting phenomenon. When a particular therapist was talking with a family, he or she would 'discover' a certain type of game, while another therapist would see, perhaps, a different one. A third therapist would see a third one. So we realized that the game depended not solely on the family but also on the therapist. Perhaps, there was no 'real game' after all. The game was something that emerged from the relationship between the therapist and the family. With this observation, we began to doubt the idea of 'discovery.' For a long time we thought that to 'discover' was our job as scientists/clinicians. Only after a good and reliable discovery could we do something that would be medically and ethically correct. But now we faced the contradiction that what we discovered depended on the 'discoverer' and on the type of questions that were asked. In essence, what we discovered was what we had co-constructed with the family.

Shifting Focus: Family to Therapist

Thus, we were compelled to make another shift. Our focus of attention moved from 'the family' to 'the therapist.' For a long time, we never discussed the observer, but now, finally convinced that what we 'discover' depends ultimately on the observer, we began to watch ourselves. We had a lot of help from our students. Students training at our Center had always shown more interest in what we, the therapists, were doing than in the families' games.

We were asking families a lot of questions about their organization while the students were asking a lot of questions about what we were doing. Two foci emerged in our attention to the therapist: the idea of hypotheses and the stance of curiosity.

From Truth to Hypotheses

As we shifted our focus toward ourselves, we became aware that we always had an hypothesis in mind. Before entering a session, or during the session, we had an idea about what was going on. This could create some tension with the family because if we liked our idea (hypothesis) too much, we inadvertently tried to impose it on the family. We thought that, perhaps, if they could see things our way then the problem would disappear.

It took some time to find out that it was not the quality of our hypothesis that made a difference. Rather, the difference was made by the contrast (the relationship) between our hypothesis and the family's or between the different hypotheses that emerged during the conversation. We struggled to give up our hypotheses even though they were very attractive and looked like the truth. Again, the hypothesis was a way of constructing a connection with the system and not a step towards the discovery of a 'real' story. We could then work for half an hour to develop a beautiful hypothesis which included all the elements in the system, a good systemic hypothesis, and then discard it in a few minutes if it revealed itself to be useless.[1]

The hypothesis is a way to contribute to the construction of a therapeutic relationship. It is the base for starting a conversation. By talking, the therapist reveals his or her own ideas about what is going on and engages with the family in a manner that resonates for all participants. This kind of resonance (a combination of body messages, verbal utterances, ideas, and hypotheses) is the ticket to participate or an invitation to create a new system. The value of the hypothesis is not in its truth but in its ability to create a resonance with those involved. I imagine that someone could enter in resonance even without talking but only with analogic conversation. However, humans use words to caress each other. Thus, words and hypotheses are a way to get in touch with each other in spite of their content. In summary, the hypothesis is a way to create a resonance with the system, regardless of its value as truth or its validity as explanation.

From Neutrality to Curiosity

Neutrality, an idea central to the Milan systemic approach (Selvini et al., 1980; Cecchin, 1987) also comes from warfare language.

Since we cannot take sides in the struggle we are observing, we choose to be neutral. In some way neutrality puts the therapist in a position of 'power.' How can we avoid this type of contradiction? It took some time to see that neutrality could be seen somehow as a 'state of activity' (cf. Cecchin, 1987). The effort of the therapist to look for patterns and to search for the fit and not for 'whys' or causes of behavior is what makes up the 'action' of being neutral.

In this circumstance, two theoreticians came to our help. Starting from the description of biological organizations, Maturana and Varela (1987) came to the conclusion that different biological units do not influence their reciprocal behavior in a direct way, but through structural coupling. In other words, different units simply fit with one another and any attempt to explain their interaction in a causal way is only a story constructed by an observer. This story could be useless and even misleading. What we see as a system is the fit of its members with one another. Fit, then, becomes an aesthetic quality of interaction. What we see happening could not *not* happen. If some event did not fit, it would not be there. This aesthetic way of seeing generates a sense of curiosity. If people are unhappy with their current situation but are, nevertheless, immersed in it, there must be some sort of 'fit.' This fit does not imply 'goodness' or value but does indicate a connection. To become curious about this connection can be useful in the construction of more viable forms of relatedness. Curiosity, as a therapeutic stance, provides the opportunity for the construction of new forms of action and interpretation.

The Irreverent Therapist as Social Constructionist

What I have described above is the position of the observer-therapist who uses his or her responses as an instrument to enter a system. But there are other possible ways for therapists to enter into a story. Anderson and Goolishian (1988) suggest that the therapeutic conversation is a way to engage with a family. I would like to offer another suggestion. As therapists, we become participant actors in the therapeutic story. The separation between 'participant actor' and 'conversationalist' is arbitrary. However, for the sake of clarification I will artificially separate these two positions. As a conversationalist, a therapist attempts to 'unblock' the logical restrictions that maintain the 'stuck' state of the system (cf. Sluzki, 1992). This is often accomplished through the use of circular questions (Selvini et al., 1980). As a participant actor, the therapist utilizes the particular role that emerges in the interactive context to take action, give prescriptions, become a 'social controller,' or even a 'moralizer.' The therapist can do this and remain loyal to a systemic epistemology only if two apparently contradictory principles are kept in mind.

First, the therapist must remember that several different relationships contribute to the construction of the therapist as a moralist, a social controller, and so on. Thus, if the therapist adopts a moralistic stance with a family where incest has been a problem, the therapist acts 'morally' only to the extent that a variety of other contexts and relationships provide the opportunity for such constructions. Some relevant relations include the therapeutic relationship (therapist to client) as well as the institutional, cultural, and historical conditions that come to bear on the therapeutic moment. Also needing consideration is the orientation of the therapist that emerges from his or her personal history, theoretical orientation and so forth. These relational concerns couple with the personal histories of the clients themselves.

Secondly, the therapist must also remember that his or her position, as constructed in the complex interactive moment, is a *co-construction*. Thus, the therapist shares responsibility for the context that emerges in therapy. So too, for those working with teams, it must be remembered that collectively the team members participate in the therapeutic situation that develops. All participants become active members in the conversation (even when they appear to be passive) and thus, all participants can be seen as continually selecting particular actions and interpretations. However, it is important to keep in mind that making a selection does not imply the viability of any construction. In order to be viable, an interpretation or action must be granted coherence within the significant interactive context. This requires a form of *social* choreography. Additionally, the selection of any particular interpretation or behavior by a therapist or client is always constrained by the possibilities that emerge in the therapeutic situation itself. In similar fashion, making a choice to act in a particular manner does not ensure a predictable outcome, because our activities are always joined with those of others, thereby providing the opportunity for unintended consequences to materialize (Shotter, 1987).

An illustration will help to clarify this second point. Suppose a therapist closes a session with the following comment, 'I cannot avoid thinking that many problems in your family stem from the fact that your behavior seems to be ruled by a patriarchal pattern that tends to oppress women. Some of the stories you told me succeeded in convincing me of this interpretation. Therefore, I will give you some instructions with the hope of breaking this pattern. Some of my colleagues behind the mirror, however, warned me that it is not proper to interfere with how families are organized, no matter how inappropriate we might think the organization is. I had a long argument with them and we came to the conclusion that I will follow my conviction, but only for five therapeutic sessions. I cannot avoid trying to do what I think is right as a therapist – even if my colleagues disagree.'

Here, the therapist takes responsibility for his or her convictions, puts them in a cultural context, offers an alternative interpretation (loyalty to patriarchal patterns), is careful to put the conviction in a time frame (five sessions), and makes clear that these convictions are not a truth independent of the observer and the context but are the result of ethical standards which stem from the therapist's personal history, cultural context, and theoretical orientation.

If you believe in action too much, you can become a manipulator. If you believe too strongly in letting the system just 'be,' you could become irresponsible. If you believe strongly in the oppressive aspects of systems, you can become a revolutionary. If you believe too passionately in the controlling aspects of therapy, you can become a social engineer. However, since it is impossible *not* to take a stand, it is exactly this reflexive loop between our taking a stand and immediately thereafter putting this stand in a larger context that creates the 'becoming' and not the 'being' of a therapist. Such a position also permits the therapist to achieve that healthy state of mild irreverence towards his or her own 'truths' no matter how much hardship it took to conquer them.

I believe that a social constructionist therapist may, at different moments, follow many different leaders, but never obey one particular model or theory. He or she is always slightly subversive towards any reified 'Truth.' In this sense the therapist illustrates a postmodern sensibility wherein the relational context is recognized as providing the therapeutic constraints and possibilities. These cannot be pre-determined by virtue of a model's validity or theoretical superiority. And yet, the irreverent therapist does not enter any therapeutic relationship void of ideas, experience, or privileged constructions. Just as clients come to therapy with their versions of reality, so too with therapists. The challenge is the negotiation and co-construction of viable and sustainable ways of being that fit with the family, the therapist, and the culturally sanctioned ways of being.

Finally, therapists become responsible for their own actions and opinions. They dare to use their resources to intervene, to construct rituals, to reframe situations, behaviors, and ideas for both the client and themselves. Those resources are, after all, the only things the therapist has. He or she cannot rely any more on 'truths' out there. Becoming free from the co-optive nature of consensual belief, he or she can also help the clients become more opinionated while simultaneously taking responsibility for their opinion.

By maintaining a position of 'irony,' the therapist attempts to understand the stories and patterns observed. Clients, themselves, observe the therapist's ironic position and can also begin, through modelling, to utilize this perspective. Clients might become more opinionated while simultaneously taking responsibility for their opinions and not reifying them as 'truisms.' Such a position promotes flexibility and creativity in both therapist and client.

Therapy is a fascinating challenge. The challenge is slowly to demolish the old story while moving toward a co-authored new story that opens up new possibilities for clients. The story of family therapy as a field follows this same narrative pattern. It is the unavoidable contradictions and dissonances that provide the opportunity for the construction of a new position, a new explanation, or a new story about what we are doing.

Note

1. Once it was established that we could change hypotheses many times, a new question appeared: 'Where are the hypotheses coming from?' Since the hypotheses are made by the observer in relation to other observers/participants, it is obvious that it is the accumulated experience of those observers that allows them to formulate any idea, concept, or hypothesis. Basically, it is their 'biases' that construct the hypothesis. The observers' biases come from their cultural background, education, and training. For the average family therapist, the major source of ideas is psychoanalysis. For example, look at the beautiful stories that come out of the Oedipal complex. From the triangulation theory of J. Haley (1964), came the boundary theory developed by Minuchin (1974) and the lifecycle explanation, and Selvini et al.'s (1989) theory of psychotic game, and so on. We usually tell our students, 'You should keep in mind 24 hypotheses, 50 stories and utilize the one that comes to your mind when you talk to a family.'

References

Anderson, H. and Goolishian, H. (1988) 'Human systems as linguistic systems: preliminary and evolving ideas about the implications for clinical theory', *Family Process*, 27 (4): 371–93.

Bateson, G. (1972) *Steps to an Ecology of Mind*. New York: Ballantine.

Cecchin, G. (1987) 'Hypothesizing, circularity and neutrality revisited: an invitation to curiosity', *Family Process*, 26 (4): 405–14.

Haley, J. (1964) *Strategies of Psychotherapy*. New York: Grune & Stratton.

Maturana, H. and Varela, F. (1987) *The Tree of Knowledge*. Boston, MA: New Science Library.

Minuchin, S. (1974) *Families and Family Therapy*. Cambridge, MA: Harvard University Press.

Selvini, M., Boscolo, L., Cecchin, G. and Prata, G. (1978) *Paradox and Counter-paradox*. New York: J. Aronson.

Selvini, M., Boscolo, L., Cecchin, G. and Prata, G. (1980) 'Hypothesizing – circularity – neutrality: three guidelines for the conductor of the session', *Family Process*, 19 (1): 3–12.

Selvini, M., Cirillo, S., Selvini, M. and Sorrentino, A.M. (1989) *Family Games: General Models of Psychotic Processes in the Family*. New York: Norton.

Shotter, J. (1987) 'The social construction of "us": problems, accountability, and narratology', in R. Burnett, P. McGee and D. Clarke (eds), *Accounting for Personal Relationships: Social Representation of Interpersonal Links*. London: Methuen.

Sluzki, L. (1992) 'Transformations: a blueprint for narrative changes in therapy', *Family Process*, 31.

Watzlawick, P., Beavin, J. and Jackson, D.D. (1967) *Pragmatics of Human Communication*. New York: Norton.

7

A Proposal for a Re-authoring Therapy: Rose's Revisioning of her Life and a Commentary

David Epston, Michael White and Kevin Murray

In the social sciences at least, it is now generally recognized that it is not possible for persons to have direct knowledge of the world; that an objective description of the world is not available to us, and that no one has a privileged access to the naming of reality, whatever that reality is.[1] And it is generally accepted that what we know of the world, we know only through our experience of it; our experience of the world is all that we have, and that is all that we can know. We cannot even know another person's experience of the world. The best that we can do is to interpret the experience of others; that is, the expressions of their experience as they go about the business of interpreting it for themselves.[2] 'Whatever sense we have of how things stand with someone else's inner life, we gain it through their expressions, not through some magical intrusion into their consciousness. It's all a matter of scratching surfaces' (Geertz, 1986: 373). And to interpret the expressions (and thus the interpretations) of others, we have to rely upon our own lived experience and imagination. The most we can do is to 'identify' our own experience of the experience as expressed by others. Thus 'empathy' is a critical factor in the interpretation or understanding of the experiences of others.

So this is all we have – our lived experience of the world. But this turns out to be a great deal. We are rich in lived experience. To quote Geertz, 'We all have very much more of the stuff than we know what to do with, and if we fail to put it into some graspable form, the fault must lie in a lack of means, not of substance' (1986: 373).

Certain questions are raised by any serious consideration of this proposal about the world of experience.

- Given that what we know of the world we know through our experience of it, what is the process by which we develop an understanding of our experience and give meaning to it?
- How do we make sense of our experience to ourselves, and how do we make sense of our experience to others?

- If we are perpetually involved in an attempt to articulate our lived experience to ourselves and to others, what processes are involved in our interpretation of it?
- What is it that facilitates the expression of our experience?
- And how does the expression of our lived experience affect our lives and relationships?

These questions focus our attention on an investigation of the ways in which we make sense of our lives to ourselves and to others; they focus our attention on the processes through which we interpret or attribute meaning to our experience.

In order to give meaning to our experience, we must organize it, frame it, or give pattern to it. To understand an aspect of our experience, we must be able to frame it within a pattern of experience that is known to us; we must be able to identify aspects of lived experience within the context of known patterns of experience.

Stories or Narratives

Those social scientists (J. Bruner, Gergen, and Harré in psychology; E. Bruner, Geertz, Clifford, V. Turner, and R. Rosaldo in anthropology; H. White, Mink, Gaillie in history, to name but a few) whose work is oriented by the 'interpretive method' and who embrace the text analogy propose that the 'story' or 'narrative' provides the dominant frame for live experience and for the organization and patterning of lived experience. Following this proposal, a story can be defined as a unit of meaning that provides a frame for lived experience. It is through these stories that lived experience is interpreted. We enter into stories; we are entered into stories by others; and we live our lives through these stories.

Stories enable persons to link aspects of their experience through the dimension of time. There does not appear to be any other mechanism for the structuring of experience that so captures the sense of lived time, or that can adequately represent the sense of lived time (Ricoeur, 1983). It is through stories that we obtain a sense of our lives changing. It is through stories that we are able to gain a sense of the unfolding of the events of our lives through recent history, and it appears that this sense is vital to the perception of a 'future' that is in any way different from a 'present'. Stories construct beginnings and endings; they impose beginnings and endings on the flow of experience. 'We create the units of experience and meaning from a continuity of life. Every telling is an arbitrary imposition of meaning on the flow of memory, in that we highlight some causes and discount others; that is, every telling is interpretive' (E. Bruner, 1986a: 7). In considering the vital role that stories have in relation to the organization of experience, it can be argued that:

1 It is the stories in which we situate our experience that determine[3] the meaning that we give to experience.
2 It is these stories that determine the selection of those aspects of experience to be expressed.
3 It is these stories that determine the shape of the expression that we give to those aspects of experience.
4 It is these stories that determine real effects and directions in our lives and in our relationships.

Performance as Shaping

In the foregoing discussion, we have argued that experience structures expression. But it can also be argued that expression structures experience. To quote Dilthey: 'Our knowledge of what is given in experience is extended through the interpretation of the objectifications of life and their interpretation, in turn, only made possible by plumbing the depths of subjective experience' (1976: 195). Thus, the stories that we enter into with our experience have real effects on our lives. The expression of our experience through these stories shapes or makes up our lives and our relationships; our lives are shaped or constituted through the very process of the interpretation within the context of the stories that we enter into and that we are entered into by others.

This is not to propose that life is synonymous with text. It is not enough for persons to tell a new story about themselves, or to assert claims about themselves. Instead, the proposition carried by these assertions about the world of experience and narrative is that life is the performance[4] of texts. And it is the performance of these texts that is transformative of persons' lives; however, these performances must be before relevant audiences or made known by some form of publication. [T]he participants must have confidence in their own authenticity, which is one reason cultures are performed. It is not enough to assert claims; they must be enacted. Stories only become transformative in their performance' (E. Bruner, 1986a: 25). Thus the idea that lives are situated in texts or stories implies a particular notion of authenticity – that a person arrives at a sense of authenticity in life through the performance of texts. This notion of authenticity may be affronting to many a cherished belief that carries propositions about the 'truth' of personhood or of human nature; those beliefs that suggest that, under particular and ideal circumstances of life, persons will be 'released' and thus become truly who they are: authentic.

Indeterminate Nature of Stories

If persons' lives are shaped through the storying of experience and through the performance of these stories, and if there is a limited stock of familial stories about who we might be and of cultural knowledges about personhood, how is it that we are not replicas of one another? Perhaps this question is best approached by considering the interaction of readers and literary texts. To do so would be to extend the text analogy in our attempts to understand more fully the processes involved in the ascription of meaning, and to liken life as lived under the guidance of stories to the reader's experience under the sway of the literary text. And since good stories are more transformative of the reader's experience than poor stories, this consideration could bring us to a review of the structure of texts of literary merit.

In following this premise, we believe that Iser, a literary theorist, assists us to find an answer to the question, 'How is it that we are not replicas of one another?'

> fictional texts constitute their own objects and do not copy something already in existence. For this reason they cannot have the full determinacy of real objects, and indeed, it is the element of indeterminacy that evokes the text to 'communicate' with the reader, in the sense that they induce him to participate both in the production and the comprehension of this work's intention. (1978: 21)

It is readily apparent that all stories are indeterminate.[5] There is a degree of ambiguity and uncertainty to all stories, and, as well, there are inconsistencies and contradictions. This fact will be appreciated by those who have read a novel that was particularly engaging and then gone to a movie of the same novel, only to find, to their dismay, that the movie director had got it wrong! In such circumstances, what is clear is that the director arrived at a different interpretation of the story through his or her unique negotiation of its indeterminacy.

So literary texts are full of gaps that readers must fill in order for the story to be performed.[6] And, in likening the interaction of readers and literary texts to the interaction of persons and the stories they live their lives through, we become more aware of our need to fill the gaps in daily interaction. Just as these gaps in literary texts recruit the lived experience and the imagination of the reader, so do the gaps in the stories that are 'lived by' recruit the lived experience and the imagination of people as they engage in performances of meaning under the guidance of the story.

Thus with every performance, persons are re-authoring their lives and relationships. And every telling encapsulates, but is more than the previous telling. The evolution of lives and relationships of persons is akin to the process of re-authoring, the process of persons entering into stories with their experience and their imagination, and the process of taking these stories over and making them their own.

The indeterminacy of texts and the constitutive aspect of the performance of texts provide good cause to celebrate. Clifford Geertz quotes Lionel Trilling's lament, 'How come it that we start out Originals and end up Copies?' Upon situating our work in the world of experience and narrative, and in accepting the idea that we must start with a story in order to attribute meaning and give expression to our experience, we would have to reverse Trilling's question, 'How come it that we start out Copies and end up Originals?' To this question Geertz finds an answer that is 'surprisingly reassuring: it is the copying that originates' (1986: 380).

We have little choice but to start out with copies. We cannot perform meaning in our lives without situating our experience in stories. Stories are, in the first place, given. However, it is the relative indeterminacy – the ambiguity and uncertainty – of all stories that we can only negotiate through recourse to our lived experience and our imagination. And this requires that we engage in a process of 'origination'.

So what might be the effects on a person's interpretation of events in his or her life, if the story that framed, selected, and determined the meaning given to those events was oppressive and authored by perpetrators of child sexual or physical abuse? Kamsler (1990), referring specifically to child sexual abuse, noted a number of 'story-telling' practices associated with it that deny the abused their own 'story-telling rights':[7]

> (1) it is usually the case that the perpetrator of the abuse has overtly or covertly conveyed to the victim the message that she was to blame for being abused. . . . (2) the perpetrator will often actively promote secrecy by enforcing it with the child or young woman so that she is divided from other family members, (3) and the various ways in which perpetrator exerted control over the child . . . may promote the development of habitual responses of fear and panic in intimacy relationships when she becomes an adult. (1990: 17–18)

And furthermore, what difference would it make if a person who had been situated in an oppressive 'story' – being told – found herself either to be entitled to her own 'story-telling rights' or to have them restored and be enabled to tell her own life and become her own author?

Rose's Revisioning of her Life[8]

From here on, Rose and I request that you prepare yourself for a different set of 'reader responses' as the genres become blurred. If fact and fiction are read differently, how best might you approach 'faction'? The following is an example of a 're-authoring therapy' but that process will be briefly described elsewhere so as not to intrude. So reader, can you find some way that suits you to divest yourself of those 'reader responses' required by academic texts? Perhaps you might set this book down for a while in order to break your train of thought and return to it later. For Rose and I offer you the opportunity of having an experience of your own as you engage with her experience of entering her life's events in an 'alternative' story, a frame of reference at great variance with the 'dominant' story of her life. Louis Mink argues that 'It is clear that we cannot refer to events as such, but only to events *under a description*; so there can be more than one description of the same event, all of them true but referring to different aspects of the event or describing it at different levels of generality. But what can we possibly mean by "same event"?' (1978: 145–6). What we could possibly mean by the same event was more than just a historiographical problem for Rose and me. For how Rose 'reads' her life – under the guidance of either the 'dominant' story or the therapeutically co-created 'alternative' story – will prove to have considerable bearing on whether she lives or takes her life, and how she lives that life she chooses to keep.

The re-authoring will be represented to you, reader, by way of those 'letters' I (David Epston) provided for her summarizing our meetings, and excerpts from the transcript of the fourth and final meeting six months later. I have taken some liberties here, deleting many of my questions and linking some of her answers. So, reader, are you ready to proceed with my account of Rose's revisioning of her experience as it is brought to life through language?

Rose's employer rang me. I was informed that despite her compunctions and regret, she had no other option than to terminate Rose's employment as a receptionist/video-camera operator at a busy advertising agency. She only too willingly acknowledged that Rose possessed obvious capabilities. Still, it seemed that whenever Rose was required to attend to a request in addition to an uncompleted task, she would 'crack up' and dissolve into tears.

Her employer drew my attention to the fact that Rose had a genius for food preparation, something she was required to do during a 'shoot'. She had endeavoured to find Rose alternative employment in catering until it dawned on her how impossible that would be. Catering is a task, she commented, that would subject Rose to both urgent and multiple demands. She also told me that Rose had a long history of losing jobs for the same reason. Rose's employer was ringing because Rose had become inconsolable on being dismissed and she was very concerned for her well-being. I suggested she provide Rose with my phone number and that I would do my best to meet with her immediately.

Rose and I met a day later. There was a sense of quiet desperation about Rose as she recounted her dismal employment history. She did acknowledge that she had a long-standing ambition to become a chef but discounted that, given the demanding nature of the work. She seemed so forlorn that I asked if there was anything more to her 'problem' than that. She grinned ruefully and nodded. 'There's more to it. I don't have a base inside myself.' I inquired, 'Do you feel like a fake person, hollow on the inside?' She greeted this description enthusiastically as if the linguistic resources I proffered her came as something of a relief. I went on to say, 'There must be a story behind this. Do you feel like telling me about it?' She sighed and grinned at the same time, 'That's what I've come for. . . . I just can't go on any longer like this.' We embarked upon a story-telling with the role of narrator-reflector shared between us. My reflecting questions and her answering led her story through time in addition to disengaging her from entering into her father's story.

His authorship over her experience of his physical abuse had been compelling, given his hegemonic parenthood in addition to his moral sanction as a parish minister in a fundamentalist Christian church. The latter particularly confounded her as his parishioners would regularly comment after church services on her good fortune to have such 'a good and kind man' for a father. Her mother was a bystander to this violence, who defended her silence as the only way she had available to her to contain her husband's violence towards their children. Still Rose felt very bitter towards her, even though she acknowledged that her mother took the action to divorce him when she was thirteen, insisting that Rose be sent away to a distant boarding school. This action was without precedent among her co-religionists.

An 'alternative' account was written up from my notes, taken during the meeting and forwarded to her by post.

Dear Rose,

It was a very pleasing experience to meet up with you and hear some of your story, a story of both protest and survival against what you understood to be an attempt to destroy your life. And you furthered that protest yesterday by coming and telling me that story. I would imagine that you had not been able to tell anyone for fear of being disbelieved. I feel privileged that you shared it with me and hope that sharing it relieved you of some of its weight. I can see how such a history could have left you the legacy you described – a sense of not seeming 'to have a base'. How could you under the circumstances of your growing up when your home – most people's base – was the site of your father's attempt at disappearing you? No wonder you are currently finding life difficult and have mixed feelings about trusting relationships with men. I consider this inevitable under the circumstances. And no wonder, despite all your abilities, talents, and personal attributes that are so obvious to others with whom you have come into contact in the course of your life, you feel somewhat hollow and 'fake' on the inside. No wonder you feel like caving in when you experience other people's demands on you!

You tell me that you were the third of four children, born to a father who 'didn't want children' and since he had them, insisted on 'obedience' to his rule and the Victorian child-rearing policy that 'children should be seen but not heard'. From the beginning, you had some life force that refused to buckle under and submit to his authority. You paid dearly for your vocal nature and were physically beaten for it. Still you refused to deny yourself, even though you came to feel that he was out to destroy you. From what you tell me, he was mood-controlled, violent, self-important, and holier than Thou. In some ways, it must have been a relief to get sent away to boarding school, even though that resulted from your parents' separation.

It seems to me that you are entitled to your resentments towards your mother for not protecting you more. However, I suspect that you don't know the full extent to which your mother endured violence and intimidation. After a certain degree of abuse, the abused person often starts to believe they deserve it. Also your father had a moral sanction, arising from his work. Some day, I believe your mother will confide in you more suffering than you know. And she may have been right that the only course open to her was to silently sit by because if she opposed him, he would have redoubled the severity of your beatings. I wonder if she has some story that is too terrible to reveal, perhaps even to herself?

Despite your father's attempts to rub you out, you ruthlessly opposed him. You did this in the face of his public image as 'a good man'. You could easily have taken his opinion of you and dismissed your own. If you had, my guess is that you would not be here today. Some special wisdom must have informed you that he was bad, not you. If not, how were you able to see through his hypocrisy?

At 18, you returned to your father, thinking perhaps he would now be able to appreciate you, an appreciation you so richly deserved. You were to discover, probably not surprisingly, that 'you can't expect anything approaching a caring father–daughter relationship'. Still, you were able to distinguish between his inadequacies and your self. This was a critical distinction, one that I believe has been life saving for you.

Although it must have been very difficult, you were able to create for yourself a very good personhood. You must have had a lot of courage to travel abroad for 4½ years and 'survive', as you put it. Surviving in such circumstances proved to you once and for all that you had 'grit'. You were able to experience some pride in yourself for having managed so well. You said that when 'I am up against the wall, something makes me get going . . . a survival instinct'. I believe that your 'survival instinct' is your life force, a force that never submitted to your father's disciplines and ruthlessness. That life force added a lot to itself during your travels. I wonder if it was then that you became more substantial as a person and started believing in yourself?

Was it then that you started seeing yourself through others' eyes rather than through your father's eyes? When was it that you no longer accepted your father's definition of yourself as 'garbage'?

It must have happened sometime or other; otherwise, you would have gone around looking for garbage collectors and a dump for them to throw you on! Somehow or other, you were able to keep your own picture of yourself alive.

And you rejected that widely shared myth that women solve their problems by being 'rescued by men'. I guess you must have found that difficult to swallow, given your history with your father. I was also impressed by your unwillingness to seek sympathy or special concessions. You have determined to see your own way through this and to make yourself up into the person you want to be. It was interesting to note that you start appreciating yourself most when you are on your own.

I wonder if seeing your two older siblings make up their own lives, despite the violence they suffered at your father's hands, has inspired you with the hope necessary for you to do the same? Obviously they had some advantages in finding partners at an early age who must have really appreciated them, so they could appreciate themselves.

I suggested that you might like to be curious how your older siblings were able to construct viable, loving relationships, ones in which they were able to realize themselves as 'good' persons. Another question you might like to entertain is this: Why didn't you fall for your father's type?

I look forward to meeting you again to assist you to write a new history of the events in your life, a new history that could predict a very different kind of future than your old history.

Yours sincerely,
David

We met a month later. Nothing could have prepared me for what had transpired in the interval. Two days after receiving the letter, Rose had applied for a job as a *sous-chef* and was not only successful but so impressed the owner/chef that he had invited her to take over sole responsibility while he took his holidays. On his return, she had been made head chef. She now felt her life was 'on the right track' and that she 'had made a start on it'. She had renewed her relationship with her mother and now felt both a sympathy for her and a new connectedness. She had also rung up all her siblings and met with them, one at a time, over the letter. They all legitimated her experiences of physical abuse, and took her side to the extent that they advised her to break off all contact with their father, as the two eldest siblings had done. She took her own advice here and decided to keep her relationship with her father open. Rose was radiant and witty as she contemplated her future, a future she was now anticipating. This meeting was summarized in the following letter.

Dear Rose,

Reading the letter, which provided you with a different story, seems to have led to 'a sense of relief . . . it was normal I had problems . . . it wasn't my fault . . . I had previously felt weak and vulnerable . . . and that I should have got it all together by now.' Instead, you began to appreciate more fully that 'I felt I had made a start . . . I was definitely on the right track.' And I suspect now that you are realizing that you have been on the 'right track' for some time now; if not, as you put it, you would have become 'disillusioned . . . and ended my life'. Well, there is a lot of life in you and it is there for all to see!

In a spectacular advancement several days after we met, you applied for a job as a chef and in no way permitted 'terror to stop me', put yourself on the line, and discovered much to your satisfaction, that you are very competent, so much so that you were requested to take over the restaurant while your employer has been on holiday. You feel you have been able to learn a lot in a short time and that this may be the career you have been looking for. As you put it, 'I'm realizing I have all these opportunities . . . and I am just beginning.' I can see that you have just opened a door and there is a lot of room to explore there.

Feeling so accomplished, you were then able to appreciate your mother's contribution to your abilities. She too 'had an enquiring mind . . . an appreciation of other cultures . . . it was something from within her'. Despite this, 'she still didn't have much self-confidence' but then again, what would she have become if your father, as you put it, didn't 'treat her like a door mat?'

You were also able to discuss some personal matters with your brother and sisters and they concurred with the letter. Their advice to you was to reject your father as they have. I believe your approach is more courageous and will have more embracing results. Still, it must have been satisfying for them to side with your story and perhaps, because of this, you have obviously been able to see yourself through others' eyes. The result of that is for you to appreciate yourself more and to develop a more comfortable relationship with yourself.

From here, you proposed that 'I feel I have to take some time out and work on Rose . . . I want her to grow . . . I want her to be strong and independent.' You proposed a month of consolidation rather than further experiment, especially in relation to your competence in your new career, to develop more self-appreciation, to experience fully your success and that degree of success is 'enough for now', and to resist the temptation of loneliness to drive you into an unsatisfactory relationship. Here you will have to challenge yet again the cultural myth that women complete themselves in relationship to men.

I will be very interested to meet you next time to hear of your further adventures. It was a very pleasing experience for me to hear how much you are pleasing yourself and how far you have come in such a short time.

Best wishes,
David

We met another month later and Rose was more full of life than ever. She had taken charge of the restaurant and had expanded her range of catering abilities. She expressed great caution about a relationship with a man she had met, as she reported her determination to fashion a different kind of relationship from her previous ones, in which she had 'felt drained'. 'I understand what mistakes I've made. I have been giving my power away and making myself available for abuse by not taking responsibility for myself.' She said she had decided to evaluate this relationship as it went and to sustain her self-respect by communicating her own needs and desires: 'I am going to decide if this relationship is positive for me as a person. . . . I no longer will be diminished. I am actively working at not letting it happen. I feel so much better about myself.'

Six months after our first meeting, I invited Rose to join me as 'a consultant to others' and followed the protocol outlined in Epston and White (1990).

> Therapy is concluded with an invitation to persons to attend a special meeting with the therapist so that the knowledges that have been resurrected and/or generated in therapy can be documented. The knowledges will include those alternative and preferred knowledges about self, others and relationships and those knowledges of problem-solving that have enabled persons to liberate their lives. (1990: 29)

'A consultant to others' implicates an audience, and those audiences that are recruited contribute to the authentication of the person's preferred claims derived from rendering his or her life's events meaningful according to the 'alternative' story. And reader, you have become a member of that audience. Rose herself was provided with both audio-taped and transcribed versions of this consultation, from which the following is an edited excerpt.

DE: Can I ask – what difference did it make to you having your story available to you, do you think?

Rose: It helped me understand what had happened and possibly why it had happened . . . my reactions to what had happened and the end result. Looking at it and following it through gave me a sense of relief and understanding. . . . It was a relief that it wasn't my fault . . . that there were things that had happened to me as a child and I had been basically reacting ever since. . . . A lot of the negative feelings I had about myself had been enforced when I was younger by a parent figure (father?). And I took that attitude, consciously or unconsciously, and continued to think that way about myself. Having the story gave me a point of reference to look back at, to read it through, to think about it and form my own opinions from what we had discussed and draw my own conclusions. I remember getting the letter from the letter box, making myself a nice cup of tea, sitting down and reading it. I had feelings of 'Yes . . . that's it . . . that's the *whole* story!' Thinking about it, re-reading it . . . and feeling a lot better about myself, possibly understanding myself and possibly what direction I wanted to go in. Without it, I think I'd still be confused . . . I know I'd still be confused and have the same feelings of inadequacy as a person and not knowing why I felt the way I did.

DE: How did having your own story validate you? If you had felt you were a fake, phoney, hollow, nothing inside of you, not a true person, how did you legitimate yourself so quickly?

Rose: It was a number of things. I think I had all these suspicions floating around and I wasn't too sure what was real, what was right, what was following through and what wasn't. Possibly having my own story helped me to find out my own attitude and thoughts. And from that so much grew . . . I just immediately started feeling so much better about myself. I started feeling I had validity. And that I had so many untapped opportunities that I had been too frightened to look at or thought I didn't have a right to them. Basically feeling so much better about myself allowed me to consider a very different kind of future for myself. If this hadn't happened, I would have remained a very unhappy person. I had got to the stage that I didn't want to go out there again and compete and have another go at finding employment. I'd got to the point where it was make or break about living. Either I did something about it . . . or I'd pull the pin and forget about living. . . . Ultimately, I think because I separated myself, in my case, from my father's opinions of who I was and formed my own opinion of who and what I was. I realized the danger of being made up by others. I had to make myself up although I think other people contributed to it. They weren't the people I expected or counted on and there is a real sense . . . a lot of feelings about all that – anger, resentment . . . a lot of pain. Somewhere along the line, you've got to accept . . . accept? Accept isn't quite the right word . . . understand and leave it behind.

I summarized this 'consultation' once again by letter:

Dear Rose,

I am just writing to thank you for sharing your 'knowledge' with me and for your willingness to make it available to others. It has also added to my stock of 'knowledge' and has certainly encouraged me to pursue further the idea of the significance of people having their own 'story' rather than their abuser's 'story'. I can't tell you how struck I was that once you had a 'story' that was truer to your own experience of the events in your life, you filled in yourself that 'base' that you had described to me earlier as lacking. To some extent, I see you as having made yourself up and having done so, were then able to realize many of those abilities that were there for everyone to see, but invisible and unavailable to you. Once you saw yourself through your own eyes, you started to see yourself as others see you. It was very pleasing for me to have witnessed you taking up a more comfortable relationship with yourself and to see you realizing many of your capabilities. As time goes by, I would imagine that there will be more of this. If you have the wish to keep in touch with these developments, I would be glad to hear from you.

Best wishes for a future of your own design.

Yours sincerely,
David

A Re-authoring Therapy: Premises and Practices

This therapy is premised on an idea that lives and relationships of persons are shaped by the very knowledges and stories that persons use to give meaning to their experiences, and certain practices of self or of relationship that are associated with these knowledges and stories. A re-authoring therapy intends to assist persons to resolve problems by: (1) enabling them to separate their lives and relationships from knowledges/stories that are impoverishing; (2) assisting them to challenge practices of self and relationship that are subjugating; and (3) encouraging persons to re-author their lives according to alternative knowledges/stories and practices of self and relationship that have preferred outcomes.

Externalizing the problem[9] as one of living according to her father's story of her, Rose and I soon came to realize that a great deal of her lived experience could not be accommodated by the 'dominant' story. Many events in her life, seen through her eyes or the eyes of others, just wouldn't fit and thus Rose had been unable to acknowledge or register them. The translation of experience into meaning was 'pre-figured'[10] by the extant narrative with certain events ascribed as meaningful and others unregistered as meaningless. The performance of her life according to the 'dominant' story led her to self-reproach and self-blame in relation to herself as a person and to fear and self-doubt in relation to the enactment of her own capabilities. An 'alternative' story became very plausible as 'unique outcomes' were identified and new meanings performed around them and the 'dominant' story began to be revisioned.[11] Rose recruited her own audiences for purposes of authentication, as did the 'consulting to others' meeting.

Commentary

'Take charge of your life', 'Be the person you've always wanted to be', 'Declare your independence'. The slogans of popular psychology books can be seen to grant the potential to mould oneself into the person one desires to be, in spite of what one imagines others think.[12] Is re-authoring therapy another version of this culture of self-reconstruction? Some consideration of this question is important in placing this clinical practice in a broader social realm.

The first obvious difference between re-authoring therapy and popular psychology concerns their respective media. Though re-authoring therapy draws on the power of textual documents, it is carried out under the gaze of the therapist as a helping *service*, whereas popular psychology appears to be largely a consumer *product* that is taken home and performed in the private act of reading. This is a difference between a *dialogical* process, in which oneself is reflected in the eyes of the other, and a *monological* process, in which the only audience for oneself is oneself.[13] This distinction is a little blurred: the reader of popular psychology texts does have some relationship with the author, albeit an abstracted one. None the less, the author of a self-help manual is unlikely to respond to the ways in which the book's advice is taken up by a particular reader. The presence of a person who witnesses one's own responses is what seems here to distinguish psychotherapy from the self-analysis of reading popular psychology. The significance of this difference rests on the necessity of having one's change recognized by a legitimate audience. In popular psychology, it is enough to introduce the book's themes into one's own private narrative, whereas re-authoring therapy partly involves setting up an audience in which forms of change can be authenticated.

For example, in David Epston's letter to Rose he writes: 'it must have been satisfying for them [Rose's family] to side with your story and perhaps because of this, you have obviously been able to see yourself through others' eyes. The result of that is for you to appreciate yourself more and to develop a more comfortable relationship with yourself.' Here a family is organized as a mirror in which to compel the client to accept a more powerful self-narrative.

This dimension of practice in re-authoring therapy raises particular questions for an understanding of what is involved in practices of self-transformation. To what degree does re-authoring therapy diverge from recent developments in psychoanalysis which place emphasis on the reconstruction of self-narratives?

Over the past two decades, American psychoanalysts have been introducing the phenomenon of narrative into their understanding of the therapeutic process. Roy Schafer and Donald Spence are two psychoanalysts in the forefront of this development. Schafer (1978) has examined how psychoanalysis is constituted in narrative form – as comedy, romance, tragedy, and irony. According to Schafer, narrative form provides a vehicle for fundamental dimensions of human nature, such as the malleability of character, the compatibility of individual and society, and potential for happiness in life. What the introduction of narrative does for psychoanalysis in Schafer's theory is to make those assumptions appear as matters of choice rather than essential components of theory. Differently narrativized versions of psychoanalysis may suit different contexts: for example, comic psychoanalysis suits a social work situation, whereas ironic psychoanalysis is more appropriate for long-term analysis. For Schafer, anyone who employs psychoanalysis chooses more than a picture of reality – they also implicate themselves in an ethical vision.

As a theorist Spence (1982) is less concerned that Schafer with the formal narrative structures involved in the therapeutic process. His emphasis is on the skills of the analyst in finding the appropriate structures in language for expressing the unconscious anxieties of the analysand. Spence names this quality 'narrative truth'. Narrative truth is not a literal representation of the past, but rather it is a picture that by virtue of its 'aesthetic finality' gathers unrecognized experiences into a manageable whole. Spence presents a truth that is measured by its therapeutic effect, rather than its accuracy. This introduction of narrative brings to the fore the creative skills of the analyst in making up a good story.

The narrative psychoanalysis represented in the world of Schafer and Spence concerns itself with a refusal of the classical paradigm of historical truth within psychoanalysis. Rather than a specific set of truths revealed in analysis, it is the particular 'form' in which that truth emerges which is seen to contain the healing potential. It is this form which most sharply distinguishes narrative psychoanalysis from 're-authoring therapy'. The factors at play in the psychoanalytic setting are limited to the clinic. This limitation is at one with the general framework of psychological healing which is to see the problem mainly 'in the head' of the client: if you look at the problem differently, it will be alleviated. Though this interpretation does not do justice to the sophistication of the narrative psychoanalytic approach, it does form a major difference between it and 're-authoring therapy'. The emphasis in Spence on the use of psychoanalysis in finding a 'home' for experience in language looks at language outside of its everyday dialogical setting – it doesn't seem to matter if no one else but the analysand and the analyst understand the problem.

One can argue that the approaches of both narrative psychoanalysis and popular psychology are fundamentally limited to this narrow context. If one looks at agency as a resource that is distributed by others – being granted the right to speak – then what others think of oneself must be taken into account; it is not sufficient simply to change one's own picture of oneself privately; one must in addition have a convincing picture to show others.[14]

It is this dialogical principle which also conditions the nature of re-authoring therapy. To a certain degree, the ideology of such a therapy stresses the *freedom* of the individual to construct his or her own life. Such therapy states as one of its ideological principles that it is giving *freedom* to the individual to construct his or her own life story.[15] With all freedoms there is necessarily some exclusion that makes them possible: a negative makes a positive. This limitation can be found in the dialogical context. One can ask: why is it that their new story is credited by their conversational group? What do others have to gain from this accreditation? These are questions which seem to rest an inch from the nose of most accounts of therapy yet, because of that, pass largely unnoticed. The criteria by which an audience will accept a client's claim to have changed through therapy is a form of what Gergen (1989) calls 'the conditions of warrant'. Change in this sense is a licence that must be purchased from an audience in forms of currency that are seen as legitimate. Personal change is a restricted economy. It is one of the sparks of genius particularly to re-authoring therapy that it recognizes the power of the text to authenticate forms of personal change.[16]

This development creates a space in which other forms of family therapy might follow. What is primary is a sensitivity to what it means for a person to 'change' in the group context. In certain Australian families, for instance, the experience of being overseas is seen to provide a legitimate demonstration of the capacities of its members (White and Epston, 1990). Travel here operates as a rite of passage that is customized by families according to their social location. At its extreme, a child is not acknowledged to be capable of an independent life until he or she has been able to return home with stories of trials in foreign settings. Such stories usually make a point that relates to the conversation between members of that family about human nature. For instance, one conversation might concern the question of whether deep down people are the same or different. A child who returns home with evidence about this in his or her experience of exotic peoples can be seen to contribute to the conversation that maintains the family.[17] The child participates in what Bruner (1987) describes as the 'meshing' that incorporates different points of view within the kind of conversation that brings families to the same table.[18] Here it is possible to examine change within the dialogical context provided by the family: change is acknowledged when it contributes to the moral picture of the family. The implication of this for family therapy is to extend the kind of sensitivity to the dialogical setting evident in re-authoring therapy to the importance of understanding the narrative ecology that already exists within the family – it is to use the family not only as audience, but also as editors and script-writers.

Re-authoring therapy exists as a licence to move outside the abstract relations which typify established therapeutic interventions. To this extent, it is not just telling a story, it is also listening to the audience.

Notes

The introductory discussion and Rose's narrative are by David Epston and Michael White; the commentary (pp. 109–12) by Kevin Murray.

1. This is excerpted from M. White (1989/90).

2. Victor Turner wrote that these expressions are 'the crystallized secretions of once living experience' (1982: 17).

3. By arguing for the proposal about the extent to which stories determine the meaning attributed to experience, we are not suggesting that the context of our lives is single-storied. Rather, we believe that the context of our lives is multi-storied. There is a range of alternative stories for the interpretation of experience in which we and others may situate our lives. Also, despite this assertion about the story-determined nature of meaning, it turns out (as discussed later) that all such stories are, in fact, indeterminate.

4. When discussing the performance aspects of ritual process, Turner states: 'The term "performance" is, of course derived from Old English *parfournu*, literally, "to furnish completely or thoroughly". To perform is thus to bring something about, to consummate something, or to "carry out" a play, order, or project. But in the carrying out, I hold, something new may be generated. The performance transforms itself' (1980: 160).

5. Turner (1980), when discussing the ritual process, relates indeterminacy to the subjunctive mood of verb: 'Indeterminacy is, so to speak, in the subjunctive mood, since it is that which is not yet settled, concluded, or known. It is all that may be, might be, could be, perhaps even should be. . . . Sally Falk Moore goes so far as

to suggest that "the underlying quality of social life should be considered to be one of theoretical absolute indeterminacy."' The relation of indeterminacy to the subjunctive mood is also discussed by J. Bruner (1986).

6. For further discussion of those aspects of the structure of stories that encourage the reader to enter the story, to take it over and make it their own, see J. Bruner (1986).

7. This phrase is taken from Shuman, 1986.

8. For another case study that has parallels to the following, see Epston (1989b) with a 4½-year follow-up 'consultation' (Epston, 1989a).

9. 'Externalizing is an approach to therapy that encourages persons to objectify and, at times, to personify the problems that they experience as oppressive. In this process, the problem becomes a separate entity and thus external to the person or relationship that was ascribed as the problem. Those problems that are considered to be inherent, as well as those relatively fixed qualities that are attributed to persons and to relationships, are rendered less fixed and less restricting. . . . The externalizing of the problem enables persons to separate from the dominant stories that have been shaping their lives and relationships. In so doing, persons are able to identify previously neglected but vital aspects of lived experiences – aspects that could not have been predicted from a reading of the dominant story. Thus, following Goffman (1961), I have referred to these aspects of experience as 'unique outcomes' (White, 1989a,b). . . . As unique outcomes are identified, persons can be encouraged to engage in performances of meaning in relation to these. Success with this requires that the unique outcome be plotted into an alternative story about the person's life.' (White and Epston, 1990: 38–41)

10. Hayden White (1973) makes a historiographical case that histories are 'prefigured' by their narratives. E. Bruner makes a similar point on doing ethnography: 'In my view, we began with a narrative that already contains a beginning and an ending, which frame and hence enable us to interpret the present. It is not that we initially have a body of data, the facts, and we then must construct a story or theory to account for them. Instead . . . the narrative structures we construct are not secondary narratives about data but primary narratives that establish what is to count as data. New narratives yield new vocabulary, syntax, and meaning in our ethnographic accounts; they define what constitute the data of those accounts' (1986b: 143).

11. Patraka defines revisioning from a feminist perspective: 'Rich defines "Re-Vision" as "the act of looking back, of seeing with fresh eyes, entering an old text from a new critical direction" until women can "understand the assumptions in which we are drenched" in order to know ourselves (1979: 35). To give speech to what has been requires describing, naming and reinterpreting past reality. To change what is calls for an analysis of the sources of that reality and the reasons for its persistence' (1983: 1).

12. For a more detailed discussion of the values of popular psychology texts, see Murray (1986).

13. This difference is articulated at length in the discourse of the Russian theorist Mikhail Bakhtin (1981).

14. The work of Erving Goffman (1968) in mental institutions can be used as a demonstration of the role of the audience in controlling the kind of agency one has in a situation.

15. The most significant principle that seems to inform the practice of 're-authoring therapy' is self-fashioning. This is a concept initially popular in the

dramaturgists of the Renaissance and now re-discovered by readers of Foucault's histories of sexuality. Its most extreme form is found in the performances of artists, who shape their lives into a work of art. Rather than see a life, as under Freud, as being a quest for a certain knowledge about oneself, which when found transforms one's existence, a life is looked at as a material to be fashioned according to whatever aesthetic or ethical principles seem fit. One of the criticisms of this principle is that it assumes that our condition of being is one of complete freedom. As such it ignores our debt to structures of meaning such as myths and language.

16. White and Epston (1990) contains reports of the seriousness with which clients took the therapist's letters – carrying them around and showing them off to others.

17. This claim is based on thus far unpublished research on travel talk (K. Murray, 'Life as fiction: the making sense of personal change', Ph.D. thesis, University of Melbourne).

18. Jerome Bruner's (1987) account of the conversational dynamics of the 'Goodhertz' family provides a subtle example of how a family might develop a discursive ecology which both individuates and binds family members.

References

Bakhtin, M.M. (1981) *The Dialogical Imagination: Four Essays*, tr. M. Holquist and C. Emerson. Austin, TX: University of Texas Press.

Bruner, E. (1986a) 'Experience and its expressions', in V. Turner and E. Bruner (eds), *The Anthropology of Experience*. Chicago, IL: University of Illinois Press.

Bruner, E. (1986b) 'Ethnography as narrative', in V. Turner and E. Bruner (eds), *The Anthropology of Experience*. Chicago, IL: University of Illinois Press.

Bruner, J. (1986) *Actual Minds: Possible Worlds*. Cambridge, MA: Harvard University Press.

Bruner, J. (1987) 'Life as narrative', *Social Research*, 54: 11–32.

Dilthey, W. (1976) *Dilthey: Selected Writings*, ed. H. Rickman. Cambridge: Cambridge University Press.

Epston, D. (1989a) 'Marisa revisits', in D. Epston, *Collected Papers*. Adelaide: Dulwich Centre Publications.

Epston, D. (1989b) 'Writing Your History', in D. Epston, *Collected Papers*. Adelaide: Dulwich Centre Publications.

Epston, D. and White, M. (1990) 'Consulting your consultants: the documentation of alternative knowledge', *Dulwich Centre Newsletter*, 4.

Geertz, C. (1986) 'Making experiences, authoring selves', in V. Turner and E. Bruner (eds), *The Anthropology of Experience*. Chicago, IL: University of Illinois Press.

Gergen, K.J. (1989) 'Warranting voice and the elaboration', in J. Shotter and K.J. Gergen (eds), *Texts of Identity*. London: Sage.

Goffman, E. (1961) *Asylums: Essays in the Social Situation of Mental Patients and Other Inmates*. New York: Doubleday.

Goffman, E. (1968) *Asylums*. Harmondsworth: Penguin.

Harré, R. (1983) *Personal Being: a Theory for Individual Psychology*. Oxford: Blackwell.

Iser, W. (1978) *The Act of Reading*. Baltimore, MD: Johns Hopkins University Press.

Kamsler, A. (1990) 'Her-story in the making: therapy with women who were sexually abused in childhood', in M. Durrant and C. White (eds), *Ideas for Therapy with Sexual Abuse*. Adelaide: Dulwich Centre Publications.

Mink, L. (1978) 'Narrative form as a cognitive instrument', in R.H. Canary and H. Kozicki (eds), *The Writing of History: Literary Form and Historical Understanding*. Madison, WI: University of Wisconsin Press.

Murray, K. (1986) 'Finding literary paths: the work of popular life constructors', in T.R. Sarbin (ed.), *Narrative Psychology: the Storied Nature of Human Conduct*. New York: Praeger.

Patraka, V. (1983) 'Introduction', in V. Patraka and Louise A. Tilly (eds), *Feminist Re-visions: What Has Been and Might Be*. Ann Arbor, MI: University of Michigan Press.

Rich, A. (1979) *On Lies, Secrets, and Silence: Selected Prose (1966–1979)*. New York: Norton

Ricoeur, P. (1983) *Time and Narrative*. Chicago, IL: University of Illinois Press.

Schafer, R. (1978) *Language and Insight*. New Haven, CT: Yale University Press.

Shuman, A. (1986) *Story-telling Rights*. Cambridge: Cambridge University Press.

Spence, D.P. (1982) *Narrative Truth and Historical Truth: Meaning and Interpretation in Psychoanalysis*. New York: Norton.

Turner, V. (1980) 'Social dramas and stories about them', *Critical Inquiry*, Autumn: 141–68.

Turner, V. (1982) *From Ritual to Theatre*. New York: Performing Arts Press.

White, H. (1973) *Metahistory: the Historical Imagination in Nineteenth-Century Europe*. Baltimore, MD: Johns Hopkins University Press.

White, M. (1989a) 'Family therapy and schizophrenia: addressing the "in-the-corner lifestyle"', in M. White, *Selected Papers*. Adelaide: Dulwich Centre Publications.

White, M. (1989b) 'The process of questioning: a therapy of literary merit?' in M. White, *Selected Papers*. Adelaide: Dulwich Centre Publications.

White, M. (1989/90) 'Family therapy training and supervision in a world of experience and narrative', *Dulwich Centre Newsletter* (Adelaide), Summer.

White, M. (1990) 'The externalization of the problem', in M. White and D. Epston, *Narrative Means to Therapeutic Ends*. New York: Norton.

White, M. and Epston, D. (1990) *Narrative Means to Therapeutic Ends*. New York: Norton. (Also printed as *Literate Means to Therapeutic Ends*, 1989, Adelaide: Dulwich Centre Publications.)

PART III

CONSTRUCTION IN ACTION

8

Therapeutic Distinctions in an On-going Therapy

Karl, Cynthia, Andrew and Vanessa

What follows is a joint report[1] of some therapeutic distinctions that emerged during a series of family therapy sessions with one family. The original draft was written by the therapist (Karl) after he reviewed his clinical records and engaged the family (Cynthia, Andrew, and Vanessa) in some clarifying discussions. The focus of these discussions was to clearly identify and affirm those distinctions that were most helpful to the family in the therapeutic process. The draft was then shared with the family and revised on the basis of their feedback.

Such discussion and feedback could be a sufficient basis for co-authorship with the family. However, the decision to co-author this report was not based on this collaboration alone. It was also a result of the therapist's awareness of the indispensable contributions of the family in triggering his reflections to produce the therapeutic distinctions that he introduced in the course of therapy. The openness and honesty of family members in consistently presenting their problematic experiences and their unresolved concerns enabled the therapist eventually to respond with the kinds of distinctions that were helpful. Without such persistence and patience on the part of the family, the therapist could not have generated the distinctions that eventually had a therapeutic influence. This issue, the degree to which clients help their therapists be therapeutic in relation to them, is not adequately acknowledged in the literature. Thus, it seemed reasonable to invite the family to co-author this chapter as a tangible step toward such an acknowledgement. Finally, the commitment to this collaboration was also based on the hope that, by jointly clarifying and validating the distinctions that seemed to have been useful in therapy, those distinctions would be strengthened and reinforced. As a result, they might endure a bit longer in the minds of family members and perhaps remain more readily available to them to help cope with possible problems in the future.

Theoretical Comments

The notion of a 'therapeutic distinction' is central to this chapter and deserves some explanation.[2] The most fundamental aspect of this notion is the concept of a distinction itself. Thus, before trying to specify when a distinction is therapeutic, an explanation of the concept of a basic 'distinction' will be provided.

As conceived of here, a distinction is a linguistic discrimination that influences the lived experience and behavioral orientation of the person who makes the discrimination. It is an observation articulated in language that is employed as a description either to oneself or simultaneously to someone else. A distinction has meaning, implicitly as well as explicitly. Thus, the distinctions we make in day-to-day living have a major influence in channeling our experience and in organizing our behavior. All distinctions exist in language and arise through conversation. As such, they are grounded in the social interactional dynamics that give meaning to whatever is distinguished.

From a theoretical point of view, it is assumed that the awareness of a distinction, while experienced as an individual phenomenon, is actually the result of social interaction between human beings. This derives from the assumption that human consciousness, observing, describing, explaining, and deciding all arise through a process of language (Maturana, 1988). Language itself is seen to arise in evolution through coordinated social interaction and is sustained and elaborated through interpersonal conversations. Individual thinking is regarded as a process of internalized conversing: a person is implicitly talking to himself or herself. In other words, the perspective being adopted here is that the 'human mind' is fundamentally a social phenomenon and only secondarily a psychological phenomenon (Bateson, 1972; Maturana and Varela, 1980). Thus, even though a distinction is experienced psychologically as a discrimination in one's own conscious awareness, it is assumed to be rooted in social process.

The significance of this assumptive social origin is that any distinction may be amenable to further social interaction. 'Outer' *interpersonal* conversations become 'inner' *intrapersonal* conversations (in the form of conscious awareness and thinking) which support further outer conversations that modify inner thought, and so on. It follows that the social interaction of a therapeutic conversation in family therapy may be employed to modify the distinctions being used in a family. Typically, altogether new distinctions also are brought forth. As a result of modified and new distinctions, the patterns of conversation in the family may be altered, and the experience and behavior of individual family members may change.

A more detailed description of what is entailed in drawing a distinction may be helpful in understanding such change. To draw a distinction is to differentiate an entity, an event, a pattern, or some other phenomenon from a background. In terms of the familiar *Gestalt* relationship of figure and ground, the 'distinction' is the specific linguistic 'figure' that is differentiated from a general 'ground' of undifferentiated awareness and other potential discriminations. What usually happens in the process of thinking (or in the course of an interpersonal conversation) is that a conscious focus emerges from a general background of undifferentiated experience and awareness. As this focus takes shape it becomes a specific distinction. To use a concrete example, 'a smile' is the distinction of a certain constellation of facial muscle movements that is differentiated from a background of on-going facial activity. Every facial movement is not distinguished and sometimes no facial expression is distinguished at all. If one does not 'see' the smile, one cannot respond to it (at least not consciously). The distinction 'captures' in language the original undifferentiated visual experience. In so doing, it temporarily 'arrests' the specific event and separates it from an on-going background stream of events, so that it can be attended to, reflected upon, and perhaps responded to. In the process of becoming conscious the original experience is given some form or meaningful shape and, hence, the experience is modified in the act of drawing the distinction itself

What is of special interest from a therapeutic point of view is that different distinctions may be drawn from the same background of human interaction and undifferentiated experience. The precise 'shape' of the distinction that is actually drawn makes a significant difference to one's conscious experience and to one's disposition to respond. It is this shape which determines the 'properties' attributed to the distinction and in so doing determines its meaning. For instance, the same smile could be distinguished as a 'friendly smile,' an 'affectionate smile,' a 'patronizing smile,' a 'nervous smile,' a 'wry smile,' a 'phoney smile,' a 'contemptuous smile,' or some other kind of smile. The meaning associated with the smile is generated by the specific shape of the original distinction. Sligh differences in the shape of the smile that is distinguished lead to quite different experiential and behavioral responses in the observer. Consequently, the subsequent interaction with the person who smiled might proceed in differing directions depending on the particular form of smile that was distinguished.

What is also of special interest is that different observers have a propensity to observe or 'bring forth' different distinctions. This is a result of differing perceptual and linguistic habits. These habits, in turn, are largely determined by a particular observer's history in prior social interaction. For example, a person who has a strong history of interpersonal acceptance and respect would probably be inclined to distinguish a 'friendly smile' or an 'affectionate smile.' A second person who has been deeply hurt by repeated betrayal is perhaps more likely to distinguish a 'phoney smile,' while a third person who has been exposed to a great deal of interpersonal blame may distinguish a 'contemptuous smile.' In other words, drawing a distinction is an activity performed by an idiosyncratic observer. At the same time, however, these distinctions are not fixed and immutable. Interacting observers readily influence one another by articulating their distinctions and discussing them in conversation. Thus, the first person could influence the second and third to distinguish the 'friendliness' in the smile by describing it vividly and giving significance to a context of trustworthiness. Alternatively, the second and third persons could influence the first to distinguish the 'phoniness' or 'contemptuousness' and invite that person to feel less trustful.

However, drawing a distinction implies more than just passively observing an entity or phenomenon (or being influenced to bring a certain observation into focused awareness). It also entails actively adopting a certain position, a behavioral stance, or a 'posture' in relation to the entity or phenomenon distinguished. This latter aspect of the process of observing – that is, of an observer automatically positioning himself or herself in relation to the observation made – is often overlooked. Yet, it is extremely significant in the moment-to-moment politics of human experience and social interaction. For example, the act of distinguishing the gaze of another person as 'disapproving judgement' entails bringing forth an experience of dread and a behavioral orientation of rejection or avoidance of the other. In contrast, distinguishing the gaze as a 'compliment' on one's appearance implies an experience of pleasure and an orientation of acceptance and approach. The specific behavioral disposition or orientation adopted by the observer is associated with the additional experiences attributed to the distinction through its properties or meaning.

The importance of the behavioral orientation/disposition adopted in the process of drawing distinctions becomes more apparent when one acknowledges that distinctions are, in fact, political. Distinctions may be regarded as political in the sense that they have power over the person who makes them (by triggering a certain disposition) and secondarily over others who are influenced by that person on the basis of the distinctions made. Generally speaking, we are more conscious of the distinctions we make than we are of their political implications. The politics involved in the distinctions employed in ordinary conversations tend to remain non-conscious until they are drawn to our attention. A major cultural example of this phenomenon is the traditional distinction of 'mankind' to refer to the human species. Most of us failed to recognize the political implications of this male-centered distinction prior to the feminist critique of language.

One reason for focusing on the process of drawing distinctions in this chapter is to invite the reader to become more mindful of this political aspect of making observations. If a person chooses to use a certain description (rather than other descriptions which could have been employed in the same situation) that person has implicitly chosen a particular political position in relation to the phenomenon being described. This is also true for us in writing this chapter. For instance, the first author deliberately chose the term 'distinction' because it implies an active involvement in creating the distinctions he used, as opposed to the term 'observation' which tends to connote greater distance and passivity on behalf of an anonymous observer.[3] One desirable political implication of distinguishing distinctions as *actively generated* is that all of us as observers may be influenced to take more personal responsibility in our observing. One political implication of distinguishing distinctions as *political* is to contribute to the realization that the dynamics of interpersonal power always are involved in the generation and use of distinctions. The politics of drawing certain distinctions and not drawing others (that is, in making some observations and not others) is extremely important in any field, but it deserves deliberate and careful attention by therapists because of their responsibility to be therapeutic.

Given this perspective on distinctions in general, a *therapeutic distinction* now may be defined simply as *an observation that orients the observer in a healing direction*. In other words, for a distinction to qualify as therapeutic, a second distinction must be possible about a healing direction as a result of the behavioral disposition produced by the original distinction. The second distinction is drawn on the consequences of the first. It discloses the power politics that are operating in the context of the original distinction. The observer making both the primary and secondary distinctions may be anyone: a therapist, a client, a family member, or an outsider (including a researcher or theoretician). The healing direction may be away from pain, suffering, restraint, and constraint (that is, away from 'problems'), and/or towards happiness, joy, greater options, and new possibilities (that is, toward 'solutions'). For example, the distinction of 'oppression' in connection with a female client who presents with 'depression' is likely to be therapeutic because it implicitly orients a therapist in the direction of liberating her from oppressive conditions in our patriarchal culture that are probably contributing to her experience of depression. To distinguish 'positive intent' behind 'blaming' also can be therapeutic by orienting a therapist to remain affirming of a client (as a person with the intention to correct a problem by pointing out what went wrong) yet offer the client feedback about the problematic effects of the blaming itself. Without this distinction of positive intent, the therapist simply might 'blame the client for blaming,' and inadvertently add a further complication to the problem.

Many examples of therapeutic distinctions actually used in the therapy with this family will be presented below. But before concluding this section, it is important to point out the existence of pathologizing distinctions and to realize that the distinctions made by therapists do not automatically orient them and their clients in healing directions. Indeed, therapists are actively invited into making pathologizing distinctions by their clients on a regular basis. This occurs when clients share with therapists the kinds of self-pathologizing descriptions in which they are immersed. For instance, clients who are depressed will likely describe themselves as ineffective, resourceless, unmotivated, and so on. If a therapist is recruited into these pathologizing views and acts in accordance with them, the therapist is liable to contribute to further elaboration or stabilization of the depression. Such recruitment is rarely intentional on the part of the clients, yet it does occur. Thus, therapists need to learn how to listen empathically to a client's distinctions of their painful experiences but also to attend carefully to the 'exceptions' to these descriptions in order to begin generating therapeutic distinctions.

There are many other sources of pathologizing distinctions. These include well-intentioned family members, friends, relatives, neighbors, work colleagues, professionals, and even therapists. Indeed, many observations and distinctions made in traditional patterns of psychiatric assessment are more pathologizing than healing (Tomm, 1990). If therapists are not mindful of the possible effects of the distinctions they introduce, they inadvertently contribute to more pathology. For instance, to distinguish an adolescent as 'rebellious' is to orient oneself to restrain the rebellion and/or to support the application of parental controls. However, the effort to exert external control upon an adolescent developing autonomy usually has the effect of intensifying oppositional thought and behavior. Hence, the problems tend to become worse. In such a context, 'rebelliousness' constitutes a pathologizing distinction because it orients the clinician and other authority figures in a pathologizing direction. In another context, the same distinction could be therapeutic (for instance, when rebelliousness is carefully connected to specific behaviors, the adolescent is committed to building a reputation for cooperation and maturity, and uses the distinction of 'rebellious' to separate the self from those kinds of behavior). Since it may not be clear what political impact a certain distinction is having at any particular moment, it is important to draw a second distinction about the direction that has been embarked upon in having drawn the initial distinction. The participation of the family in writing this chapter was especially helpful in connection with drawing this secondary distinction with some degree of authenticity.

In summary, drawing distinctions may be said to 'direct' the course of therapy. The observations that are made implicitly set clients and therapist in one direction or in another. It is therapists' responsibility to be selective in bringing forth distinctions that are therapeutic, in order to orient themselves in a healing direction. Clients obviously participate in the process, but therapists should bring some special expertise to the encounter. Part of this expertise entails generating a secondary distinction about the directions that are being set by primary distinctions. Once a therapeutic distinction is clear, it can be shared with clients so that they can adopt healing initiatives on their own.

Case Presentation

Cynthia, Andrew, and Vanessa were referred to Karl by a psychiatric colleague in March 1988. The colleague was treating Cynthia with medication and psychotherapeutic support for symptoms of serious depression, anxiety, and paranoia. He was aware of marital conflict between Cynthia and her husband, Andrew, but it was Cynthia's concern that this conflict might harm the development of their daughter Vanessa, that finally prompted the referral for family therapy.

At the time of the first family interview, Cynthia was thirty-three, Andrew thirty-four and Vanessa two and a half. The couple had been married three years after a relatively brief courtship. Both Andrew and Cynthia were the youngest of two children in their families of origin. Andrew had an older sister by five years, who lived in another city. He was not particularly close to her but was quite attached to his aging parents who lived in town. Cynthia and her older sister by four years were both adopted as infants. Her sister lived in the same town, but there was absolutely no contact between their respective families. The break occurred after a dispute over Cynthia's allegations of some incestuous behavior by her father. Immediately following the allegations, which were denied by the father, Cynthia's parents moved to another city. Subsequent contacts between Cynthia and her adoptive parents were extremely tense on the rare occasions that they took place.

By the time of the initial family therapy session, Cynthia had already been in psychiatric care with various professionals over a period of sixteen years. She had had several hospital admissions for various emotional crises and had been burdened with a variety of psychiatric diagnoses. At referral, she was living at home as a full-time mother and homemaker. Andrew had had no previous involvement in psychotherapy. He had, however, had some significant trouble at work because of 'stubbornness' which resulted in some employment difficulties and financial concerns. He felt that he had learnt from these experiences and was quite hopeful that similar problems would not arise in his new job. Both Cynthia and Andrew were deeply devoted to their charming daughter, Vanessa, who was a great source of joy to both of them.

The therapy entailed about fifty sessions over a period of two and a half years. Because babysitters were not readily available, Vanessa came along to most of the sessions, where she usually played quietly throughout the interview. Thus, approximately half of the sessions were with the whole family. Most of the remainder were 'individual' sessions with Cynthia, while Vanessa played. There were a few sessions with only the couple, a few with Cynthia alone, a few with Andrew alone, one session with Andrew and his parents, and one with Cynthia and her parents.

Distinguishing Interpersonal Patterns

The first major distinction drawn by the therapist in this case served to set him in an important direction with respect to his on-going work with the family. He distinguished a complementary interaction pattern between the couple that appeared to be having a strong negative impact on Cynthia. In other words, it was pathologizing her as a person and consequently undermining the marital relationship itself. The pattern included a tendency for both members of the couple to 'cooperate' in seeing Cynthia as 'the problem.' Not only did Andrew see Cynthia as being 'the problem' and described her in negative terms, but Cynthia saw herself as being 'the problem' and described herself as such as well. Each listened to the other's negative descriptions of Cynthia and, for the most part, affirmed each other in them. Their 'cooperation' in this pathologizing pattern was unintentional and outside their awareness (until it was distinguished and explicitly described by the therapist).

The resultant process, however, of both members of the couple continuously monitoring Cynthia's behavior and experience for problems, appeared to be deeply entrenched in the couple's interaction. This entrenchment was understandable given the traumatic events in Cynthia's early family experience and given her long history of psychiatric treatment. But the degree to which the pattern of 'Cynthia gazing' was pathologizing her within the marital relationship itself was not clearly evident to the couple. Fortunately, Cynthia intuitively experienced the injustice of being the sole focus of negativity. Hence, she protested from time to time and became quite angry with Andrew. Unfortunately, however, her protests were usually disqualified, and her anger sometimes escalated into episodes of uncontrolled yelling with occasional hitting, which convinced everyone, including herself, that she was the problem after all. In other words, her efforts to protest against the pattern resulted in a reinforcement of it. This occurred as a result of the political consequences of various individuals (family members and professionals) distinguishing the 'shape' of her protest behavior as problematic rather than potentially liberating.

For a therapist to distinguish an interaction pattern as 'pathologizing' is automatically to adopt a political stance *against* the persistence of that pattern. To distinguish the pathology as located in the *interaction* orients the therapist against the pattern itself rather than against the persons participating in the pattern. In addition, to distinguish participation in the pattern as 'inadvertent' opens space for the therapist to maintain genuine compassion towards the persons enacting the pattern while still being opposed to the pattern itself. Thus, the distinction of inadvertent pathologizing interaction patterns can be extremely useful clinically. Furthermore, pathologizing interaction patterns may be coupled conceptually with healing interpersonal patterns which are intended to serve as specific antidotes to the former. Thus, when operating within this pathologizing/healing framework (Tomm, 1991), to distinguish a pathologizing interaction pattern is implicitly to create an invitation to distinguish a possible healing pattern which could replace it. When certain interaction patterns are distinguished as 'healing,' the therapist is clearly oriented towards affirming and supporting them.

In practice, when one tries to create a distinction of a possible healing interaction pattern one begins by identifying behaviors that have opposite meanings to the behaviors entailed in the pathologizing pattern. Sometimes the exact opposite behavior is not feasible or would not clearly contribute to a healing pattern, but the behaviors distinguished for inclusion in a potential healing pattern must be mutually exclusive from those identified in the pathologizing pattern. In other words, the healing behaviors (for example, affirming the other) and the pathologizing behaviors (such as disqualifying the other) must be incompatible and therefore could not be enacted at the same time. To construct a healing pattern that is likely to be enacted *and endure*, the component healing behaviors of the interactants need to be mutually reinforcing. For instance, affirmation of a valued response invites the enactment of further such responses, and valued responses, in turn, invite further affirmation. If a therapist is able to open space for such a healing pattern to emerge, the pathologizing interaction could no longer be active at the same time. Thus, the distinction of pathologizing interaction patterns and of healing interaction patterns provides a dual foundation for guiding a therapist's contributions in a therapeutic conversation.

With this particular family, the therapist's first major intervention was based on the distinction of a possible healing pattern that could replace the pathologizing pattern initially distinguished. It was designed to counter the gross imbalance in attributing so many negative qualities to Cynthia and implicitly leaving all the positive qualities with Andrew. The therapist suggested a task for the couple between the first and second sessions. He asked them selectively to notice (distinguish) Cynthia's positive qualities, and to identify some of Andrew's chauvinistic habits. This intervention intuitively felt 'right' to the couple and solidified their original engagement with the therapist. The response to the therapist's initiative was very positive, but efforts to sustain a substantive shift away from the original pathologizing pattern proved to be quite difficult. Healing alternatives needed to be discussed again and again before the therapeutic distinctions became part of the family's own conversations. On one occasion, the therapist's attempt actively to counter the process of 'Cynthia gazing' resulted

126 Construction in Action

in a rather heated exchange between Andrew and Karl! Fortunately, Karl was able to distinguish the 'enthusiasm' for his own 'therapeutic distinction' as counter-therapeutic on that occasion and his distinction of Andrew's 'resistance' as pathologizing and was able to back off enough to avoid rupturing the therapeutic relationship. Nevertheless, the basic stance of trying to avoid an exclusive focus on Cynthia's problems, but preferentially to distinguish her resourcefulness instead, remained a useful theme throughout the course of therapy.

As time went on, Andrew gradually became more and more comfortable in acknowledging some of his own problems. Occasionally, he spontaneously brought them up himself in the course of the interviews. More significantly, however, he began citing Cynthia's competencies and successes quite regularly. Indeed, he did so in increasingly concrete ways by giving examples so that she could experience the authenticity in his positive remarks. Thus, Andrew's contributions to the original pathologizing pattern were gradually deconstructed while his contributions to a healing pattern were constructed and reinforced. Cynthia began to internalize the constructive feedback and, hence, became more affirming of herself as a person with positive qualities and legitimate entitlements. She gradually became more self-confident. Thus, the couple began a 'new form of cooperation' in shifting away from the amount of time spent enacting the pervasive pathologizing pattern of gazing at Cynthia's problems, toward spending more of their interaction time living within a more balanced healing pattern.

There appeared to be several other, more specific distinctions that helped the couple escape the intensity and dominance of the original pathologizing pattern. One was to distinguish Cynthia's problems as separate from her person; that is, as distinct from her personal identity. For instance, in the course of therapeutic conversations she was re-described as 'a person under the influence of a yelling habit,' rather than being 'a yeller.' She was also distinguished as 'a person who fell into the grip of paranoid thoughts' or 'a person who slipped into paranoid fears' rather than being 'a paranoid person.' This process of externalizing problems (White, 1988) opened space conceptually between Cynthia and her problems. She began to experience herself as separate from these problems and could visualize herself interacting with them. In other words, once the problems were distinguished as entities in themselves and as clearly distinct from herself, she could adopt a position in opposition to them. It became easier for her to experience some personal agency in having some influence over them. There were still times when she felt helpless, and passively submitted to the influence of problems, but at other times she could take initiative to diminish their influence in her lived experience. For example, she discovered that going for a brisk walk outdoors often made it possible for her to shed the grip of certain paranoid thoughts and fears.

These externalizing distinctions had a positive impact on Andrew as well. About half-way along the course of therapy he spontaneously remarked that he had noted a shift in his experience of Cynthia when she was 'symptomatic.' He found himself becoming frustrated with the (externalized) problems and their historical origins rather than with Cynthia herself. This shift constituted a significant breakthrough in therapy in that Cynthia and Andrew could then work together in their efforts to strengthen her as a person and her ability to escape the influence of the problems. It made it easier for Andrew to see how he could become more supportive for Cynthia.

Another pathologizing interaction pattern between the couple was distinguished at about six months into therapy. In his efforts to be helpful, Andrew began minimizing Cynthia's problems. Rather than being reassured by this, Cynthia felt that the depth of her inner pain was being disqualified. Thus, she responded by emphasizing her difficulties in an effort to have her experience validated. However, Andrew experienced this as her exaggerating her problems so he intensified his minimizing. The escalating reciprocity of this complementary pattern of 'minimizing and maximizing' generated a great deal of turmoil until the pathologizing pattern was distinguished and explicitly described so that a healing antidote could be proposed. The healing interaction pattern entailed Andrew's acknowledgement of her painful experiences and past trauma coupled with Cynthia's acknowledgement of his positive intent when he was trying to reassure her. These two patterns were juxtaposed not only verbally but also visually on a blackboard for further clarity (see Figure 8.1).

There was a particularly important occasion when Cynthia felt strongly validated and supported by her husband in dealing with some paranoid thoughts. It occurred after a long and difficult struggle. Cynthia had had recurrent fears that she might have broken the law and had committed a serious crime. Andrew felt these were unrealistic paranoid thoughts which she simply should ignore. But Cynthia felt invalidated and disqualified by this response. Consequently, frequent arguments took place over the issue and the fears persisted. An in-depth inquiry (which actually took place during one of the discussions to revise this chapter) revealed some basis for these paranoid fears. Cynthia's memory

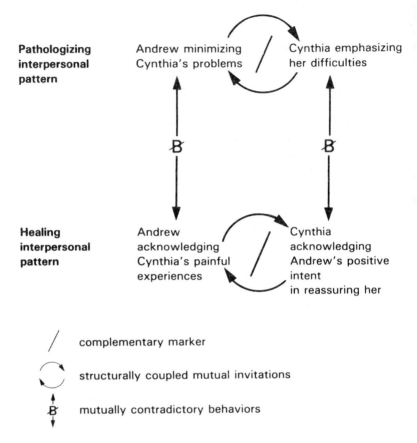

Figure 8.1

was not clear about her own actions during some of the upsetting events she had experienced in the remote past. On one occasion during her early psychiatric history, she passed out after drinking some alcohol (which was potentiated by the medication that had been prescribed). When she recovered consciousness she found that she had sustained major physical injuries, including a dislocated shoulder and a damaged spine. She did not know how these injuries had been inflicted. She became preoccupied about whether she had hurt someone else in an altercation of some sort. She worried that if she had, in fact, done something seriously wrong, this could be used against her with respect to her rights to mother Vanessa. Cynthia wanted to visit the police station to see if she had a criminal record. Andrew stubbornly refused to allow her to do so. But finally after a particularly intense argument, rather than simply reassuring her and minimizing her experience, he agreed to take her to the local police station to check out her record. The police officers were very cooperative and took her request seriously. They found no record of her being charged for any offense or of her being a suspect in any crime. Cynthia was understandably relieved. She was also very surprised that Andrew could become so supportive. As a result of this experience these particular paranoid fears diminished. Given this outcome, it was possible to distinguish the event as a significant milestone in Andrew's emerging willingness to take Cynthia's experience seriously, and a milestone in Cynthia's emerging confidence in Andrew's growing flexibility. Indeed, in reading an early draft of this chapter Cynthia came to realize more fully how significant this whole experience had been for her.

Interpersonal Crises as Unique Opportunities for Change

An interesting crisis emerged a few months after therapy began. Cynthia was afraid that Andrew would not follow through on an agreement to pay for some cosmetic surgery which she was scheduled for in the summer. Her repeated requests that he affirm the earlier commitment triggered some evasiveness on his part. His evasiveness simply invited further demands for confirmation from her which invited further refusals from him, and another pathologizing interpersonal pattern emerged. As she worried about the possibility of having to cancel the surgery, she became extremely agitated and upset, even to the point of struggling with serious suicidal thoughts.

A therapeutic conversation in response to the suicide threat yielded some additional background information which made possible the creation of some healing distinctions. There were important memories of prior unfulfilled promises that supported Cynthia's fears. For instance, Andrew had failed to give her an engagement ring as promised and had failed to arrange a promised honeymoon. Andrew acknowledged that he had difficulty fulfilling some prior promises and, thus, was reticent to affirm the recent commitment because of financial uncertainty. The therapist introduced a distinction of Andrew's existing 'reputation for unreliability' (in her lived experience) along with distinctions of 'a unique opportunity' to take a step in a new direction by building 'a new reputation for reliability' in fulfilling important promises. Andrew could see the psychological and relational benefits in making an 'investment' during this crisis (by taking out a loan if necessary) and clearly backing his earlier commitment. When he began talking this way during the interview, Cynthia's anxiety visibly diminished and the crisis began to subside. Andrew ultimately did, in fact, follow through and provide the funds. The whole episode became a constructive turning point for the relationship, and served to provide an opportunity to distinguish his growing reputation for reliability and for his increased sensitivity to what was important for Cynthia.

Another crisis, this time with some physical violence, erupted unexpectedly in February 1989, about a year into the therapy. Over the prior few months, family patterns had been improving in a number of areas and Cynthia had reduced her medication in consultation with the referring psychiatrist. However, for a number of reasons, tension began building for each family member. Andrew was under an extraordinary amount of stress at work because of a major new project. Cynthia had been feeling increasingly vulnerable in the marriage because of a lack of sexual intimacy between the couple. There was also some tension between Vanessa and her mother because the daughter had been soiling herself and was refusing to use the toilet.

The incident of violence began when Vanessa was playing with her father and was being physically affectionate with him. Andrew responded positively to his daughter's display of affection, and did so in a way in which he did not respond to Cynthia (who was observing the interaction between father and daughter). Cynthia felt deprived and devalued. She protested against the interaction between Vanessa and Andrew, angrily pulling Andrew's hair. This led to a scuffle in which each spouse struck the other and Cynthia pulled Vanessa's hair as well. In retaliation, Andrew punched Cynthia quite hard on the shoulder, which shocked her. The physical violence stopped at that point, but Cynthia's symptoms returned 'with a vengeance' (according to the family doctor who saw her two days later).

During the subsequent family interview, the emotional tension was extremely high. The therapist's efforts to invite Andrew and Cynthia to understand the experience of the other during the episode were unsuccessful. Each continued to feel angry, bitter, and resentful toward the other. When the therapist eventually shifted to explore the positive 'learnings' that could come out of the unfortunate event, the anger began to dissipate. For instance, Andrew learned about the importance of showing physical affection to Cynthia and that physical retaliation made things worse rather than better. The therapist also offered an explanation of a 'normal' sequence of development in the personal management of frustration and anger. The steps described were moving from (1) blind rage in which one strikes out at anything, to (2) physically attacking the perceived source of the frustration, to (3) directing the attack toward physical objects rather than persons, to (4) attacking verbally, by yelling and screaming, rather than attacking physically, to (5) expressing anger in sarcastic statements or hostile, non-verbal gestures, to (6) imagining angry actions or statements in one's fantasy but not acting on them, to (7) anticipating frustrating situations and preparing adequate responses, and to (8) accepting the injustices and inequities in life that cannot be changed. The therapist explained how individuals may 'regress' back down the developmental sequence when the degree of frustration overwhelms their immediate capacity to cope.

This session ended in a brief conversation with Vanessa about the issue of soiling. The therapist distinguished 'Sneaky Poo' as that 'messy stuff that sneaks up on you and pops out when you're not expecting it'. Vanessa was able to identify with this distinction quite easily. It served to externalize the soiling problem from her as a person and to offer her an experience of personal agency in possibly 'putting Sneaky Poo in its place' (see Tomm, 1989, for more on this method).

When the family returned a month later there were improvements all around. Andrew was sharing more with Cynthia about his work, which made her feel included. She had taken initiative to be more positive with his parents, which he appreciated. Vanessa had taken to using the toilet and had 'put Sneaky Poo in its proper place,' which made both her parents very happy.

Disentangling Cynthia from Internalized Pathologizing Patterns

One source of intense emotional pain for Cynthia was the inner turmoil she experienced when she recalled the incestuous behavior of her adoptive father. Although there were no episodes of actual intercourse, she experienced his seductiveness and sexual touching as a profound betrayal of her childhood trust in him. Her sense of betrayal was intensified when, as an adult, she finally felt strong enough to confront him, he denied any such sexual initiatives and she was ostracized by the whole family. The therapist legitimized and supported her frustration and anger in relation to her abuse, but Cynthia did not want to address the issue again (with anyone in her family of origin) lest doing so would aggravate their already tenuous relationships. Furthermore, her father was now ailing with serious heart problems and she did not want to aggravate his health. As an alternative, the therapist suggested she write, but not send, a letter to her father saying all the things about her experience that she wanted him to understand and acknowledge. This proved to be a very healing exercise for her, since in writing the painful experiences 'out of her system' by getting them on to paper, she felt that she was able to 'get him off her chest.'

Cynthia also had internalized some patterns of interaction with her adoptive mother that were very destructive to her self-esteem and her self-confidence. One of these had to do with her mother's high expectations for her. When Cynthia was growing up she felt her mother's disapproval very strongly whenever any of her mother's expectations were not fulfilled. This occurred not only throughout her childhood but also when Cynthia became an adult. For instance, her mother desperately wanted her to become a nurse (which apparently was the mother's own unfulfilled career dream), and let Cynthia know how profoundly disappointed she was when Cynthia dropped out of nurse's training. It was not surprising that Cynthia had internalized (and was still carrying) her mother's disappointment and disapproval inside her.

This pattern was distinguished in the therapeutic conversation as continuing interaction with her mother that had been internalized and elaborated as a powerful 'inner critic.' There were many situations in which this inner critic could easily be reactivated (in the course of ordinary social interaction). In other words, she became exquisitely sensitive to the expectations (imagined or real) of anyone, including the various psychiatrists that she saw. Sometimes efforts to encourage her, such as to try a part-time job in order to develop some adult companionship, could quickly become counter-productive as she experienced them as excessive expectations. Indeed, high expectations had become more and more elaborated within her so that she often expected 'the ideal' from herself and also expected 'close to perfection' from others. For instance, a statement of reassurance by a professional that 'things would get better' was taken as an authoritative promise, and became associated with feelings of betrayal when the 'promise' did not come true as she expected. The fact that her marriage was still troubled at times and 'not perfect' left her feeling terrified that it would fall apart and that she would lose her daughter. Thus, the distinction that 'things are not yet better' took on major significance and kept her paranoid fears alive.

Distinguishing the form of her expectations as 'an enemy' rather than 'a friend' enabled Cynthia to reconsider her commitments to them. Identifying the 'inner critic' as an externalized personification and embodiment of this enemy allowed her to separate the expectations from herself and to question their influence over her. Another useful distinction in this context was that of being 'good enough' rather than needing to be 'ideal.' For instance, it was a relief to her to have 'a good enough marriage' since then she did not have to be as afraid that it would fail because it was not perfect. Nevertheless, the issue of 'poisonous expectations' is still a source of significant turmoil for her, and remains a focus for continuing work.

Concluding Comments

This account of therapy is obviously limited. It describes many, but not all, of the therapeutic distinctions that were introduced during the course of this therapy. It does not describe any of the major changes initiated by the family on their own outside of therapy. For instance, they sold their old house and moved into a new home in a district that was more suitable for the family as a whole. Relationships with the prior neighbors had been tense and problematic. On their own initiative Andrew and Cynthia set aside Tuesday evenings as their 'couple night' and another evening as Cynthia's night out. The family took up swimming together as a family outing. Vanessa began kindergarten and started making friends of her own.

Although an enormous amount of progress has been made, further therapeutic work is anticipated. Cynthia is still on medication and feels vulnerable in many social situations. Andrew still submits to habits of domineering and stubbornness at times. But both are much more open and willing to share their experiences with each other. Their disagreements can be handled more easily than before and they can 'turn things around' when they have 'a slip' into pathologizing patterns, to make a recovery in a shorter time. Perhaps most significant, however, is that Vanessa is growing up in this family context to become a very sensitive, yet articulate and strong, little girl.

The effects of collaboration in the writing of this chapter were that the therapeutic alliance between therapist and family seems to have been strengthened. Both Cynthia and Andrew felt affirmed in the constructive changes they had already made. Although it was painful for them to reflect on some of the difficulties of the past, they were able to see more clearly how they had, in fact, come a long way in a healing direction. They were also able to identify more clearly the therapeutic distinctions that seemed to have been instrumental in some of the changes they had made. This increased clarity became a source of increased hope for them; namely, that they would be able to work through the issues that remained problematic for them.

The discussions about therapy, that were oriented toward authenticating the therapeutic distinctions described in this chapter, were also helpful to the therapist. They enabled him to clarify his understanding of the family's dynamics and of the process of therapy with them. As a result, he began generating some new therapeutic distinctions. For instance, it became clearer that Cynthia's vulnerability to paranoid thoughts was fostered by her dependence on the 'outer authority' of her husband, of her parents, of her psychiatrists, and of the therapist himself. It became apparent that this needs to give way to her 'inner authority' about her own experiences, her entitlements, her preferences, and her own future. If her personal authority continues to be nurtured and is given the space to grow, perhaps some day she may exercise it as the first author of a sequel to this chapter.

Notes

1. The primary author, Dr Karl Tomm, is a Professor in the Department of Psychiatry and Director of the Family Therapy Program at the University of Calgary. The family would like to preserve their anonymity. Dr Carol Liske, Family Therapist at the University of Calgary, and Dr Winnie Tomm, Coordinator of Women's Studies at the University of Alberta provided useful feedback on earlier drafts of the chapter.

2. The family found this theoretical part of the chapter rather 'heavy reading' but realized it was intended for a professional audience. They preferred to skip over it and get to 'the meat' of the chapter. Other readers may have a similar experience, and the therapist offers his apology for the somewhat abstract nature of this section.

3. Using the term 'distinguisher' might be more appropriate than 'observer' for the same reason. However, 'distinguisher' is a bit cumbersome. It also seemed useful to try to associate the activity entailed in distinguishing with persons as observers to facilitate an on-going reconsideration of the notion of observing.

References

Bateson, G. (1972) *Steps to an Ecology of Mind*. New York: Ballantine.
Maturana, H. (1988) 'Reality: the search for objectivity or the quest for a compelling argument,' *Irish Journal of Psychology*, 9 (1), special issue, 'Radical constructivism, autopoiesis and psychotherapy'.
Maturana, H. and Varela, F. (1980) *Autopoiesis and Cognition: the Realization of the Living*. Boston: Reidel.

Tomm, K. (1989) 'Externalizing the problem and internalizing personal agency', *Journal of Strategic and Systemic Therapy*, 8.

Tomm, K. (1990) 'A critique of the DSM', *Dulwich Centre Newsletter* (Adelaide).

Tomm, K. (1991) 'Beginnings of a "HIPs and PIPs" approach to psychiatric assessment', *Calgary Participator*.

White, M. (1988) 'The externalizing of the problem and the re-authoring of lives and relationships', *Dulwich Centre Newsletter* (Adelaide).

9

History Becomes Her Story: Collaborative Solution-Oriented Therapy of the After-Effects of Sexual Abuse

William Hudson O'Hanlon

Due in part to publicity surrounding the issue and increased therapeutic interest, a growing number of people are seeking help for having been sexually abused in childhood. Most of the approaches in the literature or taught in workshops, however, have an objectivist and pathological bias. In this chapter, I shall describe an alternate approach that opens the possibility for briefer treatment which does not necessarily involve catharsis or remembering the details of the abuse as a way of resolving the after-effects. I call this approach collaborative solution-oriented therapy (O'Hanlon and Weiner-Davis, 1988).

The approach I offer here suggests that therapists cannot help but influence the memories and views the client has while in therapy, as it is important to influence clients in the direction of empowerment and moving on as rapidly as possible. I am suggesting also that each person is different – everyone is an exception – so one cannot have general principles that hold true for everyone. Treating the after-effects of sexual abuse may involve short- or long-term treatment, it may involve remembering feelings or forgotten and repressed memories, or it may not. It may involve helping the person move on and focus on the present and the future. The principles I describe below are the ones I most often bring to the table in my collaboration with clients. I stand for orienting toward solutions and competence rather than problems and pathology; for acknowledging people's experience and points of view without closing down the possibilities for change; focusing therapy on achieving the client's goals; and negotiating solvable problems. These stances interact with the values, experiences, responses, and ideas of my clients so that in therapeutic conversations, we collaboratively construct our therapeutic reality and solutions in the course of our therapeutic conversation.

A basic component of this approach is that assessment is an intervention; clients and therapists co-create the problem that is to be focused on in therapy (O'Hanlon and Wilk, 1987). I think this is the case whether the therapist is aware of it or not, so it is incumbent upon the therapist to take care in the kind of problem he or she is co-creating. Not all problems are created equal. Some will take quite a long time to resolve, and some a much briefer course of treatment. Some will empower people to be the experts on their problems and to have a sense of personal agency, and some will invalidate and discourage clients.

Current approaches to the treatment of the after-effects of sexual abuse hold that they are discovering and uncovering the truth about clients' childhoods. They also imply that the only way to help clients resolve these issues is to remember, feel, and express the feelings and incidents they repressed involving the abuse.

In this chapter, I will provide the transcript of a brief therapeutic intervention with a woman who has been suffering after-effects from being sexually abused. I will also provide some principles for doing this work in the form of charts and commentary on the case.

Solution-Orientation

If different problem definitions can be negotiated from the raw material clients bring to therapy, then it is incumbent upon the therapist to choose ways of thinking and talking in therapy that allow for the creation of problems that are solvable. Beyond that, the therapist can create problems that are solvable quickly and with only the resources that clients have available to them.

Most therapists have conversations with clients that lead to the view that they are suffering from some pathological, psychological, emotional, neurological, or biochemical disorder. Focusing so much on what is wrong with people can have a discouraging effect. People tend to see themselves as sick and damaged. They often forget the resources, strengths, and capabilities they have.

What I am suggesting is that the therapist deliberately have conversations for solutions with clients. There are many aspects of human behavior and experience, then, that one could focus on in therapy. Where we put our attention and direct our inquiries will inevitably influence the course of treatment and the data that emerge. Since all successful therapy eventually comes around to finding solutions by getting people to do something different or to view things differently, I propose that we start pursuing these goals more deliberately from the start of therapy. In this view, clients are presumed to have resources and competence to make the changes they want to make. The therapist's job is to create a context in which clients gain access to their resources and competence. The interviewing process is designed to elicit and highlight these competences (de Shazer, 1985).

While stressing the solution-oriented aspects of this work, I want to emphasize that I do not suggest minimizing or denying people's pain or suffering or invalidating their views on their difficulties.

Acknowledgement and Possibility

In therapy, it is important that the therapist acknowledges people's pain and suffering as well as their points of view about their problems, but the fine balance that must be achieved is how to do this while keeping the possibilities for change open. Sometimes people have a view of their situation that makes it difficult or impossible to resolve.

One way to achieve this balance is to acknowledge people's feeling, experiences, and points of view without agreeing or disagreeing with them and then to open up possibilities for new views and new feelings and experiences. A common method for doing this is to use the past tense when reflecting the client's reported feelings and points of view that have been troublesome for them, and using the present or future tense when mentioning new feelings, goals and new points of view. For example, 'So you've been afraid right before having sex. When you are feeling more comfortable before sex, what do you think you will do or say differently to your partner?'

Commission and Commission-Giver

At an international family therapy conference in Ireland in 1989, I listened to some people from Sweden (Mia Andersson, Klas Grevelius, and Ernst Salamon of the AGS Institute) talk about their work. They discussed the importance of finding out what the commission is in therapy and who the commission-giver is in each case. I loved that idea. In English, this word lends itself to a nice pun. What I try to discover and create with my clients is a co-mission.

The therapist also has an agenda. Some of that agenda derives from the therapist's theories, some from his or her values, some from his or her legal, ethical, financial or agency concerns. Out of the therapist's and client's agendas come some mutually agreed-upon goals. If we do not develop some joint, mutually agreeable goals, we will probably have a rocky, 'resistant' relationship. I will be resistant to hearing them and working on their goals and they will not cooperate with my agendas.

In any particular case, there may be more than one commission-giver and more than one commission. The therapist's job, then, is to develop a mission statement that all concerned can agree upon and support.

Criteria for Satisfaction/Goals for Treatment

Steve de Shazer of Milwaukee's Brief Family Therapy Center has a nice phrase for this: 'How will we know when we're supposed to stop meeting like this?' If therapy is to come to a successful conclusion, it's a good idea to get some idea of how we'll know it has been successful.

Since I've already said that I think that therapists co-create problems with clients, I obviously don't think that having a problem is the indication for starting therapy. Many people have difficulties and never enter therapy. Therapy starts when someone is complaining about something and someone decides that what is being complained about is relevant for therapy. Of course, sometimes someone other than the person who shows up for the session is complaining (as in cases of 'involuntary' treatment, such as court-ordered treatment and parents who bring their children to have therapy when the children do not perceive a difficulty).

Therapy can end satisfactorily, then, simply when whoever was complaining about something no longer complains about it. This happens in two ways: one is when what the person was complaining about is no longer perceived as a problem. The other condition for ending therapy successfully is when what the client was complaining about is no longer happening often enough or intensely enough for the person to say it is a problem.

A goal, then, is the magnetic north that can orient the therapist's compass. One of the difficulties in the field of therapy is our inability to define what constitutes successful treatment. Goals, in collaborative solution-oriented therapy, should derive mainly from the client's vision of what constitutes success, subject to some negotiation with the therapist to ensure the achievability of the goal. Measurement of success should come from clients' reports. If clients believably say that what they were complaining about is no longer happening, then therapy has succeeded.

The chart, Table 9.1, summarizes many of the differences between this approach and traditional models and methods. What follows is a case illustration of this collaborative approach.

Introduction to the Session

This session took place during the third day of a workshop I was doing on 'solution-oriented hypnosis.' The day was devoted to

Table 9.1   *Contrasting approaches to the treatment of the after-effects of sexual abuse*

Traditional approaches	Solution-oriented therapy
Therapist is the expert – has special knowledge regarding sexual abuse to which the client needs to submit (Colonization/missionary model)	Client and therapist both have particular areas of expertise (Collaborative model)
Client is viewed as damaged by the abuse (Deficit model)	Client is viewed as influenced but not determined by the abuse history, having strengths and abilities (Resource model)
Remembering abuse and the expression of repressed affect (catharsis) are goals of treatment	Goals are individualized for each client, but do not necessarily involve catharsis or remembering
Interpretation	Acknowledgement, valuing and opening possibilities
Past-oriented	Present/future-oriented
Problem/pathology-oriented	Solution-oriented
Must be long-term treatment	Variable/individualized length of treatment
Invites conversations for insight and working through	Invites conversations for accountability and action and declines invitations to blame and invalidation

Source: Parts of this chart were adapted from Durrant and Kowalski (1990)

using hypnosis and solution-oriented therapy with people who complained about the after-effects of sexual abuse.

I offer this case to show the possibility that the treatment of the after-effects of sexual abuse can be brief and does not necessarily involve catharsis or long-term work. This woman, S, a therapist attending the workshop, had in the past few years remembered having been sexually abused in her childhood. She had connected her experience of detachment (dissociation) during sexual activity and her compulsive and unsatisfying sexual activities (often involving dangerous sex, like being beaten or having sex with a stranger in a public place) with the abuse. Consequently she had stopped the dangerous sex, but still had the experience of being detached and afraid before and during sex. We were both aware that we had only this one session to help her achieve her goals. As you shall read, we negotiated two main goals for our work. The first was to help her be more present and less fearful before and during sex. The second was to remember more of her younger sister, who had recently died of cancer. S speculated that when she had forgotten the abuse, she had also forgotten many other things from her childhood, including good memories of time she spent with her sister. Because her sister was now dead, those lost memories were more precious and she wanted help in recalling them.

I started, where I usually start, with getting an initial statement from the person about what she wants.

> *WOH*: So how may I help you? I want to start a complaint-land. Tell me so I can be oriented towards recent concerns or complaints and how you'll know when you get there, when you've achieved your goal. [*I try to orient towards recent concerns. The implicit message is that the past is not all that relevant. I also want an initial statement about a complaint so we can begin the process of focusing on creating a solvable problem and achievable goals.*]
>
> *S*: The most recent complaint I would say would be, intermittent lack of sexual desire, and then, I'll still have sex, but I don't . . .
>
> *WOH*: You won't be there totally. You won't be into it.
>
> *S*: I feel afraid right at the moment, right before and then I can kind of push through it sometimes and then other times I go into the numb state. Where I'm not really there but I'm there. And still having fairly severe menstrual cramps and . . . Hmmm . . .
>
> *WOH*: So how will you know when you get there? [*S starts to add more complaints and I try to focus by asking about goals.*]
>
> *S*: How will I know when I get there? Well . . .
>
> *WOH*: When you get through it, when you leave that behind, when that's taken care of. [*S hesitated, so I restated my request for a goal statement.*]
>
> *S*: Yeah, leave that behind and . . .
>
> *WOH*: OK Less severe menstrual cramps – that seems to be related to you or you don't know that it's related? [*I'm not sure that the menstrual cramps are relevant to the intermittent lack of sexual desire and her not getting with it when she's having sex, so I gently challenge their relevance to the problem we are to work on.*]
>
> *S*: Well I know that I guess just to give you a little background for up until the last five years I couldn't remember from 0–11 years of age. And my memory went to 11 years of age and my memory started when I had my first kiss with a boy and then through hypnosis in the past 5 years little by little and flashbacks the memory of a sexual abuse when I was 6 years old, by a cousin, that was 16. It was interesting because I was just reading a *People* magazine article about this woman that disassociated and that was when you know like you said you read a book or something and that is when it just all flooded all back up that that is what I have done all of my life is just, you know, disassociate either in sex or I have all these different parts I can be the perfect professional, the perfect daughter but still then running out and screwing a stranger in an elevator or something like that. You know, that kind of thing.
>
> *WOH*: Right. OK, so you recognized that when you read that it was like . . . WOW. [*S responds with some history. I did not ask for this*

history but since she has provided it, I'd better include and acknowledge it.]

S: Right. That that was kind of what she had done and it hit me and also it has just come up that maybe there was some pleasure involved and that's what made me perhaps forget the whole thing was the fact that maybe I had caused it . . .

WOH: That you couldn't deal with that.

S: And I have always kind of had that my whole life, appearing to be very sexual and . . . I have always called myself the elephant man because on one, I look this way on the outside, but inside I have always felt I was a different person looking out and couldn't really get too much of it . . .

WOH: Acting out.

S: So I could act things out really perfectly and pretend that I was the great seductress and everything but really I was . . .

WOH: Inside.

S: I was either not there or a scared little girl or pretending or acting. So I guess another thing would be if some memories could come back. Now I remember the abuse, although I never confronted the abuser. But I lost my youngest sister to cancer about 2 years ago and I would kind of like to bring back some memories just to have more of . . .

WOH: Sense of what growing up with her was like?

S: Right.

WOH: So to have the nicer parts of that too.

S: That would be another thing is to have the good memories come back too.

WOH: OK good. And so just to summarize for me: the work you have done over the 5 years or whenever through hypnosis. You remembered some things, a lot of the abuse, you think, or most of it, or part of it, or . . .?

S: Well, actually I remember I had a boyfriend in high school that I was laying there on a couch one time and I opened my eyes and he was standing above me with an erect penis right above me and I screamed at the top of my lungs and he couldn't understand. It was sort of that same reaction, like the woman who screamed at you, [*This was a reference to a story I had told earlier about a co-worker who had yelled at me, but was really yelling at someone else she was angry with who wasn't in the room.*] Where are you coming from? kind of thing.

WOH: Right.

S: Then as time went on all of a sudden it was the flash of like somebody turning around and I would have been like probably like waist level of him and I think that's what happened that he in kind of a gentle way came over and said 'this is my pee-pee and this is yours' and kind of made it like a game and let's do something. And I think I had a fairly dominated childhood by my mother so doing something she didn't know about that was maybe like an adult and feeling old and so. I don't really remember, you know. I'm pretty sure there was penetration because I never had uh . . . when you . . .

WOH: A hymen.

S: Right, a hymen or anything. And I always talked myself into the fact that I must have done it doing gymnastics or something. [*WOH*: Yeah, that's the sort of . . .] And then again I don't know because then why didn't I have some kind of physical ramification that I went and cried to. Also I had one flash of actually seeing my father, it happened in a barn, so maybe we would go away (it was on a farm) and play in the barn and I would see this vision of my father walking up past the door on the outside and like there was windows on the outside like there was windows on the barn door. Like something was happening we were engaged in sex and then I saw him. Then for many years I hated him. For a long time I thought he was the one maybe that had and I felt like maybe it sexually abuse but I then I thought I was making this up and then all . . .

WOH: Right.

S: . . . of these ramifications, these problems.

WOH: So, it's still not totally clear for you all that happened, but you have a sense of what happened.

S: Right, right.

WOH: OK.

S: And I don't really know how to totally resolve it. I would like to resolve it within myself whether I ever confront him about it or not.

WOH: That is something different and you may or may not do that. I just thought of something though that may be helpful for you. Sometimes I have people write a letter, not so that they are going to send a letter to that person to the cousin or to whatever it may be, not so they were going to send but write it as if they were going to send it but not sending it. And write this whole letter. Everything you would say from what you know right now or anything you. Yell at them or apologize, whatever you feel moved to do. Whatever it is. And write it all out and then if you ever did decide to actually decide to write a letter to save that letter or else get rid of it but to save the pieces of it that you would actually send in a real letter.

S: I did think of, in a nice way saying, 'Look, you know, I have worked all through this but could you just confirm . . .?'

WOH: Yeah, 'Could you just tell me what happened?'

S: Like circle *yes* or *no*.

WOH: Check *yes* or *no*. I did this on this day . . . [*Laughter*]

S: Not to tell the family or hurt anybody else or anything.

WOH: Right. Just to remember this and 'Did this happen?' and 'Am I remembering it right? Was there any stuff I didn't remember?'

S: Right.

Solution-Oriented Hypnosis

Here I start to do hypnosis. Solution-oriented hypnosis is a collaborative venture. As you will be able to read, it is a permissive, empowering, rather than authoritarian, approach to hypnosis.

The purpose of this type of hypnosis is different from traditional approaches as well. In traditional hypnosis, the hypnotherapist attempts to uncover repressed memories and feelings, to get the person to abreact or remember the sexual abuse. Or the hypnotherapist tries to counteract the negative injunctions and beliefs established during the abuse by substituting more positive beliefs, affirmations, and self-talk.

Solution-oriented hypnosis intends to evoke resources, strengths, and abilities and help people re-narrate their situation. It is a way to help people *experience* their situation differently, not just talk about it differently.

Multiple-choice options for making changes are given and new distinctions and connections are proposed. The person will not take up all the options provided, but will pick and choose among the alternatives to find the ones that fit for her. The point is not to have people abreact and express their feelings and points of view, but to *change* those feelings and points of view.

Now to the trancework.

WOH: Good, so you have been in trance before lots of times.
S: Yeah.
WOH: OK good. So let yourself go into trance and I am going to say in a way that is appropriate for you, safe for you, as safe as possible in this particular setting. To go wherever you need to go to move yourself along toward those goals, toward resolving, toward remembering just as much as you need to remember and just as little as you need to remember and you may have already done all of remembering you need to do or want to do and somehow find a way to create the room in there, the space in there for you to be validated who you are, how you are, for you to include your history, your experience, the things you have done, the things that have been done to you. To be able to leave the then time in the then time and when you are in the now time to be able to know about all the then time that you need to know about as part of your background of learnings and experience and to really be in the now time [*So far I have been acknowledging the difficulties and opening up new possibilities. One of the implicit ('history') and explicit ('leave the then time in the then time') suggestions is to put the past in the past, where it belongs.*] and to be able to give yourself permission . . . That's right [*She started to nod her head*] . . . to have felt the things you've felt and separate that from blame or approval and find some way to reconcile and connect in a way that is meaningful to you the past, to the present, to the future and to disconnect any parts that are not meaningful to you or useful for you. To know about consciously and bring into the present and the future. As we've talked all day, you have abilities, skills, resources, and strengths, coping mechanisms, ways of dealing with things, ways of not dealing with things, and you can just rearrange those in any way that you need to rearrange those. And your hand may start to lift up [*Here I am using her difficulty, dissociation, as her solution. In order to lift the hand automatically, one must dissociate it. As it continues up, I link it to the changes she is making.*

So, dissociation leads to integration and healing now.] and that may be one of those things you have done in hypnosis before and it could lift up and as it starts to lift up to your face, you can be doing the work that you need to do. It may be in terms of resolving, and it may be in terms of remembering and may be in terms of remembering to forget the things that are interfering with your good memories. The memories you would like to keep more present and future. As that hand continues to lift up, and it can lift up to your face, it doesn't have to, and it might be lifting up to your face and as it comes in contact with your face, as it does, that can be the signal for you to do whatever it is that you need to do to include within that work, any emotions or experiences you have had and that you have, that you need to have, whatever you need to know, experience at the rate of that which you could know that and you can change time to do that in a way that is right for you. You can come up with something that lets you know that these changes have occurred. And when it is time in that process, as that hand continues, up toward your face, in an appropriate way you can find the resources you need to resolve that in a way that's right for you. And after it touches your face you can at some time, when you are ready, maybe right away, maybe in a minute or two, three minutes, open your eyes and look at me when you are ready and I'm going to talk to you just briefly and find out from you if there is anything that I need to know or what I need to know. Now is there anything I need to know or to tell you to do inside or to talk to you about while you are in trance? So what is happening right now?

S: I see little boxes.

WOH: Little boxes?

S: With the then and the now, with a minus sign and an arrow taking all the hurtful experiences and leaving them and they kind of pass through the now and there was little like addition signs and they were kind of shifting around the boxes and they would superimpose on each other. And realizing that I am who I am because of them. [*After she came out of trance, in response to a question asking her to elaborate on this experience, she replied: Yeah I saw that as the sexual abuse experience as well as other poor sexual choices that I had made through the years all caught in this little box. Then I saw my present life, all the good parts of it and strengths and coping mechanisms and they were like almost like to an addition kind of like this little plus, and the future as good. But I knew I couldn't just keep it separate, so that's why I kind of moved it so it went on top of it like a super-imposition.*]

WOH: Right and it has made in a weird way it has made a contribution to who you are. That is not all bad and good in a lot of ways. OK good. All right so you close your eyes and find a way to put those things in their place and have them to be the platform which you stand to see farther into the future, to step off into the future, in a safe way so that you can feel solid grounding underneath you. And also I think it would be nice while you are in that trance to be able to find a way to make arrangements with yourself to be there for the pleasurable parts when it is safe and when it is a situation that you trust, to be there for the pleasurable parts of having sex, when it's appropriate for you. To be able to be fully in your experience and to know that what happened then was then and it had all sorts of ramifications then, had all sorts of meanings for then and as you were growing up. With the resources you have now and the understanding you have now and that you are getting as moments go on, minutes, days, months and weeks and years go on, that you could come to a new understanding and even appreciation of your history.

One of the things for me is that I used to be real depressed and real shy and very miserable and I think that kind of sensitivity to that kind of pain has been one of the things that has made me very sensitive as a therapist to other people's pain and discomfort, also to the possibilities of change. 'Cause with me, I thought I was a hopeless case and now I realize I wasn't a hopeless case and that somewhere deep inside I knew I would make it through. That somewhere deep inside there was a strength and resilience even in the midst of what looked like fragility to me like I couldn't handle anything and that I couldn't deal with anything and I was full of fear but I came to appreciate the sensitivity that gave me and to tap into the strengths. And that's one way I have come to reconcile myself with those experiences and those hurts. [*Here I offer a new frame of reference for her painful experience: that pain can lead to sensitivity to others' pain. This is relevant for her as a therapist.*]

I think it'd also be nice while you are in trance to really have something to come to your mind that's pleasant from your childhood, from your growing up, maybe something to do with your sister, I think that'd be nice. Maybe just a flash or maybe a full-blown memory or experience or maybe just a feeling. I remember my sister and I as we were little, climbing in the middle of a bunk bed that was folded up it was real tight and it felt like our fort. I don't really remember what it looked like or where it was, I just remember the feeling of that fold-away bed. And I think the body remembers those good feelings too in sort of a connection and a legacy that your sister left behind in your experience, your feelings and memories of her.

I was watching television last night, or the other night, and someone was saying, it's amazing I watched my grandchild and I can see some of the things that he does are just like my father although he never met my father and isn't interesting how these legacies get passed on. So your sister, even though she is not around, probably influenced people that you influence, that you are in contact with and connection with through the spirit and the memory of her, through those feelings. And you can bring those forward into the present and the future as well. And have a little more choice about that. Now in a minute I am going to suggest that that hand either starts to drift down or you can just put it down very deliberately, whatever is most comfortable for you. And that as it goes back down to your thigh. That's right you can begin comparing to complete this experience in trance knowing that each trance experience completion is also the beginning of other things and the opening of other things. So do that in a way that's right for you. When you are ready to come all of the way out of a trance leaving behind in trance the things that are for trance. Good. Thanks.

S: That was good. I saw her clearly.

WOH: That's great. Good. Good job.

S: A good memory just came back. [*S experienced some vivid memories of her sister while in trance.*]

WOH: That's nice. OK. Good.

[*In the discussion afterwards, S told me that the reason she had wanted to do the session right at that time was that she was getting married in a week. She had had a string of terrible and abusive relationships with men over the course of her adult life and had finally gotten into a good relationship, with a man who was not abusive and seemed pretty healthy and supportive. He knew about her abuse history and was sensitive to her fear and discomfort with sex. She wanted their marriage to start out, however, without being dominated by her abuse history and the after-effects.*]

S wrote me a letter a month later.

Dear Bill,

Just a short note to update you on my progress since our session. The first thing I noted when my husband and I had sex on our honeymoon night (1 week after the seminar – the first chance we'd had to have sex all week with all the family in for the wedding) was that I did not dissociate. I was able to feel the physical enjoyment without having to retreat. I have also noticed a total extinguishing of the pre-sex fears. All my goals were accomplished automatically.

Although I did not remember a lot of what you said specifically while in trance, I do remember you saying, 'I used to be shy and depressed.' I remember thinking for days later, 'He used to be shy? Wow! It sure doesn't show.'

I haven't written the letter to my abuser yet, but I will. I'm still floating in marital bliss.

Sincerely and affectionately,
S

Follow-up done nine months and twenty-one months later indicated that the results have held. S said that she realized that resolving what happened to her is a continuous process, but she recalls this session as the time when she turned the corner in that process.

We worked together to co-create a new view and experience for S. She had been living a life that was in many ways determined by her history, by what someone who had abused her had done to her in the distant past. She was living *his* story. We collaboratively opened the possibility for her to start to live *her* story, to take back her life and to create new chapters in the future. In summary, Table 9.2 offers some principles for using collaborative solution-oriented therapy.

Table 9.2   *Collaborative solution-oriented therapy with
survivors of sexual abuse*

Find out what the client is seeking in treatment and how she will know when treatment has been successful.

Ascertain to the best of your ability that the sexual abuse is not current. If it is, take whatever steps necessary to stop it.

Don't assume that the client needs to go back and work through traumatic memories. Remember that everybody is an exception.

Use the natural abilities the client has developed as a result of having to cope with abuse (e.g., being facile at dissociating). Turn the former liability into an asset.

Look for resources and strengths. Focus on underlining how they made it through the abuse and what they have done to cope, survive, and thrive since then. Look for nurturing and healthy relationships and role models they had in the past or have in the present. Look for current skills in other areas.

Validate and support each part of the person's experience.

Keep focused on the goals of treatment rather than getting lost in the gory details.

Do not give the message that the person is 'damaged goods' or that their future is determined by having been abused in the past.

References

de Shazer, Steve (1985) *Keys to Solution in Brief Therapy*. New York: Norton.
Durrant, M. and Kowalski, K. (1990) 'Overcoming the effects of sexual abuse: developing a self-perception of competence', in Michael Durrant and Cheryl White (eds), *Ideas for Therapy with Sexual Abuse*. Adelaide: Dulwich Centre Publications.
O'Hanlon, Bill and Wilk, James (1987) *Shifting Contexts: the Generation of Effective Psychotherapy*. New York: Guilford Press.
O'Hanlon, William H. and Weiner-Davis, Michele (1988) *In Search of Solutions: a New Direction in Psychotherapy*. New York: Norton.

10

Narrations of the Self: Video Production in a Marginalized Subculture

Annibal Coelho de Amorim and
Fatima Gonçalves Cavalcante

> The heart of the city doesn't open on Sundays, doesn't see this impunity. Children, women and men, playing, smiling, loving one another in the festival of marginality.
>
> Luiz Gonzaga, *Marginal Hearts*

Our attempt is to apply social constructionist techniques therapeutically with young developmentally disabled adults to help them reconstruct their lives in the community. More specifically, we work with groups of disabled persons who produce and perform a narrative about themselves in the format of a puppet play. By videotaping the production process it is possible to capture a revealing fragment of the life of a subculture of people forced to the margins of society by current disabling constructions. In this chapter we shall consider how stories of self, their metaphorical implications and alternatives, can lead us toward an educational device which has applications in both the mental health and the rehabilitation fields. Propelled into the search for techniques to effect social change with regard to the matter of disability, we look at this combination of constructionist narrative and puppet drama as potentially effective if used in those services where the main focus is the therapeutic community and communities as therapy.

To set the context we shall first consider puppetry and art therapy, the play element in culture, and the social constructionist therapy in modern psychology. We shall then describe *The Story of Walter A. Mess*, subtitled *It's Up to You!*, a play written and performed between June 1989 and May 1990 within a specialized organization which provides services for individuals with disabilities in the eastern United States. Here, we worked with 'narratives of the self.' They are stories of stigmatized individuals who encountered the myths of deficiency constructed and rooted in our societies.

Act I – Lights . . . Setting the Scene

Scene 1 – Introducing Puppetry

> Play is immensely exciting [because of] the precariousness of the interplay of personal psychic reality and the experience of control of actual objects.
>
> Joseph Friedman, *Therapeia, Play and the Therapeutic Household*

Many know how fascinating it is to play with puppets. Their antics are contagiously transmitted to all who dare to become involved with them. Behind the stage or in the audience the excitement is the same, and a flow of feelings arises when the puppet play begins. The result is often hypnotic, and magically carries us into the puppets' habitat: a world of never-ending stories. The puppetry technique is widely used through the world, and since ancient times puppets have expressed key cultural attitudes and social values; no matter what their origins were (religious, mystical, entertainment, and so on) playing with puppets has become a common multi-generational tradition in human societies.

The art of making and manipulating puppets has assumed different forms in various cultures (for example, Chinese shadow theater, Japanese wayangs, Japanese gidaym, Persian sehah selim, Turkish karagoes, Brazilian mamulengo, and Italian Burattini). Among these cultural diversities puppets have been brought to life by the use of strings (marionettes), hands (finger or hand puppets), by the projection of light behind them (shadow theater), by the attachments of rods (rod puppets) or by more sophisticated technologies such as animathronics. Puppetry magic has enabled puppeteers to immortalize characters such as Punchinello and Guignol (France), Punch (England), Petrushka (Russia), Raguin (Sri Lanka), João Redondo (Brazil). The puppeteers themselves have emerged as folk heroes in their own countries: Yen-Sze (China), Pierre Datelin or Brioche (France) and the poetic Cheiroso (Brazil). From ancient Greek theater to recent TV shows, puppets have delighted philosophers (Socrates and Homer), writers and poets (Goethe, Jean-Jacques Rousseau, Shikamatsu Monzamon), kings (Charles V of Spain) and ordinary people (like those who followed João Redondo in Pernambuco, Brazil).

In 1935 Bender and Woltman began to incorporate the use of puppets into psychotherapy. Since their pioneering work at the Children's Observation Ward of the Psychiatric Division of Bellevue Hospital, New York, the artistic and immortal spirit of puppetry has turned out to be a valuable and widely used tool in current therapeutic practice, both with groups and with individuals (Bernier, 1983).

Our work not only extends this technique, but draws as well from three art therapy considerations.

The puppet as an intermediary between the players and the viewers We usually find among persons with disabilities an ever-present fear of failure when a performance is socially required. North American society places a very high value on polished performance and sets unrealistically high achievement goals, thus feeding the fears of those who cannot meet these standards. In our experience, the puppets mediate and thus alleviate, to some extent, the social pressure of failing. As Jenkins and Beck (1942) put it, 'If the puppet does wrong it is the puppet, not the person that is censured or punished.' The puppet may also represent, in Freudian terms, the ego ideal and may symbolically 'restore' or 'cure' a body 'physically or mentally impaired' (ibid.). The puppet is also the persona in social interchange, allowing the players behind them to 'expand their ego by giving them a sense of mastery' (Lyle and Holly, 1941).

Puppetry as a three-dimensional art medium According to Woltman (1972) the three-dimensional quality 'gives puppetry a more realistic effect' within the context of fantasy, and the combination of realistic and fantasy characters makes it easier for the individual to enter into the identity of the puppet figure (Woltman, 1951). Puppetry, conceived by Kors as a 'miniature form of psychodrama' (Kors, 1963, 1964) enabled our puppet-player participants to reveal their conflicts while remaining invisible. Life represented on the puppet stage became an extension of the real psychodrama faced by persons with disabilities in day-to-day society. It is our conviction that myths of deficiencies can be 'played out' through the use of these intermediary 'third objects.'

At the heart of Kors' use of puppets in therapy there are three concepts: (1) 'Play your play so that the nature of the world in which you are becomes clear to me;' (2) 'Let's talk together about your play so that the world in which you are living becomes clear to you;' and (3) 'Let's try to find out why your world is so different from our common socially constructed world, that living in that common world seems to be impossible for you' (Kors, 1963). This conceptual framework is central to all of our work and we believe it has important implications for effective therapeutic interventions. Based upon play therapy applications (Axline, 1947) we can say that through the play individuals may 'talk out' their difficulties about 'being disabled,' and explore a wide repertoire of coping mechanisms for their social struggles. As we observed, through the play 'new understanding arises' and as a result, the reality contour changes. Critical to the development of such understanding are relations established among the players, between players and their parts, and the players and the play. Through *The Story of Walter A. Mess* it was possible to create a playful space in which 'disabled' individuals were no longer passive people 'receiving services' by others, but were, rather, active 'self-providers,' recasting themselves in new roles through new narratives of self.

The process of story-telling   Stories can be considered in terms of their formal aspects, their content and the psycho-social point of view. The narrative developed for our puppet show clearly revealed the way its authors 'mapped' their world. The characters were chosen to represent different degrees of activity and passivity, thus reflecting the authors' daily struggle between 'being supervised' and 'becoming independent;' their struggle with the implicit structured norms of a community placement for developmentally disabled adults. The story further encoded the conflicts between the puppet players and the community in which the play was taking place. In keeping with the observation that the narratives of this population evolve mainly from environmentally derived experiences as well as from their developing skills, the authors of this particular story chose as a theme the problems faced by the disabled person when living in the outside community. Others have suggested that in working with story-telling in this population the story-line could profitably focus on recent real-life group experiences, especially upsetting ones (see, for example, Bagel in Robbins and Sibley, 1976). We did not attempt to focus group attention on such issues but believe that Bagel's approach could be used to work out conflicts within the group and wherever the conflict of 'being or not being disabled' is apparent.

Scene 2 – Lights on Play

> In myth and ritual, the great instinctive forces of civilized life have their origin: law and order, commerce and profit, craft and art, poetry, wisdom and science. All are rooted in the primeval soil of the play.
>
> J. Huizinga, *Homo Ludens*

The importance of the 'play element' in our work can be attributed in important measure to Huizinga's *Homo Ludens: A Study Element in Culture*. Huizinga (1945) quotes Plato in describing play as 'action accomplishing itself outside and above the necessities and seriousness of everyday life.' As Huizinga put it,

'Play is a significant function where there is something "at play" which transcends the immediate needs of life.' What matters, he suggests, is 'what play is in itself and what it means for the player.' In his attempts to find other categories that might be equivalent to the essence of the 'fun' of playing, Huizinga refers to the Dutch word *aardigkeit* (which is derived from *aard*, meaning 'art') as the closest equivalent to the English word. The German word for the fun of playing, *wesen*, brings us 'essence' or the state of 'being,' a 'natural' quality of the fun element. In keeping with Huizinga, we believe that within the play element dwells an ulterior meaning, something experienced as magical or transporting which surrounds the concreteness of the play act itself. The rite (from the Greek *dromenon*) to which we refer is 'something acted.' As Huizinga suggests, 'Rite is a helping-out of the action, an action to guarantee the well-being of the world.' He points to the performances of rites in primitive societies to illustrate that there was always at play an 'indissoluble unity' between sacred, earnest and 'make-believe' or 'fun.'

In the context of our work, play represents both spontaneous and indispensable rite of passage; rite through which disabled persons attempt to transcend their current disabling status which led them to social marginalization. In so doing, the fun element of what Huizinga defines as 'with reality,' redefines the configuration of societal expectations toward disability.

While Huizinga's concepts describe a cultural perspective for apprehending play as a creative alternative for extracting meaning beyond our everyday seriousness, we articulate it with other theoretical approaches. Theorists, such as Piaget, Henri Wallon, Winnicott, and Daniel Stern, have paid much attention to the kinesthetic play experiences infants have in early stages of their lives. Daniel Stern (1985) has studied infants' experiences such as recognition of human form (face, voice, breast), and has referred to 'some kind of specialness attached to the person's vision of other persons and the self.' We believe that this 'specialness' plays a central role in the domain of our quotidian 'relatedness' in society, an ever-present process through which we construct and are socially constructed. For the purpose of our work, what specifically interests us most is Stern's (1985) question of 'how and when our constructions become related to human subjectivity, so that selves and others emerge.' It is by articulating Stern's 'some kind of specialness' with Huizinga's 'play element' that we may define the performance of the puppet play as an action which qualitatively differs from the commonplace activity of our lives. The entire production in which we engaged was an event of 'some kind of specialness,' in which the 'play element' dominated. And the 'play' was about the way a group of people socially constructed their lives. As players, we do not distinguish between 'being' and 'playing;' it is actually by playing that we all recognize 'faces' and 'voices' within the social surrounding. Thus, it is by manipulating the play elements within social life that people can realize the central role that constructionism has in their lives.

Proceeding from the theoretical to the practical, we used play elements such as order, tension, movement, rhythm, and rapture to help the puppet-play participants function in a different role from the one expected by society, the role of 'being retarded.' In the play frame, the group exercised the socially unexpected role of 'crew producers of a complex event,' the puppet play itself. In the play the participants took on a more powerful, active role than they were used to playing in the world. On what kind of cultural stage did the Walter play emerge? For decades persons with disabilities 'played' only institutionalized 'games,' kept 'out of sight and out of mind' because society defined their behavior as unacceptable. Institutions did not offer a wide variety of social contacts, and many lives became socially impoverished. With the movement to de-institutionalize this group of people, a new order of 'games' emerged. We witness new games of empowerment and self-determination like self-advocacy activities, which give people real possibilities for active social interchange.

It is in this context that we conceived the puppet games we played. In different facets of the puppet production we saw games of self-discovery, self-expression and self-resolution and, ultimately, opportunities to deconstruct the current disabling constructions and to reconstruct new and more powerful identities. Working within a highly structured educational program with clearly defined behavioral goals for its participants, we felt that it was extremely important that our puppet games appear to be special, outside, and above the necessities and seriousness of everyday life. We hoped to encourage a kind of play, a game, in which the purpose was to facilitate a creative reconstruction of reality among the 'creators' (puppeteers and/or crew) and through interactions between 'creators' and their 'creatures' (puppets, or self-projected characters). We observed a process in which aspects of their narratives helped participants see the range of their choices for living in the world; we also saw how these narratives served as a mirror for their self-concepts and helped them 'to identify' themselves to others and to themselves' (Gergen and Gergen, 1988).

Scene 3 – The Social Constructionist Takes the Stage

> Art becomes the vehicle through which the reality of life is generated. In a significant sense, we live by stories – both in the telling and the doing of self.
>
> Kenneth and Mary Gergen, 'Narrative and the self as relationship'

Having examined the play element in cultures and demonstrated the value of 'aesthetic experience' for a marginalized subculture, we now turn to our third theoretical approach, the social constructionist. This orientation stimulates an evolution in psychology in which the emphasis is placed on people's construction of their world and the effects of these constructions on their actions. Of particular concern to us in our work is the 'disabling language' used by much of society (including mental health professionals), in dealing with unusual or non-normative patterns of behavior. Also of concern is the incorporation of these beliefs into the lives of those who are thus constructed.

Most of the diagnostic categories commonly used within the mental health field imply 'implicit hierarchies' (Gergen, 1990) which have the effect of reducing persons both in status and to the labels themselves. As Gergen outlines, these labels operate 'to establish the essential nature of the person being described,' and by which we understand the person in the world. We are acutely concerned with the proliferating effects of the deficit vocabulary and maintenance of the very problems it attempts to describe. Examining Jeff Woodyard's assertion (1980) that 'segregation through institutionalization has occurred in our society as a result of many myths,' it is clear that perceiving developmentally disabled persons as 'dangerous,' 'sick,' 'burdens to society,' 'menacing,' and 'sexually uncontrollable' has been one major cause of segregation and the isolation experienced by this segment of the population. It is our concern to identify and intervene in the process through which 'handicapping language' and its 'pejorative effects' are applied both by disabled persons and those who interact with them.

Different theorists have proposed explanations for the prevalence of the language of deficiency used by mental health professionals. Thomas Szasz (1961, 1963) postulated that concepts of mental illness function mainly as 'social myths' and are used as a means of social control. Izidora Blikstein (1983) has demonstrated linguistic influences on the construction of social reality, pointing out that 'semantic or isotopic corridors' contain ideological suppositions, including some which carry negative values. Berger and Luckmann (1967) used this frame of reference to describe a reification process, by which labels applied to disabled persons cause these persons to be treated not as individuals but as objects. Erving Goffman (1963) has demonstrated the loss of personal identity attendant on this objectification, resulting in 'rituals of degradation' that led people to 'institutional careers.' Authors such as Duarte (1986) have studied from an ethnographic perspective the construction of social identities by analyzing the mental discourse of urban workers being assisted in the Brazilian public welfare system. Working from a social psychological perspective, others, like Gergen (1990), survey the 'consequences of mental language' and 'its proliferating effects in the culture at large.'

Using a social constructionist perspective in our work we have encouraged persons labeled as 'developmentally disabled' to reconstruct their personal narratives, socially re-examining the misconception and/or myth-conceptions that have caused their segregation. We have given special emphasis to Berger and Luckmann's (1967) view that 'each social role carries with it a socially defined appendage of knowledge.' When we consider the handicapped role as an 'appendage of knowledge,' we find that reconstructed narratives allow 'developmentally disabled' persons to expose myths about disability which still affect them. We see that through the self-narrative process individuals select 'self-relevant events' which may pinpoint the origins in their personal experience of the socially constructed myths. Further, since self-narratives are 'social constructions undergoing continuous alteration' (Gergen and Gergen, 1988), it is anticipated that in the process of their telling they will furnish opportunities for a healthy reconstruction of identities. We listen to the words in which persons labeled as 'developmentally disabled' socially reconstruct their past experiences. Along with them we come to see how certain internalized 'myth-conceptions' have caused their social exclusion. And with them, also, we may experience radical re-interpretations of these limiting self-concepts. Everyone grows in their ability to define themselves as an individual human being instead of with the abstraction 'disabled.' Observation of this process gives powerful new insights and tools to people who are and are not disabled.

Act II – Camera Rollin' . . . the Unfolding Narrative

Keep your voice down lady! Can't you see I'm busy?

The Story of Walter A. Mess: It's Up to You!

While much has been done to provide a variety of techniques to assist persons with disabilities in the rehabilitation and mental health fields, the use of a self-narrative video technique within a community setting is an innovative and effective therapeutic device to use with these persons. In the present case two groups of 'handicapped' individuals worked together for eleven months to produce and perform a puppet play. The group, divided in two sub-groups (one responsible for writing the script and the other for assembling the scenery), met once a week for a period of approximately two hours. Most of the situations outlined in the script resulted from a previous group brainstorm, which later on were organized into a final story-line. One of the individuals receiving services at the institutional placement came up with the 'original' theme of a 'young disabled person coping with different messy situations within a community based program.' The script title, *The Story of Walter A. Mess*, was a pun on 'What a mess!,' the expression commonly used within the culture. More generally, the main character struggles between the advice of his 'good angel' and the 'bad,' impulsive influences of a 'fallen angel.' The decision to videotape the play came as a result of two different factors. First, the group feared live performance because they could 'mess up,' and thought that an edited video would spare them any shame and give them the satisfaction of seeing themselves as they believed they could be. In our opinion the video also represents the possibility of taking away the pressure that 'disabled' persons experience when they are socially exposed. Secondly, our belief that the video strategy was appropriate and complementary to the art-therapy technique applied in our work. Let us examine some excerpts of the puppet play, as written and performed by the participants.

> *Good Angel*: Get up, Walt. It's time to go to work.
> *Walt*: Oh, I don't feel like going to work today. I think I'm sick. I'm much too sick to go to work.
> *Good Angel*: Walt, if you don't feel well enough to go to work, you should call your boss. That's the responsible thing to do.
> *Bad Angel*: Oh, Walt . . . it feels so good to be under the warm covers. You don't have to go to work. You don't even have to call your boss. He'll understand, Walt. Besides, he can read your mind.

The script was composed of three acts throughout which Walter 'messes up' with his room-mate, co-workers, girlfriends, and supervisors. In the first act, under the influence of a fallen angel, he decides not to go to work and gets fired. The excerpt above reflects some of the implicit rules that disabled persons have to confront when living in a supervised community placement, the 'necessities and seriousness' (jobs, punctuality, bosses) of their day-to-day situation.

Boss: Walt, pick up the phone!
Walt: Ah, hello, Who's calling?
Boss: Oh, cut me a break Mr Mess. You know very well who this is. Where the heck are you?
Walt: I'm sorry, but I'm . . . ah . . .
Bad Angel: Sick, sick. Say that you're sick!
Boss: Oh, come on Walt. I've heard this before. You know the rules. You can consider yourself out of a job.
Walt: But . . . but . . . Oh well, I guess I just got fired.

Life is not easy for Walt, who is pulled from side to side by his good and bad angels. Whereas the good angel advises him to straighten out his life, the bad angel urges him to 'let it all hang out' without worrying about the consequences. Processing our work, Liz (chief writer) observed that the angels represent influences which are, in fact, 'difficulties people face while making choices. It is very hard to make decisions.' Walter, in this context, is the personification of how hard life can be for individuals with developmental disabilities.

Good Angel: Walt, what are you going? You've been blasting your music all day and night. You just got fired this morning.
Bad Angel: Oh, Walt, this is so much fun. The night is young. You have nothing to worry about. Your neighbors appreciate your good taste in music. You don't have to worry about waking up early in the morning to go to work. You are a free man.
Good Angel: Walter, it is 2.00 a.m. This has gone on long enough. You really need to shape up. You need to go to bed and figure out what you're going to tell Dori.
Bad Angel: Call Dori? What a wonderful idea! This is a perfect time to call her. She's just sitting by the phone waiting for your call. Here is the phone, Walt. Dial, dial away!

The good and bad traits of Walter's guardian angels may also illustrate the hierarchies of inferiority and superiority that persons with disabilities have to face when exposed to the current mental health discourse. On the other hand, when these traits are viewed from an institutional perspective they may well represent the 'good' and 'bad' values retained in each individual's experience of independence. When living in supervised programs, persons with developmental disabilities have to balance their own needs and expectations of society. These expectations are represented here by the structure, tasks, and rules which comprise the normative culture of their residence program. Expressing themselves through the alter egos of the good and bad angels allowed the participants freely to explore decision-making options and action principles without fear of consequences or need for conforming to societal expectations. In this way, they took steps toward re-owning the enabling and disabling parts of themselves. They come to see 'good' (adaptive) parts and 'bad' (maladaptive) parts not as the essence of their identity, but as choices that they make and remake as they grow and learn. In other words, participants began to experience this dialectical dynamic as an unavoidable tension in their lives. As they develop a sense of comfort with balancing this tension, they can more objectively identify themselves.

> *Walt*: Dori, pick up the phone. This is Walt A. Mess. This is an extreme emergency. A matter of life and death. Pick up the phone, Dori, right now.
>
> *Dori*: Walter, have you looked at your clock lately? It's 2 o'clock in the morning! If you're not dying, I'm going to kill you myself.
>
> *Walt*: Dori! Ah, Dori, I just wanted to let you know that I got fired this morning.
>
> *Dori*: Walt, couldn't you have let me know about this in the morning? You had to wait until the middle of the night to call me? I had a hard day and I need to sleep. I'll discuss this with you in the morning. I'll be at your door at 9.00 a.m. Be there!

The character of Dori introduced here, like that of Mike in the last segment of the play, is of particular interest. It is noteworthy that persons whose own lives are so strictly supervised have chosen to include in their play two supervisors of their lives, in addition to a boss figure who appears later. By writing in these parts and then acting them out, the participants appear to identify with the roles of people who normally control and shape their everyday situations. In the play framework, the participants play these roles demonstrating an understanding of the other, and thereby boost their confidence that they can manage and take control of their lives effectively.

By suspending reality for a few moments, the puppet play helped the participants to act out previously unexpressed fantasies: the possibility of failing or 'being a mess' without the sharp criticism and the judgmental attitudes of society. To be behind the curtain enabled the puppeteers to dissociate themselves from the usual 'disabling' perception that confines their lives to a trapped and 'disabled condition.' At the same time they were able to experience through the puppets' characters the 'good' and 'bad' traits without worrying about the 'ideal expectation' of the everyday 'rulers.' In effect, the 'puppet meeting' – the name the participants gave to the development and production of the play – was a safe place to escape from the seriousness of profound feelings of inadequacy engendered by society's expectations. And, of equal importance, these persons were more than just participants: through their imagination and with their hands they made puppets come alive, ruling them in the way they wanted. They were 'poets' coexisting with their self-projected 'poetry.' As if they were gods creating 'man in his or her own image,' they created lives in which they had to confront the 'imperfections' and 'bad' behaviors of daily concern.

From the beginning it was clear what the group goals would be. We did not try to meet schedules of productivity, quality patterns, or the 'standards' we generally apply in the rehabilitation field. We were dealing with an expressive activity and decided that the product was not so important as the process itself. This proved to be therapeutic, because the step-by-step methodology helped the participants to discuss and to deal with the problems they were facing. A flexible production schedule allowed for such discussion. All phases of the project were planned through a group decision-making process. Everyone in their own capacity gave the best to accomplish the goals of the play's production. As a life-learning experience, what was supposed to be a minor detail of fixing a table leg on a piece of scenery could turn out to be extremely significant to some individuals. As an example of an important break-through during the work process, we recall a singular moment when the script writer (Liz) struggled with how to end the story-line, and decided to have a vote about different options. As a result, the group came up with three different choices of ending the play: (1) nothing will change in Walter's life (he will still be a mess); (2) in time he will straighten his life out; (3) a question mark. According to the group, 'it should be up' to the audience to decide which one of the choices listed would be the end of the story each time the play was enacted. Commenting later, Liz added her justification for these choices:

> We never know what's gonna happen in our lives, that's the reason why ending the play as a question mark is possible. On the other hand, it's up to everyone to decide if he or she wants to straighten his or her life out. If Walter decides to be a 'mess' it's up to him, and it is also possible to see things changing around ourselves. Then it is important to have the choice of straightening life out in time.

It is noteworthy that the voting process that took place marked a turning point in the group process. From this point on, the staff had less influence in writing the script and of building the scenery. The empowerment that the group experienced through the leadership of Liz when she showed them how to solve the great ending impasse not only excluded the staff but also demonstrated a democratic and 'risky' decision 'to be in the world on their own.' We think that their majority decision was a way of exercising a compromise that can be compared to therapeutic 'consensus points' that some groups reach in the process of identifying themselves as a collective made up of individuals.

By applying non-directive methods (such as questions related to the 'good' and 'bad' angels' lines), the staff helped the script crew to think about how the different story situations would evolve. This was an aspect extremely important in structuring Walt's performance in the play, particularly in the script-writing task, it was also helpful to bring some of the imaginative situations to a 'real'-life experienced scenario. To do this, the staff asked individuals how to solve a problem similar to that of the main characters. The combination of reality testing and imagination proved effective. In the context of developing the puppet show, these highly supervised and assisted individuals were able to use their self-narratives as the basis for independent decision-making on the part of the character they were creating. It was also a means of taking control. By creating and providing entertainment to others they were also changing their everyday experience of being provided for; we may say that they deconstructed an expected role ('people receiving services') in the course of this project, and reconstructed themselves as more capable and more proactive than they had previously been. We considered this shift a symbolic turning point in our work, and suggest that it represents a new set of possibilities for relationships between disabled persons and the people who support them.

The video production also enabled the group to examine the empowering constructions the disabled share more generally in society. It proved to be an educational device which allowed the group members to look at and listen to themselves and finally to confront and challenge the myth-conceptions. We assume that, by mixing portions of the video with discussions about the issues, disabled persons can identify their own coping mechanism and take pride in the evidence of their many abilities. Since some of these discussions were also videotaped, they may form the basis of a video which can be shown to 'non-disabled' people. We believe that such a video will serve to correct erroneous beliefs currently held by the public. We are especially hopeful that the narratives of disabled persons will promote an awareness of how the disabling language rampant in our prevailing discourse forces these people to the margins of society and effectively prevents them from realizing their own potential for independence and dignity. We especially hope that such awareness will alter the way we and our professional colleagues formulate our own therapeutic narratives, deconstructing the disabling constructions now generated in the language of our practices and reconstructing a new, more empowering and respectful discourse toward those who differ from the social norms.

Act III – Action . . . the Play Goes On

After the puppet play had been completed we interviewed Liz, and asked her if the play was really her own work. Liz said, 'Yes. These whole programs are ours. You guys are here just to support ourselves, but it is up to us to decide what we wanna do with our lives.' Now, we practitioners should ask ourselves: Does the play really come to an end? What are, in fact, Walter's choices? Is life just like a game set up with 'rules' for people like Walter? The 'self-narrative' journey does not end here; rather, it begins on a new road. The participants took a first and very important step. *The Story of Walter A. Mess* captured a slice of the lives of persons labeled 'developmentally disabled.' In their own words, 'it's up to them' to decide if they will separate themselves from the labels ('mess,' 'disabled,' 'handicapped,' 'retarded,' and so on) that have kept them distant from a real and effective participation in society.

In contrast to individual insight or catharsis-oriented therapies, we view the puppet event (including development and performance) as a process of mutual collaboration. From our perspective, Walter's three choices embody the struggle all the participants confronted in one way or another in their experience of 'being' and 'not-being' disabled. They know that the decision must be their very own and not one imposed by well-meaning outsiders. They have inherited socially constructed labels of disability; now they need to deconstruct these labels and seek to reconstruct new identities based on their own experience. We think of this process as a form of *rite de passage* that permits participants to detach from the disabling constructs they have been exposed to, and to confront more directly what they are able and not able to do in their lives. Until these constructs are clearly exposed and played out, they confuse and handicap. Once they are externalized in some form, they can be examined and re-interpreted.

Other audiences, when they see these videos, will find themselves dialectically invited to deconstruct their 'messy' reality and enter into a more daring process of reconstruction by choosing an ending. The 'question mark' listed as the third of Walter's choices itself implies a variety of open possibilities, any of which may emerge as the audience reacts to the play. Through the playing process new constructions arise. The process, from the beginning of the development of the play through the audience response to the final choices, is a dialectical one. The early narratives of self, which form the basis of the script, generate a new creature, the script, and are in turn changed by this creature. As the story is woven, it in turn weaves new stories. People may question the mental ability of persons with 'retardation' to deconstruct and reconstruct disabling constructs. The play process and the narratives of self become interlaced in such a fashion that new understanding arises. In other words, we consider the playing process as important as the content itself.

As practitioners interested in techniques for social change, we are now considering how to use this constructionist approach with other target groups; for example, families of the 'disabled.' Such techniques might offer them an opportunity of examining familial constructions, directly or indirectly related to their relationship with their offspring. Soon this method will be offered to families whose relatives are under assistance at the Pedro II Psychiatric Center in Rio de Janeiro. Staff persons can also be exposed to this self-narrative strategy as a way of assessing the polarities of 'being care-takers' as opposed to what a person with disability denominates 'support person.' Staff narrations may be particularly absorbing for those interested in institutional analysis. Groups of disabled persons can explore themes such as 'what it is like to be disabled in a non-disabled society.' This constructionist method can encourage disabled individuals to approach prejudicial attitudes they face in a highly competitive, technological society.

From an inter-institutional perspective, we want to see the use of this procedure in different kinds of community placements in order to compare self-narratives and to examine the effects of different social environments. It would be valuable, for example, to compare narratives of community placements with those of institutional settings. On an individual basis this work is a concrete tool to stimulate stigmatized persons to shatter those social myth conceptions which have been responsible for their marginalization. On a cultural perspective, this model will be applied within the Brazilian mental health system as a way of gathering a variety of narratives which will constitute data for cross-cultural studies.

We hope this chapter may positively influence other practitioners' views – and we include here our Brazilian colleagues. We think it is time to 'rewrite' some of the current practices in our relationships with the persons we call our 'patients.' It is also time to establish a *therapeia*, in Friedman's (1989) sense as a 'comprehension that what is essential is always larger than the individual, beyond his attention, will, even imagination. In this understanding we take nothing away from human achievements and failures, but simply see these as part of nature, of community.'

Notes

We acknowledge the contributions of John McGlaughlin, Vicki Schriver, Gail Germain, ATR, Virginia Briscoe, and Joan Powell. Without them this work would not have been possible.

We acknowledge our colleagues at Bancroft Institute, particularly George W. Niemann, John Tullis, Jeannette Newman, David Justice, Michael Grim, Dorian Grim, Carol Sarian, Deanna Offer, Catherine Meyers, Alan Thompson, Gloria Rowland, Pat Gerke, and Kathy Ross.

We acknowledge the early support we received from Carlos Augusto A. Jorge, Edmar de Souza Oliveira at the Pedro II Psychiatric Center, Rio de Janeiro, Brazil, Candido F. Espinheira Filho at the Hospital Philippe Pinel, Yon C. Silva at CRP Rio de Janeiro, Luiz Fernando Duarte at UFRJ, Luzilene Veras at TVE, Marcelo Cavalcanti at TVE, Rosa M.B. Fisher at TVE, Grupo Fantocheando, Angelica Ducasble at Nosso Mundo, Moacira V. Silva at CRAPSI, Ritamaria de Aguiar, Jose S.S. Filho, Carlos Eduardo C. Cunha, Virginia Schall at FIOCRUZ, Aurea Rocha at FIOCRUZ, Sergio Lizardo, Ivan A.S. Filho, Roberto Fukushi, J.A. Tauil, M. Fatima Afonso at Creche Vagalume, Ruth L. Parames. We thank João Coentro (*in memoriam*).

We acknowledge the emotional support received both from Mariah F. Gladis and Dori H. Middlemann, as well as from our colleague trainees at the Pennsylvania Gestalt Center; Ronald E. Hays, ATR and the Creative Arts in Therapy Program, Hahnemann University, Philadelphia, for helping us to find new dimensions in Art Therapy; Ralph Rosnow for introducing us to the work of Kenneth and Mary Gergen.

We dedicate this chapter to our children, to puppeteers throughout the world (thank you, Cheiroso and Jim Henson), and all marginalized persons throughout the world in honor of their struggles with the injustices of our societies, to the patients, families and staff of the Childhood Neuropsychiatric Hospital, Rio de Janeiro, and finally to the Brazilian people as a means of honoring their movements toward social equity.

References

Axline, V.M. (1947) *Play Therapy*. New York: Houghton Mifflin.

Berger, P.L. and Luckmann, T. (1967) *The Social Construction of Reality: a Treatise in the Sociology of Knowledge*. New York: Anchor Books.

Bernier, M.G. (1983) 'Puppetry as an art therapy technique with emotionally disturbed children'. MA thesis, Hahnemann University, Philadelphia.

Blikstein, I. (1983) *Kasper Hauser ou a fabricação da realidade*. São Paulo: Cultrix.

Borba Filho, H. (1987) *Fisionomia e espírito do Mamulengo*. Rio de Janeiro: MinC, INACEN.

Duarte, L.F.D. (1986) *Da Vida Nervosa nas Classes Trabalhadoras Urbanas*. Rio de Janeiro: Zahar & CNPQ.

Festinger, L. (1954) 'A theory of social comparison processes', *Human Relations*, 7: 117–40.

Friedman, J. (1989) 'Therapeia, play and the therapeutic household', in *Thresholds between Philosophy and Psychoanalysis*. London: Free Association Books.

Gergen, K.J. (1985) 'The social constructionist movement in modern psychology', *American Psychologist*, 40 (3): 266–75.

Gergen, K.J. (1988) 'If persons are texts', in S.B. Messer, L.A. Sass and R.L. Woolfolk (eds), *Hermeneutics and Psychological Theory*. New Brunswick, NJ: Rutgers University Press.

Gergen, K.J. (1990) 'Therapeutic professions and the diffusion of deficit', *Journal of Mind and Behavior*, 11: 353–68.

Gergen, K.J. and Gergen, M.M. (1988) 'Narrative and the self as relationship', *Advances in Experimental Social Psychology*, 21: 17–56.

Goffman, E. (1963) *Stigma: Notes on the Management of Spoiled Identity*. Englewood Cliffs, NJ: Prentice-Hall.

Huizinga, J. (1945) 'Nature and significance of play as a cultural phenomenon', in *Relevants*. New York: Free Press.

Jenkins, R. and Beck, E. (1942) 'Finger puppets and mask making as media for work with children', *American Journal of Orthopsychiatry*, 12 (2): 294–300.

Kors, P. (1963) 'The use of puppetry in psychotherapy', *American Journal of Psychotherapy*, 17: 54–63.

Kors, P. (1964) 'Unstructured puppet shows as group procedure in therapy with children', *Psychiatric Quarterly Supplement*, 38 (1): 56–75.

Lyle, J. and Holly, S.P. (1941) 'The therapeutic value of puppets', *Bulletin of the Menniger Clinic*, 5: 223–6.

Pepitone, A. (1949) 'Motivation effects in social perception', *Human Relations*, 3: 57–76.

Robbins, A. and Sibley, L. (1976) *Creative Art Therapy*. New York: Brunner/ Mazel.

Stern, D.N. (1985) *The Interpersonal World of the Infant*. New York: Basic Books.

Szasz, T. (1961) *The Myth of Mental Illness: Foundations of a Theory of Personal Conduct*. New York: Dell.

Szasz, T. (1963) *Law, Liberty and Psychiatry: an Inquiry into the Social Uses of Mental Health Practices*. New York: Macmillan.

Woltman, A.G. (1951) 'The use of puppetry as a projective method in therapy', in G. Anderson and L. Anderson (eds), *An Introduction to Projective Techniques*. Englewood Cliffs, NJ: Prentice-Hall.

Woltman, A.G. (1972) 'Puppetry as a tool in child psychotherapy', *International Journal of Child Psychotherapy*, 1 (1), 84–96.

Woodyard, J. (1980) *An Advisor's Guidebook for Self-Advocacy*. Kansas: Self-Advocacy Project, University of Kansas.

PART IV

REFLECTION AND RECONSTRUCTION

11

Beyond Narrative in the Negotiation of Therapeutic Meaning

Kenneth J. Gergen and John Kaye

I have reached no conclusions, have erected no boundaries
shutting out and shutting in, separating inside
    from outside: I have
    drawn no lines:
    as
manifold events of sand
change the dunes' shape that will not be the same shape
tomorrow,

so I am willing to go along, to accept
the becoming
thought, to stake off no beginnings or ends, establish
    no walls

A.R. Ammons, *Carson's Inlet*

When people seek psychotherapy they have a story to tell. It is
frequently the troubled, bewildered, hurt, or angry story of a life or
relationship now spoiled. For many it is a story of calamitous events
conspiring against their sense of well-being, self-satisfaction, or
sense of efficacy. For others the story may concern unseen and
mysterious forces insinuating themselves into life's organized
sequences, disrupting and destroying. And for still others it is as if,
under the illusion of knowing how the world is or ought to be, they
have somehow bumped up against trouble for which their favored
account has not prepared them. They have discovered an awful
reality that now bleeds all past understandings of survival value.
Whatever its form, the therapist confronts a narrative – often
persuasive and gripping; it is a narrative that may be terminated
within a brief period or it may be extended over weeks or months.
However, at some juncture the therapist must inevitably respond to

this account, and whatever follows within the therapeutic procedure will draw its significance in response to this account.

What options are available to the therapist as recipient of a narrated reality? At least one option is pervasive within the culture, and sometimes used as well within counseling settings, social work interviews, and short-term therapies. It may be viewed as the *advisory option*. For the advisor, the client's story remains relatively inviolate. Its terms of description and forms of explanation remain unchallenged in any significant way. Rather, for the advisor the major attempt is to locate forms of effective action 'under the circumstances' as narrated. Thus, for example, if the individual speaks of being depressed because of failure, means are sought for re-establishing efficacy. If the client is rendered ineffectual because of grief, then a program of action may be suggested for overcoming the problem. In effect, the client's life story is accepted as fundamentally accurate for him or her, and the problem is to locate ameliorative forms of action within the story's terms.

There is much to be said on behalf of the advisory option. Within the realm of the relatively ordinary, it is most obviously 'reasonable' and most probably effective. Yet, for the more seriously chronic or deeply disturbed client, the advisory option harbors serious limitations. At the outset, there is little attempt to confront deeper origins of the problem or the complex ways it is sustained. The major concern is in locating a new course of action. Whatever the chain of antecedents, they simply remain the same – continuing to operate as threats to the future. Further, little attempt is typically made to probe the contours of the story, to determine its relative utility or viability. Could the client be mistaken, or defining things in a less than optimal way? Such questions often remain unexplored. In accepting 'the story as told,' the problem definition also remains fixed. As a result the range of possible options for action remains circumscribed. If the problem is said to be failure, for example, the relevant options are geared around means for re-establishing success. Other possibilities are thrust to the margins of plausibility. And finally, in the chronic or severe case, the location of action alternatives too often seems a superficial palliative. For one who has been depressed, addictive, or self-destructive for a period of years, for example, simple advice for living may seem little more than whispering in the wind.

In the present chapter we wish to explore two more substantial alternatives to the advisory option. The first is represented by most traditional forms of psychotherapy and psychoanalytic practice. In its reliance on various neo-Enlightenment assumptions dominant in the sciences of the present century, this orientation toward narrative may be viewed as *modernist*. In contrast, much thinking within the *postmodern* arena forms a powerful challenge to the modernist conception of the narrative, and in doing so opens new modes of therapeutic procedure. This latter orientation is well represented by the various constructionist contributions to the present volume. However, as the present chapter unfolds, we wish to develop dimensions of the constructionist orientation not currently emphasized in the existing analyses. In effect, we wish to press beyond narrative meaning in the making of lives.

Therapeutic Narratives in Modernist Context

Much has been written about modernism in the sciences, literature, and the arts, and this is scarcely the context for thorough review.[1] However, it is useful to consider briefly a set of assumptions that have guided activities in the sciences and the allied professions of mental health. For it is this array of assumptions that have largely informed the therapeutic treatment of client narratives. The modernist era in the sciences has been one committed, first of all, to the empirical *elucidation of essences*. Whether it be the character of the atom, the gene, or the synapse in the natural sciences, or processes of perception, economic decision making, or organizational development in the social sciences, the major attempt has been to establish bodies of systematic and objective knowledge. Such knowledge should, it is reasoned, enable the society to make increasingly accurate predictions about cause and effect relations, and thus, with appropriate technologies in place, to gain mastery over the future. For the modernist, the good society can be erected on the foundations of empirical knowledge.

Empirical knowledge is communicated, of course, through scientific languages. These languages, if they have been well grounded in observation, are said to reflect or to map the world in so far as we can know it. Narratives are essentially structures of language, and in so far as narratives are generated within the scientific milieu they can, on the modernist account, function as conveyors of objective knowledge. Thus, the narratives of the novelist are labeled as 'fiction,' and are considered of little consequence for serious scientific purposes. People's narratives of their lives, what has happened to them and why, are not necessarily fictions. But, as the behavioral scientist proclaims, they are notoriously inaccurate and unreliable. Thus, they are considered of limited value in understanding the individual's life, and far less preferable than the empirically based accounts of the trained scientist. It is thus that the narrative accounts of the scientist are accorded the highest credibility, and are set apart from the markets of entertainment and everyday interaction as 'scientific theories.' From the 'Big Bang' theory of the Earth's origins to evolutionary theory within the natural sciences, and from Piagetian theory of rational development to theories of economic recession and cultural transmission in the social sciences, scientific narratives are structured stories of how things come to be as they are.[2]

The mental health profession today is largely an outgrowth of the modernist context and shares deeply in its assumptions. Thus from Freud to contemporary cognitive therapists, the general belief is that the professional therapist functions (or ideally should function) as a scientist. By virtue of such activities as scientific training, research experience, knowledge of the scientific literature, and countless hours of systematic observation and thought within the therapeutic situation, the professional is armed with knowledge. To be sure, contemporary knowledge is incomplete, and more research is ever required. But the knowledge of the contemporary professional is far superior to that of the turn-of-the-century therapist, so it is said, and the future can only bring further improvements. Thus, with few exceptions, therapeutic theories (whether behavioral, systemic, psychodynamic, or experiential/humanist) contain explicit assumptions regarding (1) the underlying cause or basis of pathology, (2) the location of this cause within clients or their relationships, (3) the means by which such problems can be diagnosed, and (4) the means by which the pathology may be eliminated. In effect, the trained professional enters the therapeutic arena with a well-developed narrative for which there is abundant support within the community of scientific peers.

It is this background that establishes the therapist's posture toward the client's narrative. For the client's narrative is, after all, made of the flimsy stuff of daily stories – replete with whimsy, metaphor, wishful thinking, and distorted memories. The scientific narrative, by contrast, has the seal of professional approval. From this vantage point we see that the therapeutic process must inevitably result in the slow but inevitable replacement of the client's story with the therapist's. The client's story does not remain a free-standing reflection of truth, but rather, as questions are asked and answered, descriptions and explanations are reframed, and affirmation and doubt are disseminated by the therapist, the client's narrative is either destroyed or incorporated – but in any case replaced – by the professional account. The client's account is transformed by the psychoanalyst into a tale of family romance, by the Rogerian into a struggle against conditional regard, and so on.

It is this process of replacing the client's story with the professional that is so deftly described in Donald Spence's *Narrative Truth and Historical Truth*. As Spence surmises, the therapist

> is constantly making decisions about the form and status of the patient's material. Specific listening conventions . . . help to guide these decisions. If, for example, the analyst assumes that contiguity indicates causality, then he will hear a sequence of disconnected statements as a causal chain; at some later time, he might make an interpretation that would make this assumption explicit. If he assumes that transference predominates and that the patient is always talking, in more or less disguised fashion, about the analyst, then he will 'hear' the material in that way and make some kind of ongoing evaluation of the state of the transference. (1982: 129)

Such replacement procedures do have certain therapeutic advantages. For one, as clients gain 'real insight' into their problems, the problematic narrative is thereby removed. The client is thus furnished an alternative reality that holds promise for future well-being. In effect, the failure story with which the client entered therapy can be swapped for a success story. And, similar to the advisory option outlined earlier, the new story is likely to suggest alternative lines of action – forming or dissolving relationships, operating under a daily regimen, submitting to therapeutic procedures, and so on. There are new, and more hopeful, things to do. And too, by providing the client a scientific formulation, the therapist has played the appointed role in a long-standing cultural ritual in which the ignorant, the failing, and the weak seek counsel from the wise, superior, and strong. It is indeed a comforting ritual to all who will submit.

Yet, in spite of these advantages, there is substantial reason for concern. Major shortcomings have been located in the modernist orientation to therapy. The scientific community has long been skeptical of the knowledge claims pervasive in the mental health professions. As it is held, mental health practitioners have little justification for their claims to knowledge of pathology and cure. Critics have also inveighed against traditional forms of therapy for their excessive concern with the individual. As it is argued, such theories are blind to the broad cultural conditions in which psychological difficulties may be significantly connected (see, for example, Kovel, 1980). Feminist critics have grown increasingly vocal in such attacks, noting that many 'female disorders' are inappropriately traced to the female mind and are the direct result of the oppressive conditions of the female in society (see, for example, Hare-Mustin and Marecek, 1988). Others have been deeply unsettled by the pathologizing tendencies of the profession. From the modernist standpoint, deviant or aberrant behavior is traced to mental pathologies, and it is the task of the mental health profession – like the medical profession – to identify and treat such disorders. Yet, in accepting such assumptions the profession acts so as to objectify mental illness – even when there are many alternative means of interpreting or understanding the same phenomena (see, for example, Gergen, 1991).

Over and above these problems, there are additional short-comings in the modernist orientation to client narrative. There is, for one, a substantial imperious thrust to the modernist approach. Not only is the therapist's narrative never placed under threat, but the therapeutic procedure virtually ensures that it will be vindicated. In Spence's terms, 'the search space [within therapeutic interaction] can be infinitely expanded until the [therapist's] answer is discovered and . . . there is no possibility of finding a negative solution, of deciding that the [therapist's] search has failed' (1982: 108). Thus, regardless of the complexity, sophistication, or value of the client's account, it is eventually replaced by a narrative created before the client's entry into therapy and the contours over which he or she has no control.

It is not simply that therapists from a given school will ensure that their clients come away bearing beliefs in their particular account. By implication (and practice) the ultimate aim of most schools of therapy is hegemonic. All other schools of thought, and their associated narratives, should succumb. Psychoanalysts wish to eradicate behavior modification; cognitive-behavioral therapists see systems therapy as misguided, and so on. Yet, the most immediate and potentially injurious consequences are reserved for the client. For in the end, the structure of the procedure furnishes the client a lesson in inferiority. The client is indirectly informed that he or she is ignorant, insensitive, woolly-headed, or emotionally incapable of comprehending reality. In contrast, the therapist is positioned as all-knowing and wise – a model to which the client might aspire. The situation is all the more lamentable owing to the fact that in occupying the superior role, the therapist fails to reveal any weaknesses. Nowhere are the wobbly foundations of the therapist's account made known; nowhere do the therapist's personal doubts, foibles, and failings come to light. And the client is thus confronted with a vision of human possibility that is as unattainable as the heroism of cinematic mythology.

The modernist orientation suffers as well from the fixedness of the narrative formulations. As we have seen, modernist approaches to therapy begin with an a priori narrative, justified by claims to a scientific base. Because it is sanctioned as scientific, this narrative is relatively closed to alteration. Minor modifications may be entertained, but the system itself bears the weight of established doctrine. In the same way biologists seldom question the basic stipulations of Darwinian theory, and psychoanalysts who question the foundations of psychoanalytic theory are placed in professional peril. Under these conditions the client confronts a relatively closed system of understanding. It is not only that the client's own reality will eventually give way to the therapist's, but all other interpretations will also be excluded. To the extent that the therapist's narrative becomes the client's reality, and his or her actions are guided accordingly, life options for the client are severely truncated. Of all possible modes of acting in the world, one is set on a course emphasizing, for example, ego autonomy, self-actualization, rational appraisal, or emotional expressiveness, depending on the brand of therapy inadvertently selected. Or to put it otherwise, each form of modernist therapy carries with it an image of the 'fully functioning' or 'good' individual; like a fashion plate, this image serves as the guiding model for the therapeutic outcome.

This constriction of life possibilities is all the more problematic because it is decontextualized. That is, the therapist's narrative is an abstract formalization – cut away from particular cultural and historical circumstances. None of the modernist narratives deals with the specific conditions of living in ghetto poverty, with a brother who has AIDS, with a child who has Down's syndrome, with a boss who is sexually abusive, and so on. In contrast to the complex details that crowd the corners of daily life – which are indeed life itself – modernist narratives are virtually content-free. As a result, these narratives are precariously insinuated into the life circumstances of the individual. They are, in this sense, clumsy and insensitive, failing to register the particularities of the client's living conditions. To emphasize self-fulfillment to a woman living in a household with three small children and a mother-in-law with Alzheimer's is not likely to be beneficial. To press a Park Avenue attorney for increased emotional expressiveness in his daily life is of doubtful assistance.

Therapeutic Realities in Postmodern Context

The literature on postmodernist culture is rapidly accumulating, and again this is an inappropriate juncture for a full review.[3] However, it is useful to emphasize a single contrast with modernism, one of central significance to the concept of knowledge, science, and therapy. Within the postmodernist wings of the academy, major attention is now devoted to the process of representation, or the means by which 'reality' is set forth in writing, the arts, television, and so on. As it is generally agreed, criteria of accuracy or objectivity are of questionable relevance to judging the relationship between representation and its object. There is no means of arraying all the events in the 'real world' on one side and all the syllables of the language on the other, and linking them in one-to-one fashion, such that each syllable would reflect an isolated atom of reality. Rather, in the case of writing, each style or genre of literature operates according to local rules or conventions, and these conventions will largely determine the way we understand the putative objects of representation. Scientific writing, then, furnishes a no more *accurate* picture of reality than fiction. The former accounts may be embedded in scientific activity in a way that the latter are not. However, both kinds of accounts are guided by cultural conventions, historically situated, which largely determine the character of the reality they seek to depict.

This reconsideration of representation does not thus reduce the importance of scientific narrative. Rather, in two major ways it shifts the site of its significance. First, rather than such narratives retaining the status of 'truth telling' – thus claiming to be predictive aids to survival – they gain their importance as constitutive frames. That is, such narratives constitute reality as one kind of thing rather than another, as good or evil in certain respects as opposed to others. And in doing so, they furnish the rational grounds or justifications for certain lines of conduct as opposed to others. Thus, if we believe with socio-biologists that human action is primarily governed by genetically based urges, the way we carry out daily life is likely to be different than if we believe, with learning psychologists, that people's actions are infinitely malleable. Each account, once embraced, invites certain actions and discourages others. Scientific narratives gain their chief significance, then, in terms of the forms of life which they invite, rationalize, or justify. They are not so much reflections of life already lived as they are the progenitors of the future.

The postmodern shift from the object of knowledge to its representation also relocates the grounds for justification. On the modernist account, scientific descriptions are the product of single individuals – scientists whose patient skills of observation yield insights for all. Individual scientists, then, are more or less authoritative, more or less knowledgeable about the world as it is. From the postmodern perspective, the factual warrant is removed from the scientist's narrative. The scientist may 'know how' to do certain things (what we might call, for example, 'atomic fusion'), but that scientist does not 'know that' what is being done *is* 'atomic fusion.' What, then, gives the scientist the right to speak with authority? In the same way that the conventions of writing permit things to be said in one way and not others, so the social conventions of the scientific community bestow on its members the right to be authoritative. That is, the scientist only speaks with justifiable assuredness within the community of those who honor those particular ways of speaking. Or to put it otherwise, scientific representations are products of the community of scientists – negotiating, competing, conspiring, and so on. Within a postmodern frame what we take to be knowledge is a social product.

This context of thought furnishes major challenges to the modernist conception of scientific narrative, and most cogently, to the modernist orientation to therapy. At the outset it removes the factual justification of the modernist narratives of pathology and cure, transforming these accounts into forms of cultural mythology. It undermines the unquestioned status of the therapist as scientific authority, with privileged knowledge of cause and cure. The therapist's narratives thus take their place alongside the myriad other possibilities available in the culture, not transcendentally better but perhaps different. And significant questions must be raised with the traditional practice of replacing the client's stories with the fixed and narrow alternatives of the modernist therapist. There is no justification outside the narrow community of like-minded therapists for battering the client's complex and richly detailed life into a single, pre-formulated narrative, a narrative that may be of little relevance or promise for the client's subsequent life conditions. And finally, there is no broad justification for the traditional status hierarchy that both demeans and frustrates the client. The therapist and client form a relationship to which both bring resources and in terms of which the contours of the future may be carved.

It is this postmodern context of thought which informs most of the contributions to the present volume. There is within these chapters a broad abandonment of the traditional narratives of therapy – at least as furnishing reliable and scientifically based accounts of pathology and cure. There is a pervasive abnegation of the role of the therapist as superior knower, standing above the client as an unattainable model of the good life. There is, instead, a strong commitment to viewing the therapeutic encounter as a milieu for the creative generation of meaning. The client's voice is not merely an auxiliary device for the vindication of the therapist's pre-determined narrative, but serves in these contexts as an essential constituent of a jointly constructed reality. In virtually all these chapters the emphasis, then, is on the collaborative relationship between client and therapist as they strive to develop forms of narrative that may usefully enable the client to move beyond the current or continuing crisis.

We strongly endorse these explorations into constructionist forms of practice. We stand as strong admirers and supporters of these efforts to realize the potential of postmodern thought. At the same time, however, the broad implications of the present endeavors are far from clear. We stand at a point of embarcation: a radical departure from traditional assumptions about knowledge, persons, and the nature of 'the real' is at hand. Substantial deliberation and experimentation will be required before the results can be assayed, and even then we shall have but additional fuel for a conversation that should ideally have no end. It is in this spirit that we wish in the remainder of this chapter to bring a sharper focus on the therapeutic narrative in postmodern context. For it is our surmise that current discussions of the construction of meaning in therapy still retain significant vestiges of the modernist world-view. And, if the potentials of postmodernism are to be fully realized, we must ultimately press beyond narrative construction. The ultimate challenge, as we see it, is not so much that of transforming meaning, but transcending it. To appreciate this possibility, it is first necessary to explore the pragmatic dimension of narrative meaning.

Narration and Pragmatic Utility

Narrative accounts in modernist frame were to serve as representations of reality – true or false in their capacity to match events as they occurred. If the accounts were accurate they also served as blueprints to adaptive action. Thus, in the therapeutic case, if the narrative reflected a recurring pattern of maladaptive action, one could begin to explore alternative ways of behaving. Or, if it captured the formative processes for a given pathology, palliatives could be prescribed. Within its knowledge frame, the therapist's narrative prescribed a better way of living. For most therapists entering the post-empiricist era, the modernist concern with accuracy is no longer compelling. Narrative truth is to be distinguished from historical truth, and when closely examined, even the latter is found to be an impostor. What then is the function of narrative reconstruction? Most existing accounts point to the potential of such reconstructions to re-orient the individual, to open new courses of action that are more fulfilling and more adequately suited to the individual's experiences, capacities and proclivities. Thus, the client may alter or dispose of earlier narratives, not because they are inaccurate, but because they are dysfunctional in his or her particular circumstances.

Yet, the question must be raised, in precisely what way(s) is the narrative to be 'useful.' How does a language of self-understanding guide, direct, or inform lines of action? Two answers to this question pervade post-empiricist camps at present, and both are problematic. On the one side is the metaphor of *language as a lens*. On this account, a narrative construction is a vehicle through which the world is seen. It is through the lens of narrative that the individual identifies objects, persons, actions, and so on. As it is argued, it is on the basis of the world as seen, and not on the world as it is, that the individual determines a course of action. Yet, to take this position is to view the individual as isolated and solipsistic – simply stewing in the juices of his or her own private constructions. The possibilities for survival are minimal, for there is no means to escape the encapsulation of the internal system of construals. Further, such an account buys a range of notorious epistemological problems. How, for example, does the individual develop the lens? From whence the first construction? For if there is no world outside that which is internally constructed, there would be no means of developing or fashioning the lens. It is simply self-vindicating.[4] And why, in the final analysis, should we believe that language is a lens, that the sounds and markings employed in human interchange are somehow transported into the mind to impose order on the perceptual world? The argument seems poorly taken.

The major alternative to this view holds the narrative construction to be an *internal model*, a form of story that can be interrogated by the individual as a guide to identity and action. Again, there is no brief for the truth of the model; it operates simply as an enduring structure that informs and directs action. Thus, for example, a person who features himself as a hero whose feats of bravery and intelligence should prevail against all odds, finds life unworkable. Through therapy he realizes that such a view not only places him in impossible circumstances but works against close feelings of intimacy and interdependence with his wife and children. A new story is worked out in which the individual comes to see himself as a champion not for himself, but for his family. His heroism will be gained through their feelings of happiness, and will thus depend as well on their assessments of circumstances and potentials. It is this transformed image that is to guide subsequent actions. While there is a certain wisdom to this position, it is again problematic. Stories of this variety are in themselves both idealized and abstract. As such they can seldom dictate behavior in complex, on-going interaction. What does the new story of self say, for example, about the best reaction to his wife's desires for him to spend fewer hours at work and more with the family, or how should he respond to a new job offer, challenging and profitable, but replete with risk? Stories as internal models are not only bare of specific information, but they remain static. The individual moves through numerous situations and relationships – a parent dies, a son is tempted by drugs, an attractive neighbor acts seductively, and so on. Yet, the narrative model remains inflexible – unbending and often irrelevant.

There is a third way of understanding narrative utility and, in our view, it is more conceptually and pragmatically adequate than the prevailing alternatives. The generative metaphor in this case is supplied in Wittgenstein's *Philosophical Investigations* (1953). As Wittgenstein compellingly argues, words gain their meaning not through their capacity to picture reality, but through their use in social interchange. We are engaged, then, in *games of language*, and it is by virtue of their use within these games that words acquire meaning. Thus, for example, what can be said about an emotion such as fear is not determined by 'the fact of fear,' but by the conventions of emotion talk in Western culture. I may say that fear is *strong* but not *sultry*, that it is *subsiding* but not *sedentary*. This is not because fear, as an object of observation, is just this way and not that. Rather, it is because of the limited ways of talking we have inherited from the past. Yet, language games for Wittgenstein are embedded within broader *forms of life*, or to extend the metaphor, *life games*. This is to say that the forms of interchange in which words are embedded, and which give them their value, are not limited to the linguistic realm alone. Such interchanges may include all our actions, along with various objects in our surroundings. Thus to count oneself as angry not only requires the use of certain words within the language games, but certain bodily actions (grinding or gritting the teeth, for example, rather than grinning) that constitute the forms of life in which the language game is embedded. To engage in anger, then, is to participate in a form of cultural dance; failing to take one's place in the dance is to fail at being angry.[5]

With this metaphor in place, let us return to the case of self-narratives. Stories about oneself – one's failures and successes, one's limits and potentials, and so on – are essentially arrangements of words (often conveyed with associated movements of the body). They are, in this sense, candidates for meaning within one or more games of language, one or more cultural dances. If they are to have utility, it is within the confines of a particular game or dance. Utility is to be derived from their success as moves within these arenas – in terms of their adequacy as reactions to previous moves or as instigators to what follows. Consider, for example, a story of failure – how one came to be lethargic and immobile. As we have seen, the story is neither true nor false in itself; it is simply one construction among many. However, as this story is inserted into various forms of relationship – into the games or dances of the culture – its effects are strikingly varied. If a friend has just related a story of great personal success, one's story of failure is likely to act as a repressive force, and alienate the friend who anticipated a congratulatory reaction. If, in contrast, the friend had just revealed a personal failure, to share one's own failings is likely to be reassuring and to solidify the friendship. Similarly, to relate one's story of lethargy and immobility to one's mother may elicit a warm and sympathetic reaction; to share it with a wife who worries each month over the bills may produce both frustration and anger.

To put it otherwise, a story is not simply a story. It is also a situated action in itself, a performance with illocutionary effects. It acts so as to create, sustain, or alter worlds of social relationship. In these terms, it is insufficient that the client and therapist negotiate a new form of self-understanding that seems realistic, aesthetic, and uplifting within the dyad. It is not their dance of meaning that is primarily at stake. Rather, the significant question is whether the new shape of meaning is serviceable within the social arena outside these confines. How, for example, does the story of oneself as 'hero of the family group' play for a wife who dislikes her dependent status, a boss who is a 'self-made woman,' or a rebellious son? What forms of action does the story invite in each of these situations; what kinds of dances are engendered, facilitated, or sustained? It is evaluation at this level that seems most crucial for the joint consideration of therapist and client.

Transcending Narrative

The focus on the pragmatics of narrative performance sets the stage for the critical argument of the present chapter. As we have seen, for many making the postmodern turn in therapy, the narrative continues to be viewed as either a form of internal lens, determining the way in which life is seen, or an internal model for the guidance of action. In light of the preceding discussion of pragmatics, these conceptions are found lacking in three important respects. First, each retains the *individualist* cast of modernism, in that the final resting place of the narrative construction is within the mind of the single individual. As we have reconsidered the utility of the narrative, we have moved outward – from the individual's mind to the relationships constituted by the narrative in action. Narratives exist in the telling, and tellings are constituents of relational forms – for good or ill. Secondly, the metaphors of the lens and the internal model both favor *singularity in narrative*; that is, both tend to presume the functionality of a single formulation of self-understanding. The individual possesses 'a lens' for comprehending the world, it is said, not a *repository* of lenses; and through therapy one comes to possess 'a new narrative truth,' it is often put, not a *multiplicity* of truths. From the pragmatic standpoint, the presumption of singularity operates against functional adequacy. Each narrative of the self may function well in certain circumstances, but lead to miserable outcomes in others. To have only a single means of making self intelligible, then, is to limit the range of relationships or situations in which one can function satisfactorily. Thus, for example, it may be very useful to 'do anger' effectively, and to formulate accounts to justify such activity. There are certain times and places in which anger is the most effective move in the dance. At the same time, to be over-skilled or over-prepared in this regard – such that anger is virtually the only means of moving relationships along – will vastly reduce one's relationships altogether. From the present perspective, narrative multiplicity is vastly to be preferred.

Finally, both the lens and the internal model conceptions favor belief in or *commitment to narrative*. That is, both suggest that the individual lives *within* the narrative as a system of understanding. One 'sees the world in this way,' as it is said, and the narrative is thus 'true for the individual.' Or the transformed story of self is 'the new reality;' it constitutes a 'new belief about self' to support and sustain the individual. Again, however, as we consider the social utility of narrative, belief and commitment become suspect. To be committed to a given story of self, to adopt it as 'now true for me,' is vastly to limit one's possibilities of relating. To believe that one *is successful* is thus as debilitating in its own way as believing that one *is a failure*. Both are only stories after all, and each may bear fruit within a particular range of contexts and relationships. To crawl inside one or the other and take root is to forgo the other, and thus to reduce the range of contexts and relationships in which one is adequate.

To frame the issue in another way, postmodern consciousness favors a thoroughgoing relativism in expressions of identity. On the metatheoretical level it invites a multiplicity of accounts of reality, while recognizing the historically and culturally situated contingency of each. There are only accounts of truth within differing conversations, and no conversation is privileged. If the therapist adopts such a view on the metatheoretical level, it would be an act of bad faith to abandon it on the level of practice. Thus, for the postmodern practitioner a multiplicity of self-accounts is invited, but a commitment to none. It encourages the client, on the one hand, to explore a variety of means of understanding the self, but discourages a commitment to any of these accounts as standing for the 'truth of self.' The narrative constructions thus remain fluid, open to the shifting tides of circumstance – to the forms of dance that provide fullest sustenance.

Can such a conclusion be tolerated? Is the individual thus reduced to a social con artist, adopting whatever posture of identity gains the highest pay-off? Certainly, the postmodern emphasis is on flexibility of self-identification, but this does not simultaneously imply that the individual is either duplicitous or scheming. To speak of duplicity is to presume that there is a 'true expression' of self that could otherwise be available. Such a view is quintessentially modern, and thus abandoned. One may interpret one's actions as duplicitous or sincere, but these ascriptions are, after all, simply components of different stories. Similarly, to presume that the individual possesses private motives, and a rational calculus of self-presentation is again to sustain the modernist view of the self-contained individual. From the postmodern vantage point, the relationship takes priority over the individual self. That is, selves are only realized as a byproduct of relatedness. It is not independent selves who come together to form a relationship, but particular forms of relationship that engender what we take to be the individual's identity. Thus, to shift in the form and content of self-narration from one relationship to another is neither deceitful nor self-serving. Rather, it is to honor the various modes of relationship in which one is enmeshed. It is to take seriously the multiple and varied forms of human connectedness that make up a life. Adequate and fulfilling actions are only so in the terms of criteria generated within the various forms of relationship themselves.

The questions persist. Does the postmodern constructionist abandon that cherished possession in Western culture, personal identity? The answer is 'yes' if what is meant by identity is the story told, the action taken, the part played. However, if one is willing to press beyond these *products* to the underlying *process* in which they are realized, it is still possible to retain a view of individual animation. James Carse (1986) provides a useful metaphor in his meditation on finite and infinite games. As he proposes, there are finite games, the purpose of which is to win, and these may be compared with the infinite game in which the purpose is to continue to play. The rules are different for each finite game; it is only by knowing the rules that one knows what the game is. However, in the infinite game the rules change in the course of play, when players agree that the play may be threatened by a finite outcome – a victory of some players and a defeat of others. In Carse's terms, 'Finite players play within boundaries; infinite players play with boundaries. . . . Finite players are serious; infinite players are playful.' In this vein, self-narration takes place within the confines of the finite game. Each portrayal of self operates within the conventions of a particular relationship. However, we may yet retain our place in the infinite game – beyond narrative. If there is identity at this level, it cannot be articulated, laid out for public view in a given description or explanation. It lies in the boundless and inarticulable capacity for relatedness itself.

Therapeutic Moves

In the light of the above, it should be clear that we reject the simple adoption of narrative reconstruction or replacement as a guiding metaphor for psychotherapy. We would argue, rather, for embedding the emphasis on narrative and narrative thinking in a broader concern with the generation of meaning via dialogue. This involves a reconception of the relativity of meaning, an acceptance of indeterminacy, the generative exploration of a multiplicity of meanings, and the understanding that there is no necessity either to adhere to an invariant story or to search for a definitive story. 'Reauthoring' or 'restorying' seems to us a first-order therapeutic approach, one which implies the replacement of a dysfunctional master narrative with a more functional one. At the same time this result carries the seeds of a prescriptive rigidity – one which might also serve to confirm an illusion that it is possible to develop a set of principles or codes which can be invariantly applied irrespective of context. It is this very rigidity which is arguably constitutive of the difficulties people experience in their lives and relationships. Just as psychotherapists may be restrained by a limiting code, so people who experience their lives as problematic seem trapped within a set of limiting precepts, behavioral codes, and constitutive conventions. Acting from these conventions, they are not only restrained from alternate punctuations but can become imprisoned in painful transactional patterns with those around them.

Heinz von Foerster has made the acute observation that we are blind until we see that we cannot see. If language provides the matrix for all human understanding, then psychotherapy may be aptly construed as 'linguistic activity in which conversation about a problem generates the development of new meanings' (Goolishian and Winderman, 1988: 139). Put differently, psychotherapy may be thought of as a process of *semiosis* – the forging of meaning in the context of collaborative discourse. It is a process during which the meaning of experience is transformed via a fusion of the horizons of the participants, alternative ways of punctuating experience are developed, and a new stance toward experience evolves. A crucial component of this process may inhere not only in the alternative ways of understanding generated by the discourse but also in the different order of meaning which concurrently emerges when our eyes are opened to seeing our blindness.

To help another toward an orientation that comes from seeing that we cannot see implies, first, a release from the tyranny of the implied authority of governing beliefs. Given the linguistic constitution of our world models, this requires in turn (1) a transformative dialogue in which new understandings are negotiated together with a new set of premises *about* meaning; and (2) the evocation of an expectant attitude toward the as yet unseen, the as yet unstoried, the 'meaning ahead of the text' (Ricoeur, 1971). In terms of Bateson's (1972) distinctions between levels of learning, it is a move beyond learning to replace one punctuation of a situation with another (Level 1), to learning new modes of punctuation (Level 2), to evolving what Keeney (1983: 159) calls 'a change of the premises underlying an entire system of punctuation habits' (Level 3). It is a progression from learning new meanings, to developing new categories of meaning, to transforming one's premises about the nature of meaning itself.

For any of these transformations to occur, a context needs to be established which facilitates their emergence. At the outset we are in full accord with Anderson and Goolishian's (this volume) emphasis on creating a climate where clients have the experience of being heard, of having both their point of view and feelings understood, of feeling themselves confirmed and accepted. It involves an endeavor to understand the client's point of view, to convey an understanding of how it makes sense to the person given the premises from which the viewpoint arises. At the same time this does not imply an acceptance or confirmation of the client's premises. It implies rather a form of *interested inquiry* which opens the premises for exploration.

This receptive mode of inquiry – with its openness to different ways of punctuating experience, readiness to explore multiple perspectives and endorse their coexistence – can, to the extent that it is experienced by the other, trigger a changed stance toward experience. By the same token it can liberate participants in therapy from an immersion in limiting constructions of the world. This is because the experiencing of receptivity – of openness to experience, together with a readiness to adopt multiple perspectives and accept the relativity of meaning itself – comprises a change in perspective.

Various ways in which a therapist can contribute to the re-forming of experience are amply illustrated throughout this book. Additional attention must be drawn, however, to the role that can be played in therapy by the exploration of experience from multiple perspectives, by sensitizing another to the relational context in which behavior is situated, and by a thorough *relativiz-ing* of experience. Toward this end, the troubled person can be invited, *inter alia*: to find exceptions to their predominating experience; to view themselves as prisoners of a culturally inculcated story they did not create; to imagine how they might relate their experience to different people in their lives; to consider what response they invite via their interactional proclivities; to relate what they imagine to be the experience of others close to them; to consider how they would experience their lives if they operated from different assumptions – how they might act, what resources they could call upon in different contexts, what new solutions might emerge; and to recall precepts once believed, but now jettisoned.

These are but a few examples of means by which people can be enabled to construct things from different viewpoints, thus liberating them from the oppression of limiting narrative beliefs and relieving the resulting pain. In this way those turning to us in times of trouble may come to transcend the restraints imposed by their erstwhile reliance on a determinate set of meanings and be freed from the struggle than ensues from imposing their beliefs on self and others. For some, new solutions to problems will become apparent, while for others a richer set of narrative meanings will emerge. For still others a stance toward meaning itself will evolve; one which betokens that tolerance of uncertainty, that freeing of experience which comes from acceptance of unbounded relativity of meaning. For those who adopt it, this stance offers the prospect of a creative participation in the unending and unfolding meaning of life.

I will try
to fasten into order enlarging grasps of disorder, widening
scope, but enjoying the freedom that
Scope eludes my grasp, that there is no finality of vision,
that I have perceived nothing completely,
that tomorrow a new walk is a new walk.

A.R. Ammons, *Carson's Inlet*

Notes

1. For additional discussions of modernism, see Berman, 1982; Frisby, 1985; Frascina and Harrison, 1982; and Gergen, 1991.

2. See Sarbin's (1986) useful volume on narrative psychology.

3. Additional discussions of postmodernism may be found in Connor, 1989; Gergen, 1991; Harvey, 1989; and Silverman, 1990.

4. For additional critique of 'the lens of cognition,' see Gergen, 1989.

5. For further discussion of narratives of the self, see Gergen and Gergen, 1988.

References

Bateson, G. (1972) *Steps to an Ecology of Mind*. New York: Ballantine.

Berman, M. (1982) *All that's Solid Melts into Air: the Experience of Modernity*. New York: Simon & Schuster.

Carse, J.P. (1986) *Finite and Infinite Games*. New York: Macmillan.

Connor, S. (1989) *Postmodernist Culture*. Oxford: Basil Blackwell.

Frascina, F. and Harrison, C. (1982) *Modern Art and Modernism*. London: Open University Press.

Frisby, D. (1985) *Fragments of Modernity*. Cambridge: Polity Press.

Gergen, K.J. (1989) 'Social psychology and the wrong revolution', *European Journal of Social Psychology*, 19: 731–2.

Gergen, K.J. (1991) *The Saturated Self*. New York: Basic Books.

Gergen, K.J. and Gergen, M.M. (1988) 'Narrative and the self as relationship', in L. Berkowitz (ed.), *Advances in Experimental Social Psychology*, vol. 21. New York: Academic Press. pp. 17–56.

Goolishian, H. and Winderman, L. (1988) 'Constructivism, autopoiesis and problem determined systems', in V. Kenny (ed.), 'Radical constructivism, autopoiesis and psychotherapy', special issue of *Irish Journal of Psychology*, 9 (1): 130–43.

Hare-Mustin, R. and Marecek, J. (1988) 'The meaning of difference: gender theory, postmodernism and psychology', *American Psychologist*, 43: 455–64.

Harvey, D. (1989) *The Condition of Postmodernity*. Oxford: Basil Blackwell.

Keeney, B.P. (1983) *Aesthetics of Change*. New York: Guilford Press.

Kovel, J. (1980) 'The American mental health industry', in D. Ingleby (ed.), *Critical Psychiatry: The Politics of Mental Health*. New York: Pantheon.

Parker, D. (1990) *The Mighty World of Eye: Stories/Anti-Stories*. Brookvale, NSW: Simon & Schuster.

Ricoeur, P. (1971) 'The model of the text: meaningful action considered as text', *Social Research*, 38: 529–62.

Sarbin, T. (ed.) (1986) *Narrative Psychology*. New York: Praeger.
Silvermann, H.J. (1990) *Postmodernism - Philosophy and the Arts*. New York: Routledge.
Spence, D. (1982) *Narrative Truth and Historical Truth*. New York: Norton.
Wittgenstein, L. (1953) *Philosophical Investigations*. New York: Macmillan.

12

Reconstructing Identity: the Communal Construction of Crisis

Sheila McNamee

What happens when we construct our lives in the discourse of crisis? Conversation with anyone who identifies a time of crisis in his or her life will be likely to invoke boundary descriptions such as, 'I felt I had no center,' 'I was on the edge,' or 'I was in a constant state of confusion never knowing what I should or should not do, think, or feel.' Other common expressions might follow the imagery of being unattached, floating, unanchored, as in, 'I lost my bearings' or 'I couldn't get a hold on myself.' Also not to be omitted are portrayals of identity that become paramount, as in the commonly heard expression, 'I wasn't myself' or 'I'm not strong enough to handle my life; I'm flawed.'

In this chapter I will examine the notion of crisis. Of specific interest is how crisis is constructed culturally and locally. Such a focus suggests that what we describe as a boundary experience actually demands full participation in the centralized, local discourse. This somewhat ironic realization helps us discuss how we *know* when we are in crisis as well as how the therapeutic context and the therapist can participate in the continuation or reconstruction (that is, change) of a client's crisis.

Individualizing Crisis

The first question we must address concerns our folk wisdom of crisis experience. In general, there are two options we might use to characterize these disruptive episodes in our lives. First, we have available for our use a conception of a person's crisis as something that *happens to* the person. This external orientation portrays an impotent individual at the mercy of situational constraints and dicta. How can one take charge of one's life given the limitations which surround one? If circumstances have *brought the crisis to the person*, how can that person muster the energy and force to change those circumstances?

An alternative version of this folk explanation is a view of crisis as a natural extension of who and what we are. In other words, a crisis is viewed as almost 'predictable' given the individual's identity. There must be something about 'me' that brings on the crises in my life. We wonder if the person in crisis is immoral, inherently 'bad' or 'evil,' or just an unlucky 'type' of person. But here again, if we *bring ourselves to a crisis*, how can we ever expect to move beyond ourselves to be other than we are?

Both these common-sense understandings of crisis give priority to the individual. Whether a crisis is inherent to the individual or brought to the individual from events in the 'real world,' people talk about their crises as some*thing* they *have*. Thus crisis is believed to be a personal possession of individuals.

Sampson argues that 'Individuals are assumed to have personal ownership of the identities they possess, including all of their attributes . . . as well as the outcomes of whatever achievements their particular abilities and motivations bring to them' (1989: 919). This perspective, which he identifies as 'liberal individualism,' focuses on 'the dynamics of the individuals whose activities create the features of human life that we encounter' (1989: 916). And, he argues, if this self-contained individual is the locus of social life, then psychology becomes the legitimate discipline from which to understand the human condition. So too, if a crisis is the 'property' of an individual – whether seen as inherent to that person or as brought to that person from external conditions – then psychology remains the appropriate avenue from which to examine crisis phenomena because it is focused on individual capabilities. But what is a crisis?

Crisis as a Boundary Phenomenon

The term 'crisis' is derived from the Greek *krinein*, which means 'to separate.' The boundary experience of crisis separates us from others in our interactive communities. To separate requires boundary setting. On a map, the separation between countries is referred to as a boundary. Similarly, when thinking of our lived experience, we mark the territory that is 'our own' and thus different from another's by referring to the 'limits of our experience.' In the family therapy literature, Minuchin (1974) conceptualizes the difference between healthy and pathological family systems as identifiable by reference to inappropriate boundaries. To him, families are in trouble if, for example, the boundaries between generations are either too diffuse or too rigid.

These examples emphasize that any idea of separation implies a boundary. But boundaries must first be drawn. This requires that a distinction be identified that separates one territory, idea, person, experience, and so forth from another. Once drawn, a boundary signifies identity; it provides a sense of what sort of 'thing' is being identified by indicating that from which it is distinguished. It is at this point that the possibility of constructing the 'other' emerges. So, too, the possibility of shifting or redefining that boundary becomes possible when the participants cooperatively negotiate the need for such a redefinition.

Boundaries also indicate distinctions between center and margin. Traditionally, we have assumed that to be in the center is to be in the culturally or locally privileged position. Terms of significance amplify this assumption, as in 'central tendencies,' 'to center oneself,' 'central administration.' Bakhtin (1981) suggests that a conception of center requires a conception of margin, periphery, otherness. This sentiment is echoed in Bateson's (1972) description of information as a 'difference.' To Bateson, we acknowledge data as 'information' only when it is placed in *relation* to other data.

With these notions, our attention shifts to the *relationship* between centers and boundaries. Rather than focus on the privileged 'center,' we now recognize the margin that allows the center to 'be.' In Conquergood's words, 'The major epistemological consequence of displacing the idea of solid centers and unified wholes with boundaries and borderlines is a rethinking of identity and culture as constructed and relational, instead of essential' (1990: 10).

If we return to the colloquial expressions indicative of a person in crisis, we notice that not only is identity in question, but the sense of being in the 'center' is deeply threatened. The crisis is defined, by its very nature, as a border experience – one on the margin of acceptable performance. A crisis could be seen as a decentralized identity, and as such is typically thought to open only two possibilities: (1) finding a route *back* to the center, or (2) moving *beyond* the border into another domain (which includes both 'healthier' non-crisis identities and the possibility of the 'abnormal' domain).

However, these two possibilities present a conceptual difficulty. How can I claim a crisis in my life – a situation that, by definition, places me on the margin – without a communal construal of my situation as such: an activity that demands my participation in the centralized, local communities of significance? How can I move *back* toward the center or *beyond* the margin if I am already firmly entrenched in the discourse that constructs my situation as a crisis in the first place? Any movement would still fall within the boundaries of this discourse. And thus, attention is drawn to discursive practices.

The Discursive Construction of Crisis

Clearly, there are well-negotiated forms of social talk that provide the resources necessary for my belief that I am in crisis. These forms of talk are communally constructed in interaction. In other words, someone is likely to think of herself as 'a person in crisis' as she engages in conversations and interactions with others who cooperatively construct such an identity with her. However, any particular behavior – such as, for example, poor job performance – does not constitute a crisis until sustained interactions direct attention in such a manner that further interactions and behaviors become identified as problematic. More important, unless a person participates in particular conversations (for example, repeated interactions with a supervisor where talk focuses on problematic performance), that individual is not likely to define the situation as a crisis. Thus, to be defined as in crisis, a person must participate just enough in the community's centralized forms of discourse to share in the construction of what counts as a crisis.

If we take a historical look, we can see many illustrations of the limits of languaging communities. The oppression of women within patriarchal society was not widely considered a crisis until shifts in the discursive realm provided the resources to discuss the inequalities between men and women. Although there were many women in the earlier part of this century who were not happy with their status in the broader community, most women did not face or even have 'knowledge' of their unmet professional, political, economic, and personal needs. However, the discourse of the time did furnish, for example, the means for identifying problems with child rearing as a significant crisis of mothering. At the same time, there were no ready means by which a woman's career interests could be discussed as a personal crisis.

As we note shifts in the discourse about women, we begin to see the development of new forms of crisis. Now a crisis can include notions of political, economic, and professional participation. In our current social context, a legitimate crisis for a woman might include the weighing of professional and family life. This was not the case, for the society at large, until recently.

Similarly, the Freudian reading of a person's problems popular in the earlier part of this century provided an array of terms and descriptions for crisis rooted in notions of competition for energy among psychic structures and early parent–child relationships. Today, with other discourses available, we are likely to explore how a person's problems are products of environmental stimuli and improper conditioning (behaviorism) or, quite different, an inappropriate family hierarchy (structuralism).

These are illustrations of crises that emerge within a particular discursive realm. To define what is 'appropriate' or 'inappropriate' requires reference to a discursive context. And, consequently, the means are ready and available for 'working through' whatever deviations have emerged in relation to the constructed, common practices. Therapy is frequently one of these already available social formations, as are institutions of education, law, medicine, and so forth.

There is a particular irony in the situation outlined above where the experience of a crisis is considered a border phenomenon by virtue of a *communally, centrally* defined notion of what counts as normal and abnormal behavior. There is an additional irony leveled on this when we recognize that the very institutions we have constructed as resources to deal with such situations (such as therapy) prevent or impede their resolution in any form other than one that maintains the privileged forms of discourse. Such an argument gives legitimacy to the therapeutic context as a viable arena for dealing with crisis. It also acknowledges therapy as a practice rooted in modernist conceptions of individuality.

Modernist and Postmodernist Orientations to Therapy

Much has been written about a modernist perspective and its influence in twentieth-century portrayals of social life (Jencks, 1986; Lyotard, 1984; Turner, 1990). Briefly, modernism assumes that individuals are inherently rational. The ability to reason, coupled with close observation of the world 'out there,' will lead to accurate descriptions of that world. The desire for correct and accurate descriptions of phenomena underscores the modernist emphasis on progress, outcomes, and goals. It is movement forward guided by clear reasoning, that will solve human dilemmas. Science, understandably, becomes a central metaphor for discussing such progress.

Much of the therapeutic literature indicates an allegiance to a modernist view of the world. In some popular forms, the task of therapy is for the therapist and client to talk through the problem episodes rationally. The shape and direction of the talk is dictated by models, stages, and methods clearly identified in texts and professional journals and books. This format approximates the rationality accredited to scientific procedures by not only clearly detailing the appropriate steps to be followed but also by illustrating compelling research that supports the effectiveness of such techniques.

More obviously related to the scientific metaphor of modernism are therapeutic approaches that rely on medical procedures. These procedures vary, but are likely to include medication, laboratory tests and observations, and an array of clinically administered treatments. Although these therapeutic approaches to diagnosis and treatment vary, they all share in the focus on individual rationality, techniques of observation, and belief in progress.

The rise of postmodernism, due largely to advances in technological capabilities, brings with it common access to diverse rationalities. In short, we now have at our disposal a variety of ways of talking about what is of value in human life, how we should act, and what counts as progress. Postmodernism is marked by a focus on language – that is, a focus on people interacting with one another in the construction of their worlds. This emphasis on language is an important shift from the modernist focus on the essential nature of 'things.' As noted above, the modernist's project is to uncover (through careful and controlled observation) the basic structure or essence of whatever is being examined so that conclusions can be drawn and principles developed. In contrast, the postmodernist's project is to examine how the process of interaction provides the opportunities for particular characterizations to emerge and dissipate. How do particular interactive contexts privilege one form of discourse while other contexts provide opportunities for vastly different discourses? This is the postmodern question.

As we can see, concern is not necessarily on the outcome of a given interaction, but, rather, it is on the ways in which a plurality of perspectives are coordinated into coherent patterns of interaction, each potentiating and simultaneously constraining particular forms of action. And, with its emphasis on language and social construction, we see that 'Under postmodern conditions, persons exist in a state of continuous construction and reconstruction' (Gergen, 1991: 7).

The emergence of postmodern thinking addresses our current, global mode of interaction and our need to attend to issues of diversity. The modernist reliance on the individual as the primary organizing principle of society is replaced in postmodernism by a communal, relational, interactive attention to understanding the social order. In a world where *local* economies depend upon world politics and trade and where *world* economies must consider and depend upon localized governments, an emphasis on self-contained individuals becomes minimally informative. Psychology, in general, has been seen as the appropriate discipline from which to study human interaction in the modern era, characterized as it is by notions of individual efficacy, intentionality, and autonomy. Is it possible to consider a postmodern form of therapy where multiplicity, diversity, and relationship become the focus? If so, how would such an approach inform our ideas about crisis and therapy in general?

If a crisis depends on living both in and at the borders of a language community, then what constitutes a crisis is identified (created) within a community. Kleinman (1988) emphasizes the local or 'significant' community within which meaning and practices emerge. We must question how that 'local life world' (Kleinman, 1988) is constructed. What beliefs about persons and about legitimate lines of action are maintained in different communities or cultures? What are the interactive domains in which certain understandings of behavior or particular interpretations are deemed viable? In other words, what meanings and actions construct the dominant or central interactive patterns in a given community and thereby define what will be considered marginal? The notion of community becomes important here because, as the following illustrations demonstrate, not all participants in a given interaction refer to the same 'local life world' or community.

Divergent Discursive Communities and Emergent Problems of Identity

The notion of a crisis, from a discursive perspective, can now be seen as a communally constructed phenomenon rather than an individual's 'problem.' For example, the definition or characterization of homosexuality as a form of pathology serves as yet another illustration of privileged forms of discourse and how modernist constructions of social institutions (such as therapy) serve to maintain this image of pathology.

Kitzinger (1989) calls attention to the social processes that ironically embrace behaviors seen as abnormal and 'fit' them into the culturally sanctioned narratives in operation. Her example addresses the issue of lesbianism, and provides a useful overview of how particular, popular (that is, centralized) descriptions of lesbianism actually serve to maintain our liberal humanist cultural orientation. Specifically, she illustrates how lesbian relationships can be described in terms of romantic love and personal fulfillment. In such descriptions, the individualist orientation of contemporary culture is reinstated by privileging relationships that enhance the self. Thus, the non-centralized politics of lesbianism and feminism are undermined – politics that embrace a sense of community and coordination. Culturally, romantic love and self-

fulfillment serve as 'legitimate' bases upon which intimate relationships are formed. To describe lesbianism in these terms, then,
suggests that lesbianism is simply another variation of the
'normative' relational form. Different ways of construing such
relationships become silenced and marginalized.

Consider polygamous relations which are not broadly sanctioned
within this society. A visit to a local therapist with complaints
about one's various spouses and their difficult relations to one
another would be unlikely to create the opportunity for a conversation in which a resolution allowing for the maintenance of the
polygamous relationship would emerge. Resolution, in such a
situation, more likely would take the form of corrective and
instructional directives on the part of the therapist concerning the
immorality of polygamy. If the client fails to accept this solution,
the crisis remains (and very likely expands). The modernist
therapist, as cultural spokesperson, will attempt to impose the
cultural constructions that contribute to the crisis in the first place.
The client who denies these constructions is further pathologized.

Yet, how do we understand these illustrations from a relational
position? How is the 'crisis' of being homosexual or polygamous
maintained and then finally transformed through discursive practice? It is not difficult to envision the maintenance of homosexuality or polygamy. However, the therapeutic context ironically
and often constructs the marginal as central by legitimating the
crisis within the sanctioned discourse, as in the case of lesbianism
cited above. The therapist, in effect, participates in *centralizing* the
crisis (otherwise thought of as the *boundary* or marginal
phenomenon).

If we recognize how particular forms of conversation sustain
identities, belief systems, and lines of action, then we can imagine
that conversations and significant interactions provide the opportunity for defining a crisis. Interactions can admittedly constrain
those participating from playing out particular autobiographies.
Often, therapist–client conversations help to create and maintain a
crisis for clients by attending to interpretations that are more
culturally 'central.' Therapeutic conversations often provide the
discursive realm in which the client's ability to 'know' the world in
a different way (for example, as a homosexual) are constrained by
the notions legitimized and privileged within a modernist
therapeutic setting.

However, attention to the notion of different discursive
communities provides a way in which to examine interactions with
one primary question in mind: How is it that what people are
doing together in this interaction provides the opportunity for

certain interpretations, explanations, descriptions, and lines of action to emerge? Of course, this question also suggests that there are lines of action, interpretations, explanations, and descriptions that are not possible – that are constrained – by the interactive process. What people do together provides the viability and sustainability of particular lines of action and interpretation (Gergen, 1990). Consequently, the constructions of identity and crisis that emerge when different discursive domains are coordinated provide potential for new ways of acting.

Participants can achieve this by continually questioning their own premises and local life worlds. Is it possible for the therapeutic context to achieve such coordination that new identity constructions emerge without co-opting the participants' varying discursive communities?

The Discursive Therapeutic Context

Some schools of therapy have emerged that attempt to take a postmodern or social constructionist focus. Here, *discursive practices* become important avenues of exploration, as opposed to the traditional emphasis on essential aspects of human behavior or motivation. And, with its emphasis on discourse, the communities within which particular forms of interaction become viable and sustainable gather attention. When our emphasis shifts to the communication process itself, the relational construction of identity (and crisis) emerges. The early work of the Mental Research Institute (Watzlawick et al., 1967) was based on this focus, and several schools of therapy have since evolved (Selvini et al., 1978; Tomm, 1987a, 1987b, 1988; Anderson and Goolishian, 1988; Andersen, 1987).

Once a therapist engages in conversation with a client, the therapist accepts the client's invitation to be in language about some topic (Anderson and Goolishian, 1988). At this moment, the topic is constructed as 'legitimate.' Once legitimized as a topic for conversation, the ability to examine premises orienting both the central *and* the marginal beliefs and actions is presented. The crisis is not centralized in social constructionist therapy by *absorbing* it into the accepted practices and beliefs of the culture. It is, instead, centralized in its own terms by the very activity of providing and sustaining a discursive space.

The relational orientation this provides presumes that the client and the therapist are cooperatively engaged in constructing a narrative about the client's crisis. It is this relational, cooperative, communal orientation that distinguishes a social constructionist approach from a modernist approach, where the therapist stands removed, evaluating and diagnosing the crisis by general, culturally significant criteria rather than locally constructed criteria.

One illustration of social constructionist therapy is the notion of circular questioning introduced by the Milan team (Selvini et al., 1978). Circular questioning is built on the idea of relational language. Rather than ask a client how important group activities are to the family's relationships (which calls forth a response that is framed as 'factual' and that simultaneously adopts an *individual's* perspective), a circular question utilizes the notion of relational information by asking a third person (perhaps a child) to comment on how important he or she thinks group activities are to someone else in the family. For example, the client could be asked, 'How important would your husband say group activities are to you?. . . How would *he* say you demonstrate your position on this issue?' These questions focus on the possible distinctions in interpretation that can be constructed within the same interactive context. By privileging the different ways each participant punctuates a situation, circular questions shift attention from what are believed to be centralized 'facts' or 'appropriate interpretations.' When used, circular questions provide the opportunity for participants to become observers of their own interactive patterns by providing the opportunity for various interpretations to emerge in a non-factual manner. Circular questions make it possible for a person to contemplate how another might describe or characterize or justify a particular action or relationship. In this way, 'problems' are less likely to be 'absorbed' into a popular narrative (either within the significant relational context or within the professional psychological discourse). Rather, a discursive space is created in which a multiplicity of interpretations and descriptions become viable.

What is interesting about the idea of circular questioning is the voice given to multiple perspectives. Divergence of interpretation becomes interesting information rather than the territory upon which debate and competition are focused. The multiple descriptions that emerge in the process of circular questioning provide the resources for new connections (relationships). 'Data' gathered through this questioning method quickly become information about connections among people, ideas, relationships, and time. Thus, information about *patterns* and *process* (not products or outcomes) emerges in this context.

Because circular questions do not engage individuals in upholding their own version of the world (including the privileged, professional, psychological version), they allow for a departure from the stories or logic that people tend to live and act daily. They provide an opening for alternative descriptions that often encompass the multiple voices that have previously been competing in the discourse. It is more likely to hear a client say, 'I never stopped to think that he would see my behavior as avoidance of family activities,' than to engage in debates concerning veracity. The relational language of circular questions provides a context where statements become curiosities rather than counter-arguments. Circular questions are only one example of therapeutic practice emerging within a relational consciousness. They provide the means for linguistically shifting the boundaries of what is 'central' and what is 'marginal.' In this way, the therapeutic conversation actively constructs the constraints and possibilities of a crisis situation.

Just as claims to identity formation and crisis definition are not individual constructions, what counts as a legitimate diagnosis and subsequent cure are also products of collaborative, interactive construction. How might a therapeutic context focused on relational forms of discourse approach these issues? Such a context would *not* generate conversation about crisis, identity, and diagnosis as individual possessions but, rather, as descriptions emerging in a context of communal construction.

To define and identify a crisis calls attention to the centrality of language in the construction of what we know. The long-held belief that language mirrors reality, known as a modernist conception, gives way to a postmodern account where language is viewed as constructing our worlds (Gergen, 1985; Shotter, 1990). This is a position consistent with Wittgenstein's (1953) notion of language games where each action is yet another move in an on-going, relationally dependent sequence. The implications of such a view are bold. What is suggested is that, rather than focus attention on what is in a speaker's mind, we orient our inquiries to the realm of discursive practices; that is, we examine what people do together in interaction and how it is that they accomplish various 'activities' all the while questioning the premises generated from within our different communities.

Conclusion

An emphasis on the relational domain in which knowledge is constructed directs our attention to the community of observers. A community of observers can be seen as those who interact with one another and who look to one another for verification of what is appropriate. In this sense, we can say that it is the community that identifies what counts as a crisis, whether that community is constituted by one's family, friends, co-workers, or professionals such as lawyers, doctors, psychiatrists, or others.

While social constructionists would argue that observation is in the domain of language because descriptions of observations are always, ultimately 'in language,' most 'observers' assume a degree of detachment and, consequently, of objectivity. Conquergood (1990: 8), following Rosaldo (1989), proposes that we replace the 'visualist bias of positivism with talk about voices, utterances, intonations, multivocality' in an attempt to shift from models of observation to models of participation in language. A metaphor of sight (gaze) implies distance and thus objectivity. A metaphor of sound implies proximity. And, as Conquergood points out, 'Vulnerability and self-disclosure are enabled through conversations. Closure, on the other hand, is constituted by the gaze' (1990: 8). In therapy, conversational participation (both verbal and non-verbal), not observation, is central. Further, many discursive domains must be negotiated within the therapeutic context.

A crisis, as a moment in a person's life, is a lived segment in which vulnerability is 'languaged' (Maturana and Varela, 1987). Is it possible to enhance the potential of such vulnerability to construct new identities, to reconstruct one's talk about the ongoing life story? Is this, indeed, what takes place in the interactive domain of therapy? If therapy is a conversational domain, then communication processes become the focus. Therapeutic contexts that consider this emphasis on the discursive aspects of crisis formation provide the context within which reconstruction emerges. Clients' problems can be seen as invitations to participate in certain kinds of conversation (Anderson and Goolishian, 1988). When conversations based on relational rather than individual meanings are pursued, what previously appeared as a crisis and thus a danger to a client's identity can emerge as an opportunity for identity reconstruction.

A crisis becomes a wonderful moment to free oneself from ideas of 'correctness,' 'objectivity,' 'acceptance,' and redesign, reconstruct one's place in the on-going narrative or life story. Yet the success or failure of such an endeavor can only be provided in the discursive realm.

Again, it is precisely this kind of *relation* between the potential and the constraint (Ceruti, 1986), between the center and the border (Rosaldo, 1989), and so too between the crisis and the 'normal' that is constructed in language. A crisis is a cooperative, communal construction.

It is useful to examine how the conversational narratives in which therapists and their clients participate become organized so that a crisis emerges, stays alive, or dissipates. Such a focus marks a shift in traditional thinking about mental health and social interaction. It marks a shift from assuming that people have problems (as if they were 'things' to be had) to examining the interactive (conversational) practices (traditions) that allow problems to emerge. It marks a shift from assuming that a good theory or method could uncover the root of the problem and thereby dissolve it, to acknowledging the discursive *practices* used by theorists and researchers – in interaction with their 'subjects' and clients and within particular cultural and ideological domains – in order to construct explanations of social phenomena. In sum, the focus is now on what people (therapists and clients) *do together* rather than on any 'essential' aspects of problems or people.

References

Andersen, T. (1987) 'The reflecting team: dialogue and meta-dialogue in clinical work,' *Family Process*, 26 (4): 415–28.

Anderson, H. and Goolishian, H. (1988) 'Human systems as linguistic systems: preliminary and evolving ideas about the implications for clinical theory', *Family Process*, 27 (4): 371–94.

Bakhtin, M. (1981) *The Dialogic Imagination*, ed. M. Holquist, tr. Caryl Emerson and Michael Holquist. Austin, TX: University of Texas Press.

Bateson, G. (1972) *Steps to an Ecology of Mind*. New York: Ballantine.

Ceruti, M. (1986) *Il vincolo e la possibilità*. Milan: Feltrinelli.

Conquergood, D. (1990) 'Rethinking ethnography: cultural politics and rhetorical strategies'. Paper presented at the Temple University 11th Annual Conference on Discourse Analysis, Philadelphia, PA.

Gergen, K.J. (1985) 'The social constructionist movement in modern psychology', *American Psychologist*, 40: 266–73.

Gergen, K.J. (1989) 'Warranting voice and the elaboration of the self', in J. Shotter and K.J. Gergen (eds), *Texts of Identity*. London: Sage.

Gergen, K.J. (1990) 'From heteroglossia to communication'. Keynote address, Temple University 11th Annual Conference on Discourse Analysis, Philadelphia, PA.

Gergen, K.J. (1991) *The Saturated Self*. New York: Basic Books.

Hoffman, L. (1981) *Foundations of Family Therapy*. New York: Basic Books.

Jencks, C. (1986) *What is Post-modernism?* London: St Martin's Press.

Kitzinger, C. (1989) 'The regulation of lesbian identities: liberal humanism as an ideology of social control', in J. Shotter and K.J. Gergen (eds), *Texts of Identity*. London: Sage.

Kleinman, A. (1988) *The Illness Narratives*. New York: Basic Books.

Lyotard, J.F. (1984) *The Postmodern Condition: a Report on Knowledge*. Manchester: Manchester University Press.

Maturana, H.R. and Varela, F.J. (1987) *The Tree of Knowledge*. Boston, MA: New Science Library.

Minuchin, S. (1974) *Families and Family Therapy*. Cambridge, MA: Harvard University Press.

Rosaldo, R. (1989) *Culture and the Truth*. Boston: Beacon.

Sampson, E.D. (1989) 'The challenge of social change for psychology: globalization and psychology's theory of the person', *American Psychologist*, 44 (6): 914–21.

Selvini, M., Boscolo, L., Cecchin, G. and Prata, G. (1978) *Paradox and Counter-paradox*. New York: J. Aronson.

Shotter, J. (1990) *Knowing of the Third Kind*. Utrecht: University of Utrecht.

Tomm, K. (1987a) 'Interventive interviewing: Part I. Strategizing as a fourth guideline for the therapist', *Family Process*, 26 (1): 3–14.

Tomm, K. (1987b) 'Interventive interviewing: Part II. Reflexive questioning as a means to enable self-healing', *Family Process*, 26 (2): 167–84.

Tomm, K. (1988) 'Interventive interviewing: Part III. Intending to ask circular, strategic, or reflexive questions?' *Family Process*, 27 (1): 1–16.

Turner, B.S. (ed.) (1990) *Theories of Modernity and Postmodernity*. London: Sage.

Watzlawick, P., Beavin, J. and Jackson, D.D. (1967) *Pragmatics of Human Communication*. New York: Norton.

Wittgenstein, L. (1953) *Philosophical Investigations*, tr. G. Anscombe. New York: Macmillan.

13

Constructionist Therapy: Sense and Nonsense

Jay S. Efran and Leslie E. Clarfield

The quest for new and potent family therapy methods persists, although few of the approaches that come along retain their therapeutic magic for very long (Schwartz and Perrotta, 1985). Some techniques lose their sparkle just moments after they are brought home from a workshop or conference. Like last year's Christmas toys, these new methods tend to fade in popularity with use. As the appeal of each diminishes, it is relegated to the bottom of the therapist's toy box, spurring the hunt for still more impressive gadgets.

It is of little surprise, therefore, that some characterize the various forms of constructionism[1] now gaining popularity in the field of psychotherapy as simply the latest craze of the fickle family and strategic therapy crowd. Moreover, they argue that when stripped of 'epistobabble' (Coyne, 1982a), such therapies are little more than recombinations of familiar 'reframing' and team observation techniques already in use. They question whether constructionist lingo will prove any more substantive or long-lived than a dozen earlier infatuations.

Recognizing that we are at a critical juncture in the appraisal of constructionist approaches, we intend to use this chapter as a vehicle for two intertwined purposes. First, we want to clear away some of the conceptual debris left behind by early interpreters of constructionism. Secondly, we intend to discuss central aspects of our own interpretation (Efran et al., 1990). For us, constructionism is neither a new type of therapy nor a snazzy set of techniques to add to pre-existing repertoires. It is a context within which to apprehend and mold the therapy contract. As such, we believe that it can lead to better and clearer designs for client–therapist interaction.

An 'Anything Goes' Mentality

The special issue on constructivism of the *Irish Journal of Psychology* (Kenny, 1988) opens with the epigraph, 'For all those jumping in the dark.' (It ends with a poem that poses the poignant question, 'Have we been fleeced?') These are public acknowledgements of the primitive and volatile state of knowledge in the constructivist domain. At the same time, the publication of that special issue testifies to the intense interest among professionals in exploring this new way of thinking. Contributors to such a volume are groping to establish a shared and workable vocabulary in this arena. However, at present there is only minimal consensus about basic terminology, and even less agreement about treatment implications. Some argue that no particular 'approved' constructivist method will ever emerge, since it is in the spirit of constructionism to consider all views and positions *equally legitimate.*

We should state at the outset that we consider this 'one is just as good as the next' interpretation of constructivism fundamentally wrong-headed. As constructionists, we are as entitled as any other professionals to choose among alternatives and to express strong preferences about what is 'right' or 'wrong' for us.

This puts us in sharp opposition to certain critics. For example, Held assumes that whenever constructivists make 'reality claims,' they violate their own philosophical dictum that one 'cannot, under any circumstances, know an independent reality' (1990: 181). Held classifies as a 'reality claim' a commitment to virtually anything, including the constructionist credo itself, since it, too, is an assertion about how the world works.

Held notes correctly that, in order to practice, constructivist therapists must entertain beliefs about why people get stuck, and what therapists can do about it. On these grounds, she accuses them of failing to practice what they preach. Ironically, we make exactly the same claim, but for diametrically opposite reasons. In *our* interpretation, the constructivist framework insists that (1) everyone has personal preferences, (2) people are entitled to express those preferences, and (3) such choices should not be 'disguised' as objective truths or realities. For us, a 'truth' is a set of opinions widely shared. As Justice Oliver Wendell Holmes, Jr, asserted, 'What is true is what I can't help believing.'

Constructionists are obliged to take responsibility for being advocates of particular positions. They are not enjoined from having them. Constructionists are even allowed to test their hypotheses using the canons of science, provided they keep in mind that science itself is a tradition involving a dialectic between the observer and the observed. It never yields value-free observations. As quantum theorist John Wheeler puts it, 'Without an observer, there is no physics' (Overbye, 1981: 66).

Unfortunately, critics of constructivism pay insufficient attention to the differences between a 'flat' two-valued logic that does not take the observer into account, and a more complex and modern self-referential logic (Brown, 1972). As Russell and Whitehead demonstrated, collapsing across self-referential logical levels always results in contradictions and paradoxes. For example, Whitehead's maxim that 'all truths are half-truths' may create problems of analysis in traditional either/or logic, but, taken on its own terms, it constitutes a perfectly sensible, understandable, and useful statement. Similarly, Bateson's well-known adage, 'Science never proves anything' (1979: 29), cannot – and need not – be proven scientifically. As Gödel's theorems make clear (see Hofstadter, 1979), the kinds of contradictions and paradoxes alluded to in critiques of constructivism can be found in *all* forms of theorizing – realist as well as anti-realist. They are inescapable. Every theory inevitably begins with a proposition that signifies an observer's preference and that cannot be defended within the framework of the theory itself. For constructivists, the proposition that one never directly gains access to an objective reality is just such a premise, and it needs neither justification nor proof. It is a starting point, and does not constitute an improper 'reality claim.'

Abstractions and Obscurities

Psychotherapy is production. The status quo is being modified. If it is successful, clients must end up in a different place from where they began. In that sense, constructionists are no exception to the general rule that clinicians have preferred methods for moving people from one place to another. We regret that some constructivists feel inclined to deny that they are in this sort of 'influence' business.

Perhaps because of their ambivalence about producing effects, much of the advice that has come from constructivist theorists has been inordinately vague, abstract, and wishy-washy. Therapists and clients are being told what to do – so softly and ambiguously that it is difficult to discern the exact nature of the message. For example, therapists may be told that they ought to 'co-construct a conversation' with their clients. Although the statement isn't meaningless, it is of limited value to a therapist about to be confronted, let's say, with a family whose teenage son has just been killed by neighborhood drug lords.

Therapists adhering to the constructivist perspective often weave a virtually impenetrable fog of abstraction. They talk about creating 'multiple conversations simultaneously,' bringing about change 'unawares,' elaborating on the 'unsaid,' and developing 'a new connectedness in language.' Descriptions of this sort fail to conjure up vivid images of an actual therapist at work. They exemplify a persistent danger in the therapy field – the tendency to create lists of principles and abstractions *post hoc*, presenting them as if they truly delineated the therapist's in-session mental processes. In our experience, there are often large gaps between what therapists do and what they later say they were doing.

By way of contrast, the popularity of the currently fashionable cognitive-behavioral framework may be linked to the willingness of those writers to provide clear and simple guidelines for solving client problems. To be sure, the approach encourages clinicians to sidestep crucial aspects of experience and relationship (for example, Coyne, 1982b, 1989, 1990). Worse yet, it relies on an outmoded and tautological theory of causality and change (Efran and Caputo, 1984; Efran et al., 1990). Nevertheless, by giving clinicians a straightforward definition of their role, and a relatively precise set of operational directives, it rescues those who might otherwise find themselves floundering in a sea of ambiguity.

Description versus Prescription

Complicating the problem of interpreting constructionist advice is the tendency of some writers in the field to slip back and forth between *descriptive* and *prescriptive* modes – a confusion of logical types. Constructionists tend to use phrases such as 'therapy as conversation' as if they were injunctions rather than descriptions. For Darwinians, 'survival of the fittest' is a fundamental way of describing life processes. However, porcupines and salamanders are not required to endorse the principle of natural selection or to go out of their way to ensure that the process works. Natural selection is a descriptive metaphor – not an exhortation or set of instructions to species members. Similarly, for constructionists, conversation is a metaphor. It isn't a set of tools that therapists should be urged to adopt, nor an admonition against giving clients direct advice, exploring past history, or avoiding counter-transference. To the constructionist, all therapies – even cognitive-behavioral approaches – will be analyzed as co-constructed conversational endeavors. Rational-emotive homework assignments and psychoanalytic dream interpretations are both forms of dialogue, although they may lead in different directions. As Varela states, 'We live and breathe in dialogue and language,' and conversation is the embodiment of the human experience 'par excellence' (1979: 268).

Conversation is nothing more and nothing less than the everyday, rough-and-tumble adaptational processes that enable us to live together on this planet. Moreover, conversations are not necessarily fragile events that require special nurturing. 'Dialogue' includes fist-fights, blood feuds, corporate take-overs, suicides, and political dictatorships. Yet some constructionists insist on defining 'dialogue' in pale and limiting terms, as if only polite discussion and an 'openness' to alternative viewpoints qualify. It is naïve and restrictive to believe that positive gains are usually accomplished through calm, rational deliberations or that only in an atmosphere of studied neutrality can clients make progress toward their goals.

Constructionists can be defined partly in terms of their preference for the conversational metaphor, just as Darwinians can be recognized by their reliance on natural selection as an organizing principle. However, constructionism does not *necessitate* running therapy sessions as open forums, consulting with team members, avoiding DSM III-R diagnoses, de-emphasizing genetic explanations of alcoholism or schizophrenia, refraining from making strong predictions, or refusing to tell clients what they ought to do. Under certain circumstances, each of these therapeutic preferences may prove defensible. None of them is basic to constructionist theory.

Hierarchy and Passivity

More than a few constructionist therapists have selected for themselves the role of 'facilitator' instead of 'coach' or 'director.' They aim to establish a supportive context rather than to prescribe change directly. They 'trust' that change will somehow happen of its own accord when the time is ripe. Some have become as non-directive in their stance as the early Rogerians.

What is disturbing in this development is that some of these therapists have become convinced that these ways of working are dictated by principles and constraints inherent in the constructivist model – as if it is somehow anti-constructionist to see people individually, to take sides, to give specific advice, to hold firm opinions, to argue, to work without co-therapists, and so on.

For many family and strategic therapists, the 'polite' version of constructionism has perhaps provided a convenient escape route from the highly manipulative and directive modes of therapy in which they were previously trained. The image of the adversarial family therapist as powerful magician and tactician has been increasingly under attack by feminist writers and by members of mental health advocacy groups. Having grown weary of attempts to outmaneuver powerful family resistances, these workers have welcomed an approach that appears to license a more egalitarian posture. Family therapists had been looking for a more 'aesthetic' format (Keeney, 1983) in which they could retain the notion of an 'invented reality' (Watzlawick, 1984) but de-emphasize power politics. Recent interpretations of constructionism have made available to them the somewhat 'softer' model they had been looking for. Our objection is not to their preference, but to the insistence that this therapeutic style represents the essence of the contructionist perspective.

In this connection, we found reader reaction to our recent book (Efran et al., 1990) interesting. Some constructivist colleagues liked (and agree with) much of what we had to say, but we were chastised for specifying in too much detail how we ran our own therapy sessions. Their point was, 'That isn't constructivism – that is you.' Of course it was us. But constructivism isn't a special method. Part of the virtue of the approach is that it *legitimizes* an unabashed presentation of who we are and where we stand. After all, how is an 'invented reality' to get itself invented, if we all sit on the sidelines, feigning neutrality and waiting for something interesting to crop up? In our view, a participatory epistemology invites participation. Constructivist books (and therapies) like our own are not required to be apolitical and impersonal. They should deal forthrightly with issues of ethics, morals, responsibilities, and visions of the future. They are allowed to advocate and teach, lead and influence. As we said earlier, constructivists are not prohibited from having and expressing preferences, hopes, and opinions. They are only enjoined from claiming that these belong to someone else, or derive from a privileged access to an outside, objective reality. Clients, too, are invited to take responsibility for their positions. We affirm Richard Bach's position, 'Your only obligation in any lifetime is to be true to yourself. Being true to anyone else or anything else is not only impossible, but the mark of a fake messiah' (1977: 59).

Maturana was once asked by a therapist at a conference why he or any person should do therapy, especially if there were no *objective* criteria by which to determine the characteristics of the good life. Maturana's answer was simple and straightforward: 'Because he or she wants to.' To the structure determinist, the ultimate reference for a human being is himself or herself. We recall the late Martha Graham's response to interviewers who asked her why she choreographed: 'So I would have something to dance.'

We are concerned that a number of Maturana's (1988) ideas – for example, the notion that each of us lives in a unique 'multiverse,' and that 'instructive interaction' is a structural impossibility – have been widely misunderstood. Misconceptions surrounding these concepts are leading some therapists to abandon potentially useful strategies. Although direct 'instructive interaction' is an illusion on the part of an observer, and not a good description of how the biological system operates, the principles of structure determinism do not imply or require that schools close or that teachers keep the fruits of their investigations to themselves. Teaching and learning remain alive and well. Maturana himself is a superb educator and has no intention of deserting the classroom any time soon, nor of withholding from students the conclusions he has reached based on a lifetime of thinking and experiencing.

Yes, it is true that every student at a lecture will be uniquely and differentially affected by the interactions that take place there. However, because students are structured similarly and share commonalities of language and heritage, there will also be points of intersection in their experiences. Moreover, in the attempt to educate others, we simultaneously enhance our own understandings and move the communal effort forward.

Cyberneticists point out that human beings – unlike so-called 'trivial machines' – are not fully predictable (von Foerster, 1981). However, this piece of cybernetic wisdom was never intended to discourage therapists from using past experience as a guide to future action. Even with non-trivial entities, it makes perfect sense to formulate plans and make educated guesses about what might come next. Expert advice is still preferable to novice opinion, although it cannot be expected to prove correct in every single instance. Some constructionist therapists act as if the absence of perfect predictability and direct instructive interaction means that they must eschew the role of expert and abandon all attempts to anticipate the future and influence outcomes. They seem to believe it is better to let change come about 'unawares,' and they sometimes act as if their aim was to celebrate the haphazard.

Fortunately, caterers and surgeons show no signs of having been troubled by these sorts of epistemological dilemmas. Thus, caterers regularly predict how much food they will need to satisfy a given crowd, and their estimates are rarely far off. Similarly, surgeons approximate where to make the first cut, and what kinds of structural changes are apt to make a difference. Both caterers and surgeons forcefully move events in particular directions and adjust their strategies when the unexpected occurs. Nothing in constructionism or structure determinism suggests that therapists should do otherwise.

Therapists who have decided to adopt a neutral stance and to eliminate elements of hierarchy from their work have generally not consulted their clients about the matter. This creates an inconsistency between 'text' and 'sub-text' akin to what happens when parents announce to their offspring that certain family issues will now be settled 'democratically.' This doesn't eliminate parental authority – it disguises it. Similarly, in the Summerhill experimental educational environment (Neill, 1960), students were permitted to hold council meetings and vote on various matters, but everyone was clear that headmaster Neill was in charge – especially since the school's licence was in danger of being revoked if matters were to get out of hand. The students voted 'freely' as long as they voted correctly or when the issues on which they voted didn't threaten core organizational values.

Some therapists have now decided that what clients want is a therapist who is neutral, and who operates in a setting that is non-hierarchical. For example, Hoffman (1985) claims she wants to de-emphasize hierarchy without blurring distinctions and boundaries. And yet, it is distinctions and boundaries that form hierarchies – you cannot have one without the other (Brown, 1972). We agree with Golann that, 'despite the good intentions of such leading theorists as Boscolo, Cecchin, and Hoffman, constructivism and the observing-system stance have not yet led to a substantially less intrusive or hierarchical family therapy practice' (1988a: 56).

In fact, the very idea that hierarchy can be eliminated in therapy strikes us as absurd and counter-productive. The client has a problem and is seeking help from someone who presumably knows something about how to improve matters. (Even when it is only our cars that need repairs, we are inclined to grant god-like hierarchical status to any auto mechanic who seems able to intervene.) Moreover, therapeutic encounters usually take place on the therapist's turf and involve remuneration. In a society such as ours, those factors alone are sufficient to fix and communicate the shape of the hierarchy.

Along these lines, a psychoanalytic teacher used to remind us that when two individuals lunch together, you can tell who is 'buying' and who is 'selling' by who picks up the check. (The hierarchy is clear, although it may be trickier to discern from a distance the particular commodities that are under negotiation.) Similarly, therapists – constructionist or not – are selling a product and running a 'shop.' They get to set shop policy. Clients vote on the arrangement by continuing to avail themselves of the services being offered or by deciding to shop elsewhere.

Therapist Neutrality

We have already alluded to the issue of therapeutic neutrality. In our view, it is a chimera. To the constructionist, no stance is apolitical or neutral (Durkin, 1981). Epstein and Loos recently suggested that the constructivist therapist 'must develop a position that simultaneously respects *all* the views of *all* the participants' (1989: 416; emphasis added). To act as if all views are equal and that we – as therapists – have no favorites among them undercuts the very sort of frank exchange we want and expect to have with our clients. It patronizes them, compromises our own integrity, and treats open dialogue as if it was an endangered species needing 'hothouse' protection.

How Many Observers are Enough?

Not all the suggestions that have been made in the name of constructionism are abstract and heady. Some writers *have* proposed procedures that are concrete and circumscribed. Unfortunately, many of these suggestions bear only a tangential or superficial connection to the constructionist principles they presumably embody. For example, because constructivists recognize that knowledge arises as a function of the activities of an observing community, some therapists have felt called upon to gather up their own special group of 'observers' and plunk them down behind a one-way mirror. The result is practically a parody of what happens when workers, filled with enthusiasm for a new philosophical insight, attempt to translate that insight directly into tangible form. It is a form of the fallacy of misplaced concreteness. Something very similar happened in the early days of family therapy. Because it was called 'family' therapy, it was assumed that all members of the family should be present. Even today, beginning family therapists sometimes ask, 'How can I do family work if the person's parents are deceased?' or 'I wanted to do family therapy but the client is living in an apartment by herself.' Even though Murray Bowen (1978), one of the founding fathers of family therapy, coached people to work with members of the family *outside* the therapy session, the notion has persisted in some quarters that family therapists must have lots of family members physically present. Many have had difficulty grasping the notion that family work is a way of thinking about life and problems, not necessarily a particular arrangement of bodies in a room.

Obviously, placing an observing team behind glass in no way ensures that the resulting work will be particularly constructionistic or will avoid the pitfalls of 'linearity' that are sometimes said to result when there is just one client and one therapist present. Moreover, the quality of the therapy is not determined by how frequently the lights and sound system are reversed, or by the schedule on which therapists flit back and forth to confer with their colleagues behind the mirror or in the next room.

It is true that Bateson (1979) wrote about the virtues of so-called 'double description,' such as when binocular vision makes depth perception possible. However, useful perspectives are not necessarily correlated with the number of individuals whose comments are sought. Edison, Einstein, Ford, Beethoven, Picasso – and, for that matter, Bateson himself – all managed to do quite nicely as solo acts. The double, triple, and quadruple description that enhanced their work did not require frequent committee meetings. Although Bateson (1972) emphasized the importance of an ecology of ideas, he was not suggesting that you had to pack the entire ecology into your car and take it to work with you.

Again, these procedures turn an idea – a description – into a concrete and potentially superficial recipe. Besides, as Rabkin (1970) points out, there is no such thing as a single therapist and a single client meeting together. People *always* represent an interface between portions of a communal 'network.' Even in individual treatment, the client brings his or her family or 'problem-determined system' (Goolishian and Anderson, 1987) into the room, and the therapist is accompanied by his or her personal and professional support system. Not everyone has to be there in person.

Letters to Go

Besides recommending the use of observers, therapists influenced by the Milan group have introduced exotic variations of procedure, such as presenting the family with a missive detailing the musings of the team, or giving cryptic instructions about what to do next. One wonders what clients make out of some of the mysterious ways in which their cases are being managed. A number of investigators have reported consternation on the part of at least some family members exposed to these procedures, and a lot of us know many more such horror stories on the basis of convention gossip and personal experience. One family member put it this way: 'I would have liked to know the purpose of the group. The whole thing was couched in such secrecy. When I asked for information about the objectives of the group, my questions were answered with other questions. . . . I never felt so used and guinea-pigged in my whole life!' Another said, 'It was very disconcerting when [Dr X] was called out in the middle of [an] emotional sequence and then comes back and repeats mechanically what [the] group says' (Mashal et al., 1989: 467). One wonders whether members of future generations will consider these procedures as distinctly quaint, the way we now view bloodletting. Fortunately for those of us who lack sophisticated audio-visual set-ups and cannot easily assemble a clinical cast of thousands, effective constructionist therapy will probably turn out to require nothing more elaborate than a therapist, a room, and one or more individuals with problems on their minds.

Special Question Formats

Some theoreticians have presumed that the 'magic' of constructionism is contained not so much in who sits where, and who writes letters to whom, but in the particular formats used for asking questions. However, in our view, neither circular questioning nor reflexive questioning are necessary devices for the constructionist therapist, and in some instances they may be counter-productive. We are not fond of pat verbal formulas for several reasons. First of all, they create an *illusion* of impartiality and fair play. Golann (1988a, 1988b) notes that such question-asking disguises the therapist's actual motives: 'It is shortsighted not to realize that asking hypothetical questions of people who are ambivalently invested in change involves the therapist in an exchange of power' (1988b: 69). And, 'if the therapist's hypotheses are invisibly communicated by the pattern that connects the therapist's questions . . . one must ask if such forms of therapy are an improvement over earlier strategic forms of practice' (1988a: 63). In our view, therapists should be more explicit about their stance and should model the taking of responsibility. Circular questioning can serve to cloak therapist intent behind a mask of general inquisitiveness.

Furthermore, clinicians tend to gain a false sense of security by following pre-determined question formats. These recipes make it all too easy for clinicians to 'go on automatic.' Trainers of Rogerian therapists used to complain that common client-centered phrasings too readily became mindless formulas. Circular questioners may launch into a formulaic succession of inquiries without having to grapple with session or treatment goals or the relevance of the content to the issues at hand. Clients, for their part, sometimes answer such questions just to be polite, without having an inkling as to their purpose.

Tomm (1988) judiciously recognizes that one cannot specify a 'circular' or a 'reflexive' question independently of context and therapist intent. However, many practitioners have managed to ignore this caution. In sample tapes we have heard, the therapist sounds more concerned with having a steady stream of questions ready to ask than with determining the effects of the questions they have already asked. The result is a triumph of technique over content. Appropriately or not, each person is asked in round-robin fashion to comment on the reactions of others. It has yet to be demonstrated that circular or reflexive formats yield any special advantage in terms of what participants gain, or that they enable clients to arrive at more sophisticated causal formulations.

Effective therapy must be continually re-created in the context of participant interaction. Otherwise it quickly deteriorates into a series of canned routines. Clinicians often report how wonderfully an intervention worked on its first trial, and how flat it fell when they tried to resurrect it for what seemed to them like a similar occasion.

Therapy and the Conversational Domain

It may be useful to remind ourselves that the word 'psychotherapy' was coined around 1889 simply by combining the words for mind (*psyche*) and treatment (*therapeia*). In the dualistic thinking of the day, it seemed apparent that if there were treatments for the body, there also should be some for the mind. Unfortunately, none had actually been invented, and to this day the term lacks unique, specifiable referents. It can be applied to almost anything clients and therapists might decide to do together, providing it isn't against the law.

From our point of view, psychotherapy is not a specific set of procedures – it is a form of education. It differs from other educational ventures mainly in terms of the nature of the curriculum and the arrangement of the student body. Clients are typically seen in offices instead of classrooms. They are not earning degree credits or expecting to achieve proficiency in specific content areas, such as mathematics, music, or chemistry. Instead, the focus of the tutoring is on living arrangements and life satisfaction. The success of the venture, as Freud suggested long ago, is usually assessed in terms of enhanced capacity to work, play, and love.

Objectivists may assume that therapy fixes broken emotional machinery, improves mental health, or roots out irrational thinking. However, constructionists are clear that they are simply working at an educational endeavor under the terms of a student–teacher contract. Authorization to proceed does not come from having discovered objective flaws in psychic machinery, but from having negotiated a satisfactory agreement between participants that adheres to the limits established by the larger community. Just as a student generally signs up for a course at a licensed institution, clients (or their advocates) hire particular therapists or agencies to tutor and coach them. The contract need not be written, but once it is in place it establishes goals, procedures, and roles for everyone involved. At the conclusion, the requirements of such contracts have either been satisfied, renegotiated, or abrogated. Obviously, the first and second options are preferable to the third.

The natural medium of therapy – as in most other educational pursuits – is language. The context is basically philosophical rather than medical, and constructive rather than simply remedial. The key to therapy as well as other forms of education is what Maturana calls 'orthogonal interaction' (Maturana, 1988). We will say more about that shortly. Language, of course, is not just verbal exchange – it is a pattern of communal activity. Words and symbols are ways of experiencing ourselves in the context of a community. Different vocabularies embody and sustain different social arrangements. It is true, for example, as Johnson maintains, that 'the language of science is the better part of the method of science' (1946: 59), and that the method of science is fundamentally a formula for organizing communal living. Religion, too, is a set of organizational guidelines. Each vocabulary generates its own set of experiences, creates an idiosyncratic brand of knowledge, and generates distinctive social imperatives (Maturana and Varela, 1987).

Moreover, in a system of language, there are no synonyms. Each word or symbol represents a unique coordination of actions and pattern of consequences. Two words may seem synonymous to an observer when he or she has no immediate interest in the dimensions along which the terms differ. However, the distinctions that an observer ignores on one occasion may become critically important on another. Diplomats quickly discover that successful relations can hinge on subtle distinctions of vocabulary and ritual to which the folks back home pay little attention. Similarly, therapists must appreciate that a choice of words dictates a form of interacting. For example, the term 'anxiety' usually creates a bit more mystery than the term 'fear.' A person is therefore more likely to seek treatment for 'test anxiety' than for fear of coming home with poor grades. Overcoming fear is apt to require achieving mastery or demonstrating courage. Anxiety, on the other hand, is more apt to require medication or relaxation training. (In our own work, we attempt to translate the mysterious into the ordinary.)

As we implied earlier, if constructivism stands for anything at all, it stands for an appreciation of the fact that 'everything said is said from a tradition' (Varela, 1979: 268). Meanings do not float around in the stratosphere, disconnected from the contexts in which they were generated. They are performances that 'live in' and maintain particular conversational settings. Reality may be invented, but it is also situated.

Because in our culture we have had a tendency to reify the distinction between words and actions, we generally underestimate the importance of the former and focus too heavily on the latter. Words constitute a specialized form of action, and, of course, are involved in virtually all other forms of activity. You can play baseball without an official field and without a glove, but not without words. It is also a mistake to assume that because constructionists emphasize language processes, they are dealing with just 'interpretations' of problems – reframings – rather than with the problem themselves. 'Real problems' *are* interpretations – they are never simply collections of facts. Moreover, interpretations are consequential – not simply epiphenomenal.

These are not 'subjective' matters. In a system of thought like constructionism in which objectivity is considered an observer illusion, subjectivity also becomes an ambiguous term. Changing the status of one automatically changes the status of the other. (When you modify the meaning of 'up,' 'down' is also affected.) Thus, constructionists replace the usual objective/subjective dichotomy with an appreciation of the nature of participation. In fact, constructionism avoids being solipsistic precisely because it emphasizes that what people think, say, do, imagine, and feel is constituted by the form of their participation. As elements of an on-going ecology, people are not free-standing units who can conceptually pack up and go wherever they like, whenever they please. They are constrained by their structures and their circumstances. Unlike the White Queen in *Through the Looking Glass*, it is not feasible for human beings to believe five or six impossible things before breakfast.

About the best we can do – and it is often sufficient – is to note the peculiar social and structural prison in which we are confined. We believe what we do, and do what we believe. We might wish that a chair were a table or that a malignant cancer were a harmless wart, but wishing doesn't make it so. We have deep structural obligations that require us to play by the rules we have devised. Constructionism is therefore *not* a license to engage in pretense or to encourage people to rely inordinately on wishful thinking. In fact, most individuals whom therapists see are already too heavily involved in fantasy and fabrication. Words represent a relatively stable – and sometimes painful – set of practices. However, few explore all aspects of the verbal terrain that are potentially available to them, and that is where a therapist may be of use.

Orthogonal Interaction

As we mentioned earlier, orthogonal interaction is the key to
therapeutic change. Consider the auto mechanic who is unhappy
with how a car is running. He removes the spark plug, adjusts its
gap with a tool, and replaces it in the engine. As a result of the
slight change in the structure of the plug, it performs its role
differently, and the entire system operates more efficiently. That is
a simple example of orthogonal interaction. The interaction
between spark plug and mechanic was orthogonal – literally,
perpendicular – to what *ordinarily* happens to the spark plug as a
component of the engine. After the spark plug is modified, it
relates differently to the other engine components, and the entire
system undergoes revision. Therapists and other educators are in a
position to interact orthogonally with members of organizations;
they provide opportunities to operate outside ordinary 'club' rules.

Fortunately, the therapist isn't a member of the same 'clubs' as
the client. Therefore, he or she can introduce novel and catalytic
patterns of orthogonal interaction. In doing so, however, it is
essential that the assumptive structure of these clubs not be
replicated in the therapy. As Maturana and Varela report, 'The
solution, like all solutions to apparent contradictions, lies in
moving away from the opposition and changing the nature of the
question, to embrace a broader context' (1987: 135). The
philosophy of constructionism is of help in this respect in several
ways. First, the constructionist therapist does not presume that
club suppositions represent immutable objective realities. The
therapist neither trivializes such communal arrangements nor takes
them to be singular truths. Many new patterns can be constructed.
We can agree with Wittgenstein's observation: 'The limits of
[people's] language mean the limits of [their] world.' Broader and
more inclusive formulations are apt to prove advantageous.
Orthogonal interaction is required to generate additional language
distinctions and thus breathe life into new alternatives. However,
constructionist therapists must not lose sight of the investment
individuals have in preserving certain desirable aspects of their
current club memberships. Emotional contradictions in living
(Mendez et al., 1988) are resolved when the new framework has
sufficient room for those older positive elements to be incorporated
into the newer relationship arrangements. For example, a person
moves into his or her own apartment, but still returns home for the
family's traditional Sunday dinners.

A client came to an initial session complaining of the 'bad week'
she just had. (Notice that in this person's language, it is the week

that was considered 'bad,' rather than certain decisions that arose from her pattern of living.) The reaction she expected from her therapist was sympathy and support, because that was how friends and relatives – her 'club members' – generally responded. Instead, the therapist inquired about why having a 'bad week' should be of concern to anyone. Besides, even if others were to care 'deeply,' would that really make much of a difference? Clients sometimes think the answer to that question is certainly 'yes,' but as they think about it at greater length, they realize that the sympathy of others obtained under such circumstances is rarely nourishing to the self.

The therapist's responses were not what the client expected, but they led to a far-reaching and fruitful discussion about the nature of the therapy contract, the meaning of life, and the linkage she had established between self-satisfaction and the approval of others. She saw how certain assumptions about what she needed from others, and what she expected to receive from them, were directly tied to severe disappointments in her social life and other relationship difficulties. After leaving the session, the client went home with renewed energy and decided to throw out an old and hated piece of furniture. The next day, she signed up for an art course at a neighborhood adult education center. Waiting for approval from others began to seem less important to her than acting on her preferences.

Conclusion

Because we are in the middle of an epistemological revolution, it would be unrealistic to expect definitive answers to every question posed about constructionist approaches. On the other hand, it is hard to avoid sympathizing with those bewildered souls on the professional firing lines who feel the need for more concrete instructions, particularly from those implying that they have been heading in the wrong direction. Clinicians need to know how constructivism might help them deal more effectively with a quarreling couple, a cocaine-addicted teenager, a suicidal husband, a house-bound agoraphobic, an obsessive hand-washer, or a high-school dropout. Some of the advice given to date seems unnecessarily abstract and idealistic. Other advice is more specific but is not necessarily derived from constructionist principles. In our view, constructionism doesn't necessitate being neutral, avoiding hierarchy, or waiting for change to happen of its own accord. Nor does it require special audio-visual facilities, teams of therapists, or special questioning techniques.

Psychotherapy is a form of education. The medium of therapy is language. Therapist and client interact 'orthogonally' in an attempt to generate more encompassing alternatives. Constructionism highlights the nature of the communal enterprise, as well as the notion that there are many possible legitimate living arrangements, only a small subset of which have been explored. It neither trivializes social interaction nor the accompanying and necessary use of words and symbols. The constructionist therapist takes responsibility for his or her opinions, values, and beliefs, and the consequences connected to them. Moreover, he or she encourages clients to do the same. Clients are tutored to see 'symptoms' as generated by and embedded in current living patterns rather than as products of mysterious outside forces or internal psychic diseases.

Notes

The authors wish to thank Elsa R. Efran, Richard J. Leffel, and Jeanne Akillas for their help in preparing this manuscript for publication.

1. In what follows we use the terms 'constructionism' and 'constructivism' interchangeably. When we are quoting or discussing a particular writer's views, we use the term used by that author.

References

Bach, R. (1977) *Illusions: the Adventures of a Reluctant Messiah*. New York: Delacorte Press (Creatures Enterprises, Inc.).

Bateson, G. (1972) *Steps to an Ecology of Mind*. New York: Ballantine.

Bateson, G. (1979) *Mind and Nature: a Necessary Unity*. New York: Bantam.

Bowen, M. (1978) *Family Therapy in Clinical Practice*. New York: Jason Aronson.

Brown, G.S. (1972) *Laws of Form*. New York: Julian Press.

Coyne, J.C. (1982a) 'A brief introduction to epistobabble', *Family Therapy Networker*, 6 (4): 27–8.

Coyne, J.C. (1982b) 'A critique of cognitions as causal entities with particular reference to depression', *Cognitive Therapy and Research*, 6: 3–13.

Coyne, J.C. (1989) 'Thinking postcognitively about depression', in A. Freeman, K.M. Simon, L.E. Beutler and H. Arkowitz (eds), *Comprehensive Handbook of Cognitive Therapy*. New York: Plenum. pp. 227–44.

Coyne, J.C. (1990) 'Concepts for understanding marriage and developing techniques of marital therapy: cognition *über Alles*?' *Journal of Family Psychology*, 4: 185–94.

Durkin, J.E. (1981) *Living Groups: Group Psychotherapy and General System Theory*. New York: Brunner/Mazel.

Efran, J.S. and Caputo, C. (1984) 'Paradox in psychotherapy: a cybernetic perspective', *Journal of Behavior Therapy and Experimental Psychiatry*, 15: 235–40.

Efran, J.S., Lukens, M.D. and Lukens, R.J. (1990) *Language, Structure, and Change: Frameworks of Meaning in Psychotherapy*. New York: Norton.

Epstein, E.S. and Loos, V.E. (1989) 'Some irreverent thoughts on the limits of family therapy: toward a language-based explanation of human systems', *Journal of Family Psychology*, 2: 405–21.

Golann, S. (1988a) 'On second-order family therapy', *Family Process*, 27: 51–65.

Golann, S. (1988b) 'Who replied first? A reply to Hoffman', *Family Process*, 27: 68–71.

Goolishian, H. and Anderson, H. (1987) 'Language systems and therapy: an evolving idea', *Psychotherapy*, 24: 529–38.

Held, B.S. (1990) 'What's in a name? Some confusions and concerns about constructivism', *Journal of Marital and Family Therapy*, 16: 179–86.

Hoffman, L. (1985) 'Beyond power and control: toward a 'second order' family systems therapy', *Family Systems Medicine*, 3: 381–96.

Hoffman, L. (1988) 'A constructivist position for family therapy', *Irish Journal of Psychology*, 9: 110–29.

Hofstadter, D.R. (1979) *Gödel, Escher, Bach: an Eternal Golden Braid*. New York: Basic Books.

Johnson, W. (1946) *People in Quandaries*. New York: Harper & Row.

Keeney, B.P. (1983) *Aesthetics of Change*. New York: Guilford Press.

Kenny, V. (ed.) (1988) 'Radical constructivism, autopoiesis and psychotherapy', special issue of *Irish Journal of Psychology*, 9 (1).

Mashal, M., Feldman, R.B. and Sigal, J.J. (1989) 'The unraveling of a treatment paradigm: a followup study of the Milan approach to family therapy', *Family Process*, 28: 457–70.

Maturana, H.R. (1988) 'Reality: the search for objectivity or the quest for a compelling argument', *Irish Journal of Psychology*, 9 (1): 1–24.

Maturana, H.R. and Varela, F.J. (1987) *The Tree of Knowledge*. Boston, MA: New Science Library.

Mendez, C.L., Coddou, F. and Maturana, H.R. (1988) 'The bringing forth of pathology', *Irish Journal of Psychology*, 9 (1): 144–72.

Neill, A.S. (1960) *Summerhill: a Radical Approach to Child Rearing*. New York: Hart Publishing Co.

Overbye, D. (1981) 'Messenger at the gates of time', *Science '81*, June: 61–7.

Rabkin, R. (1970) *Inner and Outer Space: Introduction to a Theory of Social Psychiatry*. New York: Norton.

Schwartz, R. and Perrotta, P. (1985) 'Let us sell no intervention before its time', *Family Therapy Networker*, July–Aug.: 18, 20–5.

Tomm, K. (1988) 'Interventive interviewing: Part III. Intending to ask circular, strategic, or reflexive questions?' *Family Process*, 27: 1–16.

Varela, F.J. (1979) *Principles of Biological Autonomy*. New York: Elsevier-North Holland.

von Foerster, H. (1981) *Observing Systems*. Seaside, CA: Intersystems Publications.

Watzlawick, P. (1984) *The Invented Reality: How Do We Know What We Believe We Know?* New York: Norton.

Index